Confessions
of a
Latter-day
Virgin

Confessions

of a

Latter-day

Virgin

———— ✦ ————

A Memoir

NICOLE HARDY

HYPERION
New York

Pages 105–106: "Salvador Late or Early" by Sandra Cisneros, from Woman Hollering Creek and Other Stories. *Copyright © 1991 by Sandra Cisneros, reprinted with permission.*

Page 221: Excerpt from "Advice I Wish Someone Had Given Me" by Ann Darr, from St. Ann's Gut, *reprinted with permission.*

Library of Congress Cataloging-in-Publication Data

Hardy, Nicole.
    Confessions of a latter day virgin: a memoir/Nicole Hardy.—FIRST EDITION.
        pages cm
    ISBN 978-1-4013-4186-2
    1. Hardy, Nicole.   2. Spiritual biography.   3. Ex-church members—Church of Jesus Christ of Latter-day Saints—Biography.   I. Title.
    BL73.H34A3 2013
    204.092—dc23
    [B]

                                                                2012045975

FIRST EDITION

10 9 8 7 6 5 4 3 2 1

SUSTAINABLE FORESTRY INITIATIVE   Certified Sourcing
www.sfiprogram.org
SFI-00993

THIS LABEL APPLIES TO TEXT STOCK

We try to produce the most beautiful books possible, and we are also extremely concerned about the impact of our manufacturing process on the forests of the world and the environment as a whole. Accordingly, we've made sure that all of the paper we use has been certified as coming from forests that are managed, to ensure the protection of the people and wildlife dependent upon them.

For Eric, that pusher

PROLOGUE

———— ◆ ————

"Sex isn't everything," my mother says lightly, from the kitchen of my new condo. She means to be encouraging. But I stiffen reflexively against her words, as if to defend myself. I've heard it too many times from too many people—that sentence, so reductive it's offensive.

How easy it is for my mother, who married at twenty, to dismiss what she's never lived without. I can't help but feel like she's being purposefully dense, simply refusing to consider anything beyond the surface. My first impulse is a fierce rush of frustration—the urge to roll my eyes, shout a blistering, condescending "no shit" in the direction of the kitchen, where she's unpacking boxes. *Obviously,* the problem is not just the absence of sex. Obviously, there are more complex issues at the heart of my unplanned celibacy.

But when I turn to meet my mother's eyes, I work hard to keep my voice from veering into sarcasm. "Do you think I'd be a virgin at thirty-three, Mom, if I thought sex was everything?"

As if on cue, the CD we've been listening to reaches the last notes of the final track. The silence in the room highlights the trepidation we both feel. "I know you're struggling," my mother says, resting her hands on the counter. An impotent kind of energy is humming around her. She wants to help me, I know. She's trying. For the first time, she's asking.

Seconds pass before I trust my voice not to waver, before the burn in my throat subsides. "I don't know how to fix it." Ashamed by even that admission, I hold in the heaviest secret, the sentence that frightens me at night. Outside, a container ship slowly barrels through the shipping lanes. The north end of Vashon Island is nearly obscured behind its towering mass of orange crates, its hull plowing a wake toward the breakwater below. "I don't know how much longer I can live like this," I say finally, half hoping my mother won't hear.

The Mormon Church is a system of absolutes. There is only one right way to live. One complete truth. Either I believe the doctrine of my church was revealed by God to a living prophet, or I don't. And if I believe, I must live the way I've been commanded. I must endure to the end. If I am floundering, drowning, or desolate, my faith should be the solution.

I can feel my mother's fear from across the room, the exaggerated stillness of her body. How can I tell her that over the past two years I have *willed* myself into depression? The relief of numbness, that saving grace. How can I say I am glad to feel myself withering? That I can almost stop needing what I can't have, if I don't allow myself to feel anything.

If I say no, sex isn't everything—those mechanics, that act—but it affects everything, she will say, "Be faithful." If I say sex casts a monstrous shadow over my life: the visceral wanting of it, the religious sanctions against it, the looming threat of disfellowship or excommunication, and the damaging ways I've devised to resist it, she will tell me to follow the prophet's counsel, and that of his apostles. If I say sex keeps me from getting near enough to a man to fall in love, because nonmembers are the ones who want me and I can no longer trust myself around them. If I say I'm unmarriageable in the Mormon community. If I say the crisis of celibacy is a crisis of isolation, that I am wrong in both places, judged by both sides, she will say wait for my spiritual reward. "Look to the afterlife," as if this life means nothing.

There will be no way to respond that isn't sacrilege. No prophet or apostle has lived a celibate life, is what I'd like to tell her. No one who's told me celibacy is a viable option has ever been celibate. They don't even use the word. They say "abstinent," which implies there will be an end. They don't consider what my life will be like, if I never marry. Which is likely, given who I am, and the ways I'm different. People stand at the pulpit or they come to my house and tell me not to need what every human needs. Afterward, they go home and undress. They lie down next to the person they love most, or once did. When they reach across the bed, someone is there.

The ship outside my window has traveled all the way from China. I imagine it's full of laptops, T-shirts, lipstick, or toys; I imagine a crate full of telephones or headphones—some advanced technology that could help my mother hear me. Make her understand. One of the apostles recently warned against withdrawing from others. "Such retreat," he said, "may ultimately lead to the darkening influence of the adversary, which leads to despondency, loneliness, frustration." *He's got it backward,* I remember thinking. Withdrawal is a *survival tactic.* Because if I can't get numb enough, if I can't withdraw far enough from my body and the need to feel human, I will end up clinging to a stranger on a deserted beach, again. I will find myself tangled in the arms of another somebody, anybody, on my entryway floor. It will be some weary, medicinal surrender that destroys everything. One moment of weakness is all it would take to make myself a hypocrite, or a failure.

I open my mouth to explain, or try to. But there is nothing I can say. I listen, instead, to the steady, rhythmic crash of waves against the seawall. And my mother's voice, which sounds as if it's coming from far away. "Everyone has trials, honey. You just love God. You keep the commandments, and you say your prayers." She turns back to the dishwater, as if that is all that needs to be said.

Chapter 1

And ye must practise virtue and holiness before me
continually. Even so. Amen.

—DOCTRINE & COVENANTS 46:33

———— ·•◆•· ————

Age twelve is a turning point in the Mormon Church. For me, on that portentous birthday, the heavens opened. The angels sang. Because the following Sunday I would enter the Young Women's program and would never again have to sit with the little kids in Primary, be made to sing embarrassing, babyish songs, and be talked to as if I couldn't already read at a ninth-grade level.

I'd been indignant about Primary the entire year prior—about still being categorized as a child by the hierarchies of my church. I was five foot eight, and still growing—if only because my parents ignored their doctor's dead-serious suggestion to give me growth-stunting drugs at age two. I wore a bra, if only for training. So I was more than ready to become a Beehive—the designation for every twelve- and thirteen-year-old Mormon girl.

My first Sunday in Beehives I sat in the small semicircle of folding chairs feeling fancy in a sea-green Laura Ashley dress and my first pair of heels: mauve leather pumps with clip-on bows—a feature that sealed the deal before I even tried them on and practiced walking the plush, carpeted runway in Brass Plum shoes. I wore those heels with pride, though they made me even taller than my father. I wore lip gloss and mascara, too, for the first time that Sunday. But perhaps the most obvious marker of my status as a Young Woman was our Sunday school lesson that week—the first of many to come regarding The Law of Chastity.

Sister Jepson, our teacher, stood confidently in a small classroom adjacent to the chapel. She was pale skinned and dark haired, thinner and younger than our mothers. All seven of us Beehives wanted to grow up to look exactly like her. She had six children, which was hard to believe, given her figure. The first was born when Sister Jepson was nineteen—*only seven years older than I am now*, I remember thinking.

"Today is the day you should decide," she said, looking each of us straight in the eye. "Make up your minds right now how far you'll let boys go. Then, when the moment comes, you'll never be unsure of what to do."

We watched, rapt, as she turned to the chalkboard and drew a line graph, labeling from left to right: kissing, necking, necking and petting, heavy petting, and intercourse—nouns that seemed old-fashioned, and embarrassing. Then she abruptly changed the subject, or so it seemed.

She told us how much her husband loves her hair. He'd *die* if she cut it he always says. And we agreed. It was magnificent: the kind of hair we'd soon be spending all our babysitting money trying to repli-cate, via perming, diffusing, back combing, and spraying, until Aqua Net seared our lungs like mustard gas.

Sister Jepson segued into the special bond a physical relationship creates. She assured us there is no more wonderful expression of love between a husband and wife. "Some people think it's okay to have sex before marriage, as long as you love the person," she said. "But what's wrong with that line of thinking?"

Mindy Harris, a girl wildly obsessed with Duran Duran's pompadoured drummer, Roger, was the first to speak up: "What if you fall in love with *lots* of people before you get married?"

"Exactly," said Sister Jepson. She asked Mindy to read from a recent issue of the *Ensign*—the church's monthly magazine, which includes reprints of talks from General Conference, where twice per year the living prophet and his twelve apostles speak to the membership worldwide.

"[The prophet] Alma, in the Book of Mormon, says, 'Bridle . . . your passions, that ye may be filled with love,'" Mindy read. "Bridling increases strength, increases power, increases love . . . A horse is stronger than a man, so the man bridles it, thus controlling its power . . . Passions are stronger than we are, so we bridle them, thus controlling their power and using that power to strengthen a marriage and forge it into eternity."

Sister Jepson thanked Mindy for reading, and in another unexpected turn asked us to raise our hands if we loved mashed potatoes. Our arms shot up. Our mouths began to water in a collective Pavlovian response, triggered by fantasies of Sunday dinner. We envisioned the ham, pot roast, or spaghetti that would appear, steaming, from our kitchens after this—the third and final—hour of church.

Sister Jepson combed her fingers through her curls until she caught several loose strands. She held them out, and asked which of us would eat a plate of mashed potatoes if they were laced with her jet-black hair. We groaned in disgust; Mindy Harris pretended to gag.

"Beautiful things," said Sister Jepson, "in the wrong place, at the wrong time, can cease to be beautiful." She paused, to let that idea sink in. "And the most beautiful thing about you is your virtue. I want you to make a promise to God, right now. How much will you give away before your wedding night—knowing you can never get back what innocence you've lost?"

She indicated the chalk line, clearly labeled, illustrating the slippery slope to sin and the threat of eternal punishment. God's punishment. And in the silence that followed, I promised to maintain a personal standard corresponding to the church's standard. I'd be married, given six to ten more years. Anyone can wait that long. *And besides*, I remember thinking, *is it just me, or does sex seem kind of gross anyway? I mean he pees from there.*

Eight years later, sitting in a large theater-style classroom at Brigham Young University in Provo, Utah, I'm not married or even close. I am, however, in the midst of another equally enlightening lesson about sex. Psych 101 includes a unit on human development, which—at the moment—has us knee-deep in exhibitionism, voyeurism, and frotteurism.

My professor, who teaches every day in Levi's and a white dress shirt rolled at the cuffs, flips on the overhead projector. Bullet points appear on the ten-foot screen behind him. The bulb illuminates his impeccably white rockabilly pompadour. "Frotteurism is a paraphilic interest in rubbing, usually one's erect penis, against a nonconsenting person for sexual gratification. Frotteurs are generally male, victims female," he says cheerfully.

This is all news to me, and I am *captivated*. I love the freakiness of it—not to mention the glamorous French spellings (frotteur, derived from the French verb *frotter*, meaning "to rub").

The professor's voice carries easily to the back of the room. "Although female on male, female on female, and male on male frotteurs exist."

Whoa, I am thinking. And, *ew.* I copy the salient points in my notebook, unable to help myself from imagining potential questions for our upcoming exam:

A FROTTEUR MAY ATTEMPT TO RUB YOU:
   a. In a box
   b. With a fox
   c. In a house
   d. With a mouse
   e. In the rain
   f. On a train

"Frotteurism usually occurs where the victim can't easily respond," our professor continues. "For example, on crowded trains or buses."

Suddenly, there's a commotion in the back of the room. A girl has stood up from her chair. *Abruptly.* She slams her book shut, and all two hundred of our heads track her furious, clomping journey down the linoleum-covered stairs. Just before reaching the door, she turns, takes a deep breath, and chucks her seventy-five-dollar textbook directly at our professor's head. "Here's your *sex manual!*" she declares righteously, before flouncing out of the room.

The class erupts in laughter—either at her emphatic declaration, or her wide miss—and I cover my mouth in gleeful horror. All I can think is, *Clearly, that girl has never* seen *a sex manual.* If she'd spent her fifth-grade afternoons like I had—poring over *The Joy of Sex* in my friend Jennifer's basement—she'd have known the difference. This text has no earnest charcoal renderings, no stunning puffs of pubic hair, no catalog of intriguing and/or perplexing sexual positions.

Our professor picks up the textbook from the floor and says, after a pause, "I am so grateful for that sweet sister." And then, with a wink, "Her aim was *terrible!*"

Outbursts like these—prompted by religious fervor, or some perceived sacrilege—certainly aren't the norm at BYU, but they're common enough. They're probably to be expected at one of the nation's most conservative Christian universities. But what consistently shocks *me* is how many people are shocked about sex around here—even married students, for whom nearly all sanctions are lifted.

I love talking about sex, especially when it's part of the curriculum. I want information from every appropriate source, so I'll be prepared when the time comes. I've heard too many nightmare stories of virgins who get married and literally *don't know* what to do, or who are unnecessarily guilt-ridden, unable to get beyond the idea of sin.

"God would not have created the clitoris," I overheard once on a TV talk show, "if he didn't want women to enjoy sex." I feel like that's a philosophy I can live by; I plan to put it into practice one day soon. No one ever said Mormons have to be prudes just because we practice abstinence. I may never have been to second base, but I sure as hell want to know what a frotteur is. That information could turn out to be *useful* one day—particularly if I travel by train.

Growing up, my family always talked openly about sex—which I'm beginning to realize isn't exactly the norm for Mormons. But each of my parents suffered traumas as children—in varying degrees—so it was always a priority for them to debunk whatever myths my brother and I picked up on the playground, answer whatever questions we had, and protect us—as best they could—both from predators and the religious guilt often used to promote abstinence.

"It's how adults play," my mother often said, casually. But sex has its time and its place. Our church leaders are adamant about that distinction, as were my parents: wherever, whenever, as long as you're heterosexual, married, and monogamous.

That trifecta is right in my wheelhouse. I'll get married during college, or not long after—because that's what Mormons do. The practice of abstinence speeds things along, obviously: if I were to hit it off with Mr. Dreamy in the striped sweater sitting two rows up, our entire value systems would already be in sync. We'd already have the same priorities, the same core beliefs, the same vision for our future.

If we could talk and laugh and trust each other, and if we wanted to tear each other's clothes off, what more would we need to build a life together? But beyond the urgency abstinence inspires, Mormons marry because "two of the vital pillars that sustain Father in Heaven's plan of happiness are marriage and the family."

My mom has called twice since Christmas to tell me she's had spiritual promptings regarding my future husband. I'll meet him soon, she says—any day now. Which makes me sort of nervous, honestly. I've never even really *dated*. During high school, I kissed a grand total of three guys. My longest relationship happened when I was officially too young to date: sixteen is the church-sanctioned age, and I was fifteen. Nate and I went to different schools, and his parents made it hard for us to see each other, so we stayed together months longer than we otherwise would have. After that, I had one date with a trumpet player in the high school band, and a two-week flirtation with a Mormon guy who'd recently moved from California and charmed me with his long-in-front skater haircut.

Last year, as a freshman in college, I had a four-month interlude with a guy I'm pretty sure is gay—but honestly, that didn't matter much. We weren't having sex, we weren't getting married, and he was a *really* good dancer. Since then, I've been on one date each with two different guys. Both ended with a five-minute doorstep makeout, and little interest in seeing each other again. One lived out of town, and the other, it turned out, had a thing for my roommate, Krista. That's the grand total of my romantic experience, which could be worse: it's still a far cry from rubbing up on strangers on a city bus, or running around in nothing but a fedora and a trench coat like some pervy film noir private eye.

After class, I head over to meet Krista at the Cougareat. I launch into the story as soon as we choose a booth and detray. But neither frotteurs nor book-chucking girls can hold her attention like Ty Detmer can. Krista's staring at BYU's resident hero and Heisman Trophy

winner as if his sandwich contains the clue to the missing link. I wave
my hand in front of her face.

"I hear you," she says, batting my hand away. "I'll see your frotteurs, and raise you the forty-year-old woman in my marketing class."
She pauses between bites of frozen yogurt. "Last week, she interrupts
everything to announce she can't *possibly* be expected to research misogyny in advertising. Her temple covenants would *never* allow it.
The professor had to hand her a dictionary. She couldn't be convinced misogyny wasn't a synonym for porn."

On the tabletop beside my fork I notice a pencil drawing—a
heart with a banner over it and two sets of initials, in the style of a
1940s MOM tattoo. Which makes me wonder if my mom ever sat at
this table. Met my dad between classes, shared a milkshake, talked
about the Beatles or Vietnam. It's strange to think I could *literally* be
walking in their footsteps when I'm on campus: that their feet, as
well as my brother's and mine, have slid into the same deep grooves in
the marble library stairs.

My parents met on this campus, twenty-five years ago. They fell
in love, married, and conceived my brother, all before graduation.
Five years ago, they began their campaign: promising to help my
brother and me pay for college if we chose their alma mater. I only
cared about three things: going to a big school, out of state, where
people had to be smart to get in. I was happy to come here, though
my nonmember friends can't see why anyone would attend a college
with such a strict honor code. And make no mistake. There *are* a lot of
rules: no drinking, no smoking, no sex, no porn, no drugs, no coffee,
no co-ed living. No co-ed visits in dorms, except on rare, authorized,
supervised occasions. No co-ed visits in off-campus housing, either,
except in living rooms and kitchens. On campus, skirts and shorts
must be knee length; no tank tops, no backless, no strapless, no bra-
less, no midriff, no bikinis. No extreme hairstyles or colors. Nothing
too tight, nothing low-cut. No piercings (except for girls, except for

ears—and only one pair), no visible tattoos, though even *in*visible ones would be scandalous. No beards, no grubby facial hair—though neatly trimmed mustaches are okay. No long hair for men, modest sideburns only. Nothing dirty, ragged, frayed, or patched may be worn on campus according to the dress code. Women always wear dresses for church, where regular attendance is required, and men always wear ties.

A skirt hitting a few inches above the knee or an unshaven face could bar a student from entering certain buildings. Like the testing center. During finals week. And from the pulpit, there are often pointed, embarrassing directives to the student body, in regard to remaining morally clean. Picture a sixty-year-old man saying into a microphone, without a hint of irony, "Backrubs lead to front rubs." Our bishop stood in sacrament meeting just last week to announce, "Feigned sexual intercourse with your clothes on, also known as 'dry sex' or 'Levi lovin',' is strictly forbidden."

And though the entire student congregation sat mortified, cringing at his excruciating use of Utah-based slang, we've all come to expect such things. The rules aren't anything new, nor are the lectures about them. And honestly, I probably wouldn't do anything against the BYU honor code, regardless of where I went to school. Besides, it's nice to live in a place where I don't have to listen to the "Come on, don't be uptight. You only live once. It's no big deal."

I committed—at baptism, at age eight—to a life absent of experimentation, rebellion, and risk. And 98.5 percent of the other students here are Mormon, too. Which means they also promised to suppress every physical appetite in the quest for a spiritual reward. I can't speak for all thirty thousand of my classmates, but I've kept those commitments since my baptism, and I don't feel like I've missed out. I never saw the point in derailing my life for the sake of teenage rebellion.

Obeying the Word of Wisdom—which prohibits drugs or

alcohol—meant I'd never be suspended, incarcerated, or sent to re-hab. It meant no thoughtless decisions made while I was impaired, no life-altering mistakes, the wrong ride in the wrong car on any given night. Obeying the law of chastity meant no pregnancy scare, no pregnancy actual, no "why didn't he call me, why doesn't he love me," no damage of that particular kind to my self-esteem. That's not to mention the spiritual consequences, or the fact that I had *home-work* to do. Mostly it seemed like a lot of effort to worry about abor-tion, birth control, and Chlamydia.

According to Mormon scripture, sexual sins are "most abominable above all sins save it be the shedding of innocent blood or denying the Holy Ghost." I don't even want to think about committing a sin nearly on par with murder. How terrible I'd feel after, or what consequences it would bring. So far, the worst of my spiritual offenses is an affinity for swearing—including the F word, but excluding any phrase including "God" or "Jesus." That, and occasional attendance at Brother Bell's Sun-day school class. Provo's Taco Bell is just a few tempting blocks from campus. And while keeping the Sabbath Day holy prohibits spending money on Sundays, neither Krista nor I can commit to going hungry for twenty-four hours when we've forgotten to stock the fridge.

"I need to stop by the bookstore," I tell Krista, gathering up the detritus from our lunch. "Wanna come?"

"Sorry," she says. "Study group." She walks out the door, smiling coyly, not thirty feet behind Mr. Heisman.

The bookstore, any bookstore, is one of my favorite places on earth; though this one lacks ambience, has too many strictly instructional tomes. But in the section where I spend most of my time—the as-signed aisles for the English department—the shelves are like a shrine to my truest loves. I've shared my bed with a pile of books for as long as I can remember. This week I'm shacking up with *Leaves of Grass*—for the third time, at least. I like to imagine Walt Whitman and me on a picnic, holding hands. Lolling around in the grass, picking daisies. Shaking our locks at the runaway sun—just before diving face-first into a wheel of triple-cream Brie.

In the absence of boyfriends, books have taken on the role of the beloved. In the absence of adventure, passion, and pleasure, they've always been my source. When I was a kid called to dinner, made to put my book down and take my assigned spot at the table in our split-level suburban house, my father would ask one of us to pray aloud, thanking God for our abundant blessings. If it was anyone's turn but mine, I would turn inward instead of out. I would nurse whatever tragedy, romance, death, or injustice I'd recently read about for as long as I could make it feel real. I'd sit with my head bowed, my eyes closed, savoring whatever bruise my book had left behind.

As a Mormon girl, I've been taught to "be not of the world," and also to love my fellow man. Stand apart, but love. "The natural man is an enemy to God," according to Mormon scripture. "And will be, forever and ever, unless he yields to the enticings of the Holy Spirit, and putteth off the natural man and becometh a saint through the atonement of Christ the Lord." Because I could not—*should* not—walk in others' shoes, I have read their stories instead. They're a conduit to the empathy I've been commanded to feel—and are as sacred, to me, as any sacrament or scripture.

Halfway down one of the long narrow bookshelves, I find what I'm looking for: *Refuge*, by Terry Tempest Williams. It's been on the syllabus since the beginning of the term, but the books have just now arrived. I slide a copy from the shelf and flip to the back cover, which details the story of a woman whose family is plagued by cancer—exposed to fallout from nuclear testing in the 1950s. Woven through that tragedy is an account of the catastrophic flooding of the Bear River Migratory Bird Refuge. In this book, the author's mother will die, the land will flood, and the birds will disappear.

The back cover also says the author is Mormon, and a woman. Looking at her photograph, my heart jumps to my throat. I know there are Mormon writers, obviously. One of my roommates is obsessed with the genre novels of Orson Scott Card; and what Mormon girl hasn't read *Charly*, the *Love Story* of Mormon culture? Every Deseret Book outlet is bursting with titles almost solely by Mormon authors. But mainstream literature, earning critical acclaim? A Mormon woman, doing that? I didn't know such a thing existed. *Could* exist.

Looking at the author's face, holding her book in my hands, I feel the thrum of a kindred spirit. Sister is the title I'd use if I were to meet her at church: Sister Williams. Terry Tempest Williams. Tell me everything.

I rush straight home and crawl into bed with *Refuge*. I break its thin spine and lean in for the marrow. I stay up all night, devouring her story, imagining I can feel the author's breath in my lungs as I read. That her world is mine, collapsing. I'm enthralled by the two stories woven together, but the detail I keep coming back to is a tiny, nearly inconceivable aside—an idea circling, burrowing into my consciousness for the first time.

The author says she and her husband chose not to have children. I realize, upon reading that sentence, I've never heard of such a thing. And even more strange is that I've never noticed, until now. I know Mormon women who don't have children, obviously. Who *can't* have children. But without exception, it's the trial, the refining fire, the suffering that forces the soul to grow.

I'm astonished to hear a Mormon woman say she simply chose differently—that her identity and sense of purpose spring from a different source. It seems ridiculous to say it: I didn't know a Mormon woman could *choose* that. I've never met an LDS woman who has chosen to be childless, the same way I've never met an LDS woman who has chosen not to marry.

I've only known one Mormon adult who's never been married, and it was obviously not a situation she'd chosen. Molly Cartwright babysat my brother and me the few times my parents went out of town without us. She was afraid to use the microwave and wouldn't take us swimming because she refused to be seen in shorts or a bathing suit. My brother and I couldn't go unsupervised, and I felt unjustly punished by Molly's body issues. And when I wrote letters to my parents, Molly insisted I address them to Mr. and Mrs. Van Hardy, rather than Ardith and Van. Even at age nine, I bristled at the implications therein, the syntactic lack of my mother's autonomy. Anyone who's met my mom knows she's not a Mrs. Mr. *anybody.*

Molly Cartwright's spinsterhood was no mystery to me, even as young as I was. And I was nothing like her—couldn't be, if I tried. I *loved* swimming. I wasn't afraid of shorts, or the microwave. One day I'd get my braces off and get a better haircut and would no longer be slightly chubby and way too tall. I'd be pretty, and I'd get married in college, or right after, like normal people do.

My alarm frightens me awake with its horrible electronic beeping. I slam my hand on top of it, and realize—nothing new—I'm still in my clothes, my bedside light is still on, and there's a book digging into my stomach. I brush my teeth, put on a hat, grab a banana, and hurry across the sprawling, freezing campus, anxious to talk about the poetry of Williams's language, the man-made tragedies of her life, and those of coincidence. I want to talk about the ways faith can fail us, and how it heals—what we turn toward, and turn our backs on, in the face of death.

I choose a seat at the back of the classroom, one warmed by a thick, rectangular ray of sunlight. I open my notebook to a clean, white page. I set my copy of *Refuge* in front of me, ready to be inspired. Instead, I'm caught in a firestorm.

"She's misrepresenting the church!" someone shouts the minute our professor walks to the front of the room.

"She toasted with *champagne*," another calls out, furious. "She's supposed to be *Mormon!*"

Another pipes in, "Why would you even *assign* this book?"

Our professor tries to steer the discussion back to the socioeco-
nomic, political, and environmental effects of the flood. Silence. He
asks about the loss and the resurgence of the birds, how that symbolism
works in the book.

"She put her hands on another to heal the sick!"

"She wants *women* to hold the priesthood!"

"She's preaching false doctrine!"

My head is spinning. I look around to find others, even *one* other,
who is as shocked as I am. No one will meet my eyes. *But this is
English class; this is* literature, I'm thinking. Can't we read a book
without needing it to be a parable?

My classmates have morphed into an angry mob, enumerating the
author's spiritual failures, the long list of her sins. They can abide such
things from non-Mormons: those to whom the fullness of the Gospel
has not been revealed. But this woman has been given the whole truth.
Her questioning feels, to them, like betrayal.

As Mormons, we're taught that when one disagrees in matters of
the spirit, the answer is to be obedient to God's laws, and to pray for
understanding. Obey, and wait: for clarity, or a change of heart.
Voices of dissent are not encouraged in our meetings, or even in our
culture. To divulge one's struggle publicly—if it is in opposition to
the doctrine—can be interpreted as a battle against God, a rebellion
of spirit. I know why my classmates are angry. But still, I have the
urge to stand up and shout, "She isn't preaching! Her book isn't *doctrine.*" My hands are shaking. I want them to *hear* her, a woman saying this is my story. This is how my mother died. This is what I saw,
and how I grieved.

I want them to listen—to let God judge, if judgment is required.
But I don't know how to defend the author without also being cast as
sinful, or tolerant of sin. We are taught to stand up in defense of the
church, and otherwise be humble, meek, and lowly in heart. So when
my classmates want to know how Terry Tempest Williams has not

been excommunicated from God's church, when they call for a banning, if not a burning, of her book—for the first time ever among my people—I feel afraid.

I don't know how to oppose them, or how I ended up on the outside. I don't know how to be the one person out of two hundred crazy or brave enough to stand up and interrupt, to call bullshit and walk out in the middle of class. I've never imagined I could be the person who's a joke over lunch at the Cougareat.

But it's not until I'm walking home, utterly deflated, that I realize what frightens me most. I don't want to be wrong to admire the woman who wrote *Refuge:* her impulse to act against the silence instilled in her, to speak, regardless of consequence, in defense of the desert and her mother's body, both of which were ravaged by weapons of war. I don't want to be wrong to consider, for myself, a life like hers. I look upward, into the clear, blinding blue sky. *I don't want to be wrong,* I pray. *Let it be them and not me.*

Chapter 2

My life has been the poem I would have writ . . .

—HENRY DAVID THOREAU

M y thin, harried-looking English professor is pacing at the front of the room. He's talking about *The Love Song of J. Alfred Prufrock*. About paralysis of the spirit and the dangers of avoiding what we most desire. His performance feels slightly affected, like a B-grade scene from *Dead Poets Society*, but still, the class is silent. We're interested, if not rapt, and listen intently as he recites:

> *And indeed there will be time*
> *To wonder, "Do I dare?" and, "Do I dare?"*
> *Time to turn back and descend the stair,*
> *With a bald spot in the middle of my hair—*

"I can relate to this poem," our professor says. He turns and indicates the thinning hair on the back of his head, and we laugh as if on cue. But he quickly brings the mood back down. He stands still and continues:

> *(They will say: "How his hair is growing thin!")*
> *My morning coat, my collar mounting firmly to the chin,*

My necktie rich and modest, but asserted by a simple pin—
(They will say: "But how his arms and legs are thin!")
Do I dare
Disturb the universe?

Our professor seems to relish the long silence hanging above his head, and I imagine his words suspended in a dialogue bubble. "Would it have been worth while," he continues,

To have bitten off the matter with a smile,
To have squeezed the universe into a ball
To roll it toward some overwhelming question,
To say: "I am Lazarus, come from the dead,
Come back to tell you all, I shall tell you all"—

He stops there, though he isn't finished with the poem. "Cherish this time," he says ruefully. "It doesn't come around again." He sits on the edge of his desk with a slightly exhausted air. "I love my wife. I adore my four children, but that doesn't mean I don't have regrets. That there aren't chances I should have taken, before those chances were lost."

I'm surprised by his candor, and his weariness. He can't be more than forty. I look back to the lines in front of me.

And indeed there will be time
To wonder, "Do I dare?" and, "Do I dare?"

For the third time today, I note the fluorescent green flyer on the classroom bulletin board. It seems to move toward me, though it's tacked down firmly: LONDON, STUDY ABROAD. SUMMER SEMESTER, 1993. DIVIDE YOUR TIME BETWEEN THE CLASSROOM AND LONDON'S MUSEUMS, THEATERS, CONCERT HALLS, AND HISTORICAL SITES. DAY TRIPS INCLUDING STONEHENGE, STRATFORD-ON-AVON, CANTERBURY,

OXFORD, AND BATH. I've been reading those four sentences, dreamy-eyed, every Monday, Wednesday, and Friday since the beginning of the term. When class discussions go stale, I envision myself in London: a sophisticated, cosmopolitan version of myself—one who wears beautifully tailored clothes and understands the cartoons in the *New Yorker.*

According to the flyer, the three-month course of study costs $2,550, which covers room, board, and tuition—but not travel, personal expenses, or excursions. In London, I would use words like "excursion." But my savings account balance is shamefully low, and I'm doubtful about asking my parents. Growing up, my family didn't travel, except for the week every summer we spent in the San Juan Islands—just a drive and a ferry ride away from home. Once, we went to Disneyland, and another time, Hawaii. We didn't have expensive cars, designer clothes, a boat, jet skis, or whatever other toys upper-middle-class suburban families generally collect. Evidently, I asked my mother one time if we were poor; other kids at my elementary school went to Hawaii every spring, took ski trips every winter.

It is still years before I'll realize my parents have money. They have a nice house and we've enjoyed a comfortable lifestyle, but my brother and I have both worked since it was legal for us to do so. We grew up knowing we'd always be expected to contribute to the household and to pay for at least half of our tuition and living expenses during college. I've never minded: I like having my own money, and, after I tithe 10 percent to the Lord, the freedom to spend it however I please.

I know there's little point in asking if my parents are interested in coughing up another three thousand dollars to send their only daughter to London for a summer. My dad has made no bones about planning to retire as early as possible and play golf every day for as long as he can walk upright. He's been climbing the corporate ladder—late to bed and early to rise—since he was twenty-three years old, and his funds have long been allocated. The point has been reinforced in ways I'm not likely to forget: My brother and I shared a 1975 Volvo station wagon in high school, bright orange—the polar opposite of the pristine BMWs, Audis, and Jettas that populated our high school's parking lot. We were given the car, with a caveat: If we fought over it, they'd sell it; if we crashed it, they'd junk it, and if we didn't qualify for "good student" insurance, we'd have our licenses revoked. My brother and I would pay for gas and expenses—with the exception of major repairs. But when the transmission broke and the Volvo stopped going in reverse, our parents advised us—with shrugs of amusement—to *push*. This is the story I've used to put the idea of London out of my head.

Today, however, I flip the page in my notebook and begin a letter to my parents—about London. About the necessity of going to London. I simply suddenly don't care if I sound ridiculous: "I want to walk the moors swimming in heather like Catherine and Heathcliff. I want to go to Westminster Abbey and talk to Browning and Keats and see Thomas Hardy and tell him we're related and that Tess is incredible and beautiful and tragic. I want to stand on the White Cliffs of Dover with the wind in my hair. I want to watch *Hamlet* in a real London theater and walk the streets next to people who say things like 'jolly chap' and 'pip pip.' I want to eat Yorkshire pudding. In *York!*"

What I don't tell my parents is that my interest in London is fueled by an ever-increasing sense of urgency: sometimes complete with heart palpitations, like those inspired by my professor just now. For the past two and a half years, every time I've gone to church in Seattle when home for Christmas or summer vacations, someone—or several people—will say, in regard to a road trip, or camping trip, or a late night out dancing, "You won't be able to do *that* after you get married."

Very soon, my life will be dictated entirely by the structures of church and family, my husband's job and school vacations. I am quickly approaching Time to Settle Down. I should be looking forward to meeting my eternal companion, and I do want that. I do. But the larger part of me knows I am nowhere near ready for the looming, impending TTSD. The term "settling down" implies prior upheaval—some *un*settling, some disorder, something beyond the entirely predictable life I've led up until now.

All I've done so far is chip away at life's prerequisites. I'm not a person who received a ride in a limo after high school graduation, a senior trip to Mexico, a skywritten "Congratulations!" in the midst of my commencement ceremony. High school graduation isn't an achievement, my dad says. It's the *least* important thing you'll do in life: the starting point. College, too, was a given in my family. So I haven't chosen much of anything, yet. I've been waiting for a release from the sit still and wait of childhood. The be good, pay attention, and listen of the past twenty years. Elementary school, junior high, high school, sacrament meeting, Sunday school, Young Women's, and seminary—a four-year, 6:00 AM scripture study program. And college, too—as much as I love it—is mostly about sitting, and listening.

I am ready for abandon, as much as there can be abandon within the parameters of my faith. I'm ready for daring, and dreaming—some heedless leap into life. I want to try things, go places, see things before the onset of strollers and diaper bags and feedings and changings and car seats, before the making of lunches and the daily doing of laundry and dishes. I'm only twenty; I'll get to those things. *Indeed, there will be time.* I just can't imagine settling into family life without ever having lived alone. I need a time when my life is decided only by my whims, my work schedule, and the money I've saved. And I can't imagine having never traveled. I'm not talking family reunions and Disney cruises; I'm talking *pyramids*, the Eiffel Tower, the northern lights, Santorini. As yet, the only truly foreign place I've been is Seoul, Korea, where I spent ten days traveling with my family at the end of my brother's two-year religious mission.

Immediately after my British literature class, I drop the letter to my parents in the mail and take a detour into the administrative offices for BYU's study abroad program. I pick up a glossy information packet on the BYU London Centre, which is automatically glamorous because "centre" is spelled with the *e* on the outside of the *r*. And its architecture! Two adjoining Victorian townhouses among a continuous line of Victorian townhouses lining the swank Bayswater Road. I rush home to draft my admissions essay, which begins: "I need to do *something* before it's too late to do *anything*."

Three weeks later, my heart thrills when I find, in the shuffle of bills, pizza coupons, and have-you-seen-me's on the kitchen table, my acceptance letter for the London program. My joy is raised to the power of exultation the following week, when an envelope arrives from home—including a check for $2,550 made out to the Brigham Young University Study Abroad Program. Enclosed is a note, in regard to my upcoming finals. "To My Favorite Daughter: Excel or die. Love, Dad."

When my plane lands at Gatwick, I set myself to the task of navigating the airport and money exchange and the tube and the neighborhood map, all of which make me sweaty, anxious, and hours later triumphant. I arrive on the doorstep of the London Centre miraculously still in possession of my oversize duffel bag, passport, credit card, and cash, which I have folded into tiny squares and stashed into different pockets, my bra, and my panties in case of subway robbery.

I collapse onto a sofa in the living room, which is decked out in brocade and gilt and wainscoting. In a more elegant era the room would have been called a *parlor*. I make weary small talk and size up my classmates, who trickle in over the next hour. I'll admit to an irrational swell of pride that I made the journey without once bursting into tears: an accomplishment, based on the dramatic entrances of the other girls.

Our orientation tour starts on the main floor of the Centre, in the dining room adjacent to the parlor, where all of us will eat twice a day over the following months. Beets and gherkins will be the accoutrements to every meal prepared by Fred and Mildred, the London natives who live on the ground floor. They cook and clean and offer tours of the city in Fred's hilariously tiny Mini—just like the one in the chase scene of *Oxford Blues*, wherein Rob Lowe wedges his '56 Thunderbird between the stone walls of a gothic-looking alley. Fred and Mildred promise to teach us practicalities, and slang: the vacuum is a hoover, the trunk is a boot, the hood is a bonnet, and the TV is a telly. Say "bum bag" rather than "fanny pack," they advise. Fanny is not a *nice* word, in England.

The third floor of the London Centre houses two classrooms as well as apartments for our instructors and their families. The girls' rooms are on the fourth floor, the boys' on the fifth. There are three times as many girls as boys, as I expected. I'm not surprised to find the boys too short, and not particularly attractive. But I am disappointed at having to immediately dismiss the idea of a European romance. Until I remind myself that I haven't been to church yet—where there could be any number of charming blokes lining up to give me private walking tours of the city—at dusk, where a lone violinist might serenade us from the shadow of a hundred-year-old, wrought iron streetlamp. I imagine my date pulling me into an alley for a passionate, knee-buckling kiss before rushing through the rain to hail one of London's quintessential black cabs. Which would take us home to our separate houses, obviously—but that detail is decidedly irrelevant to my fantasy.

My female flatmates take great pains with the bulletin boards installed beside our bunk beds. They cut colored paper into creative shapes, and talk about the scrapbooks they can't wait to make, upon their return to the States. They post pictures of their boyfriends, and Jesus, and earnest quotations falsely attributed to him, in the manner

of: "I never said it would be easy; I only said it would be worth it."
My bulletin board remains conspicuously blank. Because who cares
about colored paper and *pinking shears* when any day of the week I
can walk down the street, pick up a copy of *Time Out*, and use my
student ID for day-of tickets to the Royal Shakespeare Theatre or the
Barbican or the Globe, when I can be amazed by the plays themselves
and the amount of slobber flying across the stages of London's finest
theaters—not to mention the force with which it flies.

Our first Sunday in London, all of us—students and staff—dress in
our Sunday best and walk down Oxford Street toward the Marble
Arch. We'll cut through Hyde Park to attend the church that includes
the Centre in its boundaries. We'll attend the same ward, at the same
chapel, at the same time each week, and we'll be taught the same lessons, from the same manuals, as every other Mormon worldwide.

My new friend Stephanie has just told me she's here to preserve
her virginity as much as to experience London. She and her fiancé,
Taylor, thought distance might help them remain worthy of their
temple marriage, which will happen a week after she gets home.

"*Any* reason is a good reason to be in London," I say. And, doing
my impression of the stereotypical church lady, I'm wide-eyed, slow-
talking, and embarrassingly earnest. "Your virtue is the most precious of jewels." I nod and squeeze her arm.

Stephanie laughs. "Especially around here," she says, glancing at a
group of middle-aged men dressed elegantly in robes and turbans.
"I've heard there are Muslim men who will pay twenty thousand dollars for a virgin."

"Probably an urban legend. But is it twenty thousand dollars or
twenty thousand pounds? Seems like the exchange rate would help
inform that decision. And would you have to get married? Do they
want virgin *brides*, or virgins for a night?"

"The rumors are unspecific," she says. "Why, are you thinking about it?"

"I might, if he looked like a young Omar Sharif. I could repent while traveling around Europe for a year with my twenty thousand dollars. God might understand."

Stephanie laughs again. "Is Omar Sharif even Muslim?"

"No idea."

"Whoa." Stephanie points to a noisy throng up ahead. "What's going on?"

"Oh, hey," I say, excited. "It's Speakers' Corner!"

As we walk closer, it comes into focus—people standing on crates talking into megaphones, people wearing sandwich boards, shouting at whomever will listen. People squaring off a few yards from each other, debating, for the delight of their audiences. Most are tourists, there to snap pictures with disposable cameras. Others join in. Some heckle.

The news stories running in a loop on CNN are conspicuously absent from the discourse here: no one seems to care about Clinton's election, David Koresh and the Waco siege, the Menendez brothers, the Rodney King trial, the newly instated "don't ask don't tell" policy, or the Chicago Bulls' history-making three-peat. Rather, we're assailed by more global concerns. Voices assault us from all sides, shouting about the assassination of the president of Sri Lanka, the European unity pact, the UN troops killed in Somalia. Voices are raised in support of, and against, UN weapons monitoring in Iraq, Europe's Maastricht Treaty, and the imminent arrival of the apocalypse. All I can think is the last time I had a grip on issues like this was in eleventh grade, during Ms. Mukai's world hot spots class.

"The time to repent is *now!*" a man screams at Stephanie and me, with an ominous look. He's waving a sign smeared with red, drippy lettering: THE BLOOD OF CHRIST! it says, and in response, we wave and smile politely.

Once past Speakers' Corner, the park opens into a lush, green expanse, divided by the Serpentine. There are beds of bright flowers everywhere, footpaths, fountains, and couples in love—holding hands, laughing, leaning into each other. Next to me, Stephanie sighs heavily; she's missing Taylor, as usual.

Earlier in the week she asked me to take a picture of her next to a couture wedding dress in the window of a posh boutique, though she'd never be able to afford the dress—or wear it, given the restrictions of temple garments. For women, garments look sort of like white, cap-sleeve, scoop-neck T-shirts and midthigh Spanx. For men, picture boxer briefs and a T-shirt. Mormons generally begin wearing temple garments when they go on missions, or when they get married in the temple. Garments are meant to be a physical reminder of spiritual covenants, and should be covered by clothes. People don't wear them when working out, or fooling around with their spouses, but the exceptions don't extend to strapless wedding gowns. Still, of all the sights we saw that day, the dress was what moved Stephanie.

As much as I'd like to be in love, I feel glad not to be in her position: torn between where she is and where she'd rather be. This is the pull I always feel: on one hand, the wanting of love, the craving for it some days. And on the other hand, the knowledge of what love might mean. The past year has been a blur of bridal showers, each a carbon copy of the one before: girls and women gathered in a circle to watch the bride-to-be open boxes of beautifully wrapped china, small kitchen appliances, heart-shaped Le Creuset cookware, kitchen towels, and, inevitably, a bouquet of cleaning supplies: a bright-colored bucket as the "vase," upturned toilet brushes and kitchen-sink scrubbies as "flowers." Rather than envy, anticipation, or joy, what I feel when I look at the bride is a shortness of breath. I hear the echo of doors closing, as if every one of her life's decisions has just been made.

It's quiet in the flat when we return from church, even though everyone is home. Most people are napping, reading, or writing letters home. Even in London, Mormons keep the Sabbath Day holy, so there's no shopping today. There are no plays, no restaurants, and for some, no studying—depending on how they define the spirit of the law. It's during these quiet times that the Sunday blues often set in: I'm relieved to have claimed my favorite window seat, escaped the other girls, many of whom are homesick, or boyfriend-sick. One of my roommates literally, unironically, kissed the photograph of her boyfriend, a missionary who won't be home for another year. It brought to mind the way I used to practice making out with my Wham! poster when I was twelve and blissfully unaware of George Michael's preference for men, and public bathrooms.

Outside, it's too cloudy to see much of the park, but in London, even the *rooftops* are picturesque. I write:

Dear Mom and Dad:

Today was the first week of church in London. It was exactly the same as church at home—it's nice to be able to count on that. Except everything seemed fancier because of the British accents. The ward here is more international than any I've ever attended; there are members from India, and Africa, and the Caribbean. One of the men who spoke in sacrament meeting is from the Ivory Coast, here for a year on a research fellowship. I'm not even sure I've heard of the Ivory Coast; for sure I couldn't find it on a map. The bishop is British and his wife is French: he's white; she's black. They have four biracial kids who are spectacularly gorgeous. Part of me couldn't help but wonder if that kind of marriage would be a scandal in a ward back home. I assume it wouldn't be; but I can't help but wonder why there aren't couples like them at church anywhere else I've lived—is it culture, or economics; geography, or politics?

Next week we're taking a car trip to the Lake District

because my new friend Lisa wants to take a picture of a house where one of her ancestors lived. I've been promised mazes of hedges, gardens, and estates straight out of *Pride and Prejudice*; so I can't wait. Also, over the next two weeks we're going to Stratford-on-Avon, Oxford, Cambridge, Sherwood Forest, and Haworth—where the Brontë sisters lived. My plan is to pray *for weather* and walk the moors through a blustery wind shouting, "Heathcliff!" with a hand thrown across my forehead.

Next month it's Edinborough, and the castle where Mary, Queen of Scots lived; and Grasmere, where William and Dorothy Wordsworth lived, and Keats's house (wherever that is?); I am excited to see if it's true, what I once saw in a drawing—that Keats and I have the same nose. Exactly the same. Exclamation point.

In summary: the food is bad and the men are short, but I know already this trip will change my life.

Love, Nicole

I put my letter aside, and take out my journal. Because while everything I've written to my parents is true, there is a secret I don't want to tell. I open to a quotation I copied from a novel assigned last week for class: *Letters to Alice on First Reading Jane Austen*. I read the quotation again, though I'm sure I have it memorized, by now. "The inner excitement, when a writer realizes that this whole world of invention and meaning lies waiting to be explored . . . is like falling in love. The feeling of being singled out, of suddenly discovering that you are different from other people, and in some way special, is powerful."

I feel a rush of affirmation, reading those sentences. Because what I feel for books is more crucial and lasting than anything I've felt for a boyfriend. Because, more than anything, I've always wanted to write. In one of my earliest memories, I am sitting with my mother in her bed. We're both in our pajamas, watching *Happy Days*. I remember

the white covers, the creamy wool blanket in stark contrast to my
mother's crimson fingernails. She is catching up on her correspon-
dence. I know my alphabet, but not how to read or write. Still, I insist
that I be allowed to write a letter, too. My mother plays along. She
asks me what I want to say, and copies my sentences in large, exacting
print. When I'm finished dictating, she hands me a pen and a blank
sheet of paper. I copy every word, being sure to leave spaces where she
has left spaces. I work painstakingly, and proudly lick the envelope
when I am done. I don't remember what the letter said, or whom it
was for. The act of writing is what mattered: my thoughts made of
letters, sentences, and punctuation drawn onto thick blue stationery,
folded into a matching envelope, sealed with good-tasting glue.

But how can I say out loud that I indulge in fantasies of walking
into a bookstore and seeing my name printed on the spine of a novel,
of opening a slim volume of poems and seeing my words arranged
deliberately on the page? Because every time I imagine myself as a
writer, I hear the voice of our prophet in my head: *We earnestly pray
that our single sisters will desire honorable marriage in the temple to a
worthy man and rear a righteous family, even though this may mean the
sacrificing of degrees and careers. Our priorities are right when we realize
there is no higher calling than to be an honorable wife and mother.*

For Mormons, marriage is not just a commandment; it's a sacred
ordinance, required to reach the highest level of exaltation. Once married, a woman shouldn't work unless she must. Families should forgo
luxuries, should be careful about what is considered a necessity—
because what could be more important than a woman's presence in the
home? I've been taught that "there is no role in life more essential and
more eternal than that of motherhood." I don't have resistance to that
idea; I've just not *felt* it, yet. So when I picture myself sitting alone in a
silent room for hours at a time, lost in a paragraph, consumed by a chap-
ter, that vision works against what I've been told is my divine nature—
with what work I've been taught is most important in the world.

Writing feels like an indulgent dream, something I should grow out of. Like at age ten, when I pictured myself a Rockette at Radio City Music Hall, high kicking in sequined sparkle panties. I soon realized the folly of that fantasy: in real life, I can hardly touch my toes. And in real life, as well, the words of the late prophet David O. McKay are carved into the walls of the Salt Lake Temple: "No other success can compensate for failure in the home." I'm sure there are women who do both—raise families *and* write books. Who are not failures on either front. There's nothing that prevents me, necessarily, from writing. Mormon women are encouraged to be intellectually and physically engaged in the world—as long as those pursuits don't interfere with our divinely appointed role of mother. I suspect my problem is *me*. I've always felt drawn to a writing life, and never to motherhood.

And also, if writing were a valid choice for those of us who want a Mormon life, wouldn't a writing program exist at BYU—a Mormon university of more than thirty-one thousand students? If it were possible for me to have both, wouldn't I know other women, personally, who have done it? Who *are* doing it? And what if I allowed myself to pursue writing, and then felt compelled to give it my undivided attention? I can't assume the risk—especially because I came from a traditional Mormon family, and can speak wholeheartedly to the success of that model.

My mother made dinner every night, kept a beautiful house, and made sure my brother and I got our homework finished and went to bed on time. She was a faithful confidante, and provided unwavering emotional support during the years I was bullied by Rodney Fontaine—and later, that coven of razor-clawed fifth-grade girls. I have my mother to thank, in large part, for my inherent sense of worth, my confidence, my feisty sense of humor. I've never respected her less because she didn't work outside the home. I've never thought she was less smart, less capable, or less a partner in her marriage. My mother wears *pants*; there was no such thing, in our house, as "wait until your father gets home."

Besides, even if I did come home and announce that I wanted to transfer schools and study creative writing, my parents would not be able to stop themselves from expounding, for the five millionth time, on Uncle Steve's epically useless *geography* major. Teaching, on the other hand, is a noble profession, and practical. The perfect job for a woman with a family, if she ends up needing to work.

I close my journal, and start in on another letter—to Alicia, my best friend since junior high, who's studying cello at Northwestern. We keep in touch via letters that are mostly a string of stories and jokes. I tell her how one of the girls here ate so many beets her pee turned red and she went hysterical, convinced she had kidney failure. And how last week, some drunken idiot crawled in one of our windows at 4:00 AM, thinking he was at his girlfriend's house. Chad the TA bolted from his room, shrieking like a preteen girl—wearing nothing but his temple garments and a backward bathrobe.

Nighttime at the London Centre has a slumber-party feel. Sixteen of us girls share a room with eight bunk beds—so before and after lights out, it's girl-talk central. Stephanie's just revealed that her fiancé is nine years older than she is—and divorced. Divorce is allowed when you're Mormon, but it's still fairly uncommon. Particularly at our age.

"I could never marry someone who'd slept with another woman," says Ashley, from her top bunk. She leans down to look at Stephanie. "Aren't you worried he'll always be comparing you?"

Beth chimes in, having just returned from the bathroom down the hall. "Yeah, don't you think it would be more special and romantic if it was *both* of your first times?"

These two girls—every day they're either crying because they're homesick, or they're complaining that we have to read books. *Another book*, one of them will groan, looking at the syllabus. And the other will respond, "Right?! I mean, come *on*."

Stephanie rolls her eyes. "No, I don't think my relationship with my husband will mean less because he was married before. I doubt he'll spend any time wishing he were having sex with someone who made him miserable for six years."

I pipe in. "And what could be more amazing than to be *seduced*. As a rule, we don't get to have that." Seduction is at the top of my list of PG-13 fantasies: I'd consider moving some of them up to an R rating were I more aware of what there is to imagine. Besides, there isn't much point to fantasizing in that way, as the things that accompany said fantasies are strictly forbidden. "I mean there's probably something to be said for *someone* knowing what they're doing."

Stephanie laughs, and Ashley gasps in horror. "I'd hate it if he knew what he was doing! I'd be wondering who he learned with, and was she better. I don't want my husband to have ever seen another woman naked!"

"I'm sort of looking forward to the awkward fumbling," says Lisa. She's nineteen, an adorably goofy tomboy still waiting for her first kiss. "I think it'll be sweet."

Beth says, "Well, I'm just glad I'm not you, Stephanie; I don't know if I could be that brave."

"Oh, *geez*." I flop on my back in exasperation. "How is it *brave* to marry the man you love? If he wanted to be with his ex, he'd be with his ex."

"Oh, you know what I mean!" she snaps, and turns out the light.

I roll over and close my eyes to say my silent nightly prayer. I pray for patience with horrible girls like Ashley and Beth, who truly believe and even say out loud that their education is "just in case." I pray that they will become so tortured by required reading that they'll go home early. That, or be struck down with raging, debilitating cases of laryngitis.

And I pray, like I do most nights, that I will find love someday soon. That I'll find a relationship that opens life up for me, that I'll find a way to be a Mormon wife and still feel like myself. That I'll be intellectually challenged, have an adventurous, spontaneous life without thwarting what's been preordained for me.

When I was sixteen, I received a blessing from a patriarch—a Melchizedek priesthood bearer, called and ordained under the direction of the Quorum of the Twelve Apostles. My patriarchal blessing, recorded and transcribed, is a sacred, personal revelation—a guide for my life. And the blessings it promises depend on my spiritual worthiness. Mine says I will marry in the temple. I will have several spirits brought to my home. My children will look to me for wisdom, strength, and guidance—an idea further enforced when I was seventeen. That year, my mother had a vivid dream. The dream was so real, she told me, so fraught with import that it had to be a premonition. In it, there was a boy, nine or ten, standing next to me. He was my son, dark haired and handsome—willful, she could tell, by his determined, narrow shoulders. In the dream, there was also a towheaded boy, years younger than his brother. He was the mischief-maker, the love, peeking from behind my leg. I held a baby in my arms, and I was happy. A spirit child hovered above my head, waiting.

This is my future. My revealed path, I tell Stephanie on our way to the Tate Modern during our last week in London. She's getting married in ten days. Her blessing mentions kids, too, she says. But she's planning to wait two years. She wants to finish school first.

"Do you ever wish you'd met Taylor a year or two later?" I ask. "Won't it be strange to go straight from parents to college to husband?"

"No," she says. "I wish I met him sooner. Why prolong the torture of dating? Why prolong *virginity?* I love him," she shrugs. "I want to be with him forever, starting now. Starting yesterday. Two years ago."

"Okay," I say, laughing, as we enter the museum. "I get it."

"I didn't picture myself marrying at twenty," she whispers, as we join a group gathering around a blue-blazered docent. "Who does?"

Our conversation tapers off as the group begins its tour of the paintings. We don't get far, however, before Stephanie and the rest of the group abandon me. I'm left standing, mesmerized in front of a large oil painting. I can't disconnect from the woman on the canvas: a haunted beauty sitting in a small wooden boat, floating down a dark, slow-moving river

I am captivated: by her delicate face and the yearning implied in the tilt of her neck, the reach of her body pressing forward. In one hand she holds a small, rust-colored chain. The other lies gracefully in her lap, palm up—as if to offer, or receive. I ache when I look at her, though even the ache she inspires is beautiful.

The title reveals a woman, and a story, I already know. *The Lady of Shalott.* She lived in a tower on an island outside Camelot, and was cursed—forbidden to leave or look out the window. She spent her days weaving scenes from the world outside, as reflected through a mirror. And through the mirror, through the window, she fell in love with Sir Lancelot.

Half-sick of shadows, one day she fled from the tower. She found a boat on the riverbank, and sang as she floated toward Camelot. Lancelot recognized her voice, but thought it belonged to a fairy. He didn't know who she was, that she was real, or that she'd die because she loved him.

I consider her body on the canvas: weighed down, yet weightless—as if caught in the moment when the spirit takes leave of the body. She is exquisite in the act of dying. I can't read her expression. There is a question, an imperative, repeating refrain in my mind. Her mouth is partly open, as if she might turn and speak. As if she could tell me whether it is love, or fear in her eyes. Whether she is singing, or fighting to breathe.

On the flight home from London, I'm wearing red lipstick and a black beret. The male gate agent smiled archly as he handed me my boarding pass. I thought he was just being friendly, until I looked at my seat assignment. He'd upgraded me to first class, and I, after turning down the champagne and accepting, instead, a glass of orange juice, a blanket, a delicious meal, an individual movie player, and midflight steaming hot towel, am preoccupied with thoughts of home, school, friends, and studies. Am I different now, in ways more substantial than lipstick?

I am picturing the reunions I'll have with my roommates, and how we'll decorate our new apartment. I'll hang my print of *The Lady of Shalott* in my bedroom; keep her to myself. She's the one tangible thing—besides a cache of ticket stubs, playbills, and pictures—I've brought home to remind me of these months abroad. I recline my seat as far as it will go, and close my eyes. I picture waking up to her enigmatic face, illuminated by the streetlamp above my window, her eyes, and the question I feel behind them.

Chapter 3

O thou afflicted, tossed with tempest, and not comforted,
behold, I will lay thy stones with fair colours, and lay thy
foundations with sapphires.

—ISAIAH 54:11

———◆———

The summer of 1995 will turn out to be the longest, hottest summer in Chicago's history, if you believe the anchors on the six o'clock news. Already, refrigerator cars sit stacked outside the city's morgues waiting for their next rash of elderly victims, while on a sweltering patch of sidewalk outside Wrigley Field, I'm wearing long navy pants, a baseball cap, and a Cubs jersey the size of John Candy's pajamas.

I—along with dozens of other aisle vendors, all but two of whom are male—am standing in line, waiting for today's assignments. We're dripping with sweat, fatigued before we even begin to ply the twenty-five thousand fans inside with overpriced concessions. My only thought, as I inch toward the window at the front of the line, comes in the form of a prayer. *Let it be peanuts. Please, God: peanuts.* So light, and such a part of ballpark culture they're practically patriotic. Not to mention that at $2.25 a bag, I'll end up with seventy-five cents in my pocket nearly every sale. Because who wants to be the guy insisting I pass three quarters hand over hand twenty people deep in a row?

Vince—the GM of concessions—waits for us at the front of the line. He sits on a stool in an air-conditioned office inside the ballpark, assigning concessions based on a system of numbers none of us understands. A plate of glass, starting about chest-high, is all that separates us from him, though it represents a forty-degree differential in temperature.

When I finally reach the window, I have to clear my throat before asking about working White Sox games as well as Cubs. Theoretically, the union card in my pocket allows me to work any sporting event in the city, and I could use the extra money. But in the three weeks I've worked here, I've never seen *anyone* talk to Vince. I don't know if it's a real rule or an unspoken rule about the not talking.

"Come again?" Vince barks into the round metal vent that carries our voices. As usual, he's looking stereotypically Mafioso: dark glasses, a pinky ring, slicked-back hair, and a shiny shirt the color of cantaloupe. It would be hard for me to take Vince seriously if he didn't scare the crap out of me. Our heads are inches apart, on opposite sides of the glass. I'm nervous, repeating my question, hoping he isn't the type to *take the cannoli.*

"You wanna go to *Comiskey?*" He shakes his head. And in a move that takes me entirely by surprise, he reaches through the cutout in the bottom of the window to pat my hand. "Sweet kid like you? Nah, can't let you do it." Vince points a meaty finger at me. "You're a good girl. Remind me of my niece, you want the truth. South Side ain't a place for a peach like you." He slides my paperwork through the trough in the windowsill and motions for the guy behind me to step up. End of conversation.

I look down at my assignment, hoping for peanuts, or this summer's smash hit, Lemon Chill, which sells fast and is only half as heavy as Pepsi, which must be lugged in a backbreaking metal tray designed to hold two dozen twenty-ounce cups. Most dreaded of all, however, are chocolate malts, which is what I get today—the curse of the rookie employee.

Out of Vince's earshot, I groan and head into the concrete catacombs at the stadium's interior—to a cell-like room where the supervisor, a woman who can only be described as a battle-ax, hands me a blue soft-side cooler, packed full. She tells me to haul my sweet ass straight to the kids in the cheap seats, where I will sweat like Rocky Balboa in the fifteenth round, and make zero dollars in tips.

"Sell 'em before they melt!" she yells after me. But I've already learned to move faster than the three other guys selling the same thing I've got. Her voice is a constant bark in my head: "Sell, sell, sell!" and "Face your money! Turn your hat forward!" She doesn't give a *shit* if the bill obscures my peripheral vision, if I can't see the stairs.

This job would be pure torture if not for the fact that it's *baseball*. It's not that I care about the sport itself—or any sport for that matter—but I'm a sucker for the voice of James Earl Jones, which is what I hear over the sound of the organ playing "Charge!" His soliloquy from *Field of Dreams* runs in my head, punctuated by the sharp crack of a bat: "The one constant through all the years, Ray, has been baseball. America has rolled by like an army of steamrollers. It's been erased like a blackboard, rebuilt, and erased again. But baseball has marked the time. This field, this game, is part of our past, Ray."

So I climb and I shout and I shout and I climb, in rhythm with manic chants of "So-SA! So-SA!" taking part in this collective American experience. I brave an Everest of bleacher stairs—nine innings without a break—determined to fend off the heatstroke threatening to fell me before the bottom of the sixth. I'm on a mission to appease whatever die-hard Cubs fan needs one more bag of peanuts, one more hot dog, to propel him through another home run in yet another losing game.

I came to Chicago on a whim. Alicia called a month ago—just before finishing her master of strings performance—to tell me she'd landed a summer job house-sitting in a creepy, gothic Victorian where she was afraid to sleep alone. She asked me to come visit. Just for the summer she said, and I hesitated for only a second—until I realized there was no one I needed to ask. I'd just finished my student teaching in American Fork, and there were only a few weeks before commencement. By the time I boarded the plane to Chicago O'Hare, I'd have my college degree in hand—meaning I'd have met my life's minimum requirements. From there, I could do *anything*; I could live *anywhere*.

Coming to Chicago, working at the ballpark: these are the first decisions I've made that didn't require the advice, permission, or financial support of anyone else. I've been waiting for this moment—for independence—as long as I can remember. As far back as age two, according to my mother, I had a habit of breaking out of the house during nap time, running down the sidewalk buck naked, shouting, "Yippee!" Some neighbor would inevitably ring the doorbell and hand me and my clothes back over. My first—and only—full sentence was, "I can do it myself."

"Strong willed" is the nice way of describing me as a child. When made to do anything I found unfair or unfounded—at ages two through four—my response was blinding, teeth-grinding rage. The tantrums were so intense I'd bloody my elbows and knees, beating them on the sidewalk. My mother, in tears, described me to the pediatrician as *deranged*. He asked her to bring me in for an exam, after which he made the tactical error of telling me to get dressed. The ensuing tantrum was so epic that two nurses and an injected sedative were required to get me into my clothes. Before that sedative took its full effect, however, my mother will swear under oath that I managed a Houdini-like escape from my car seat and attempted to leap from our station wagon while it was speeding down I-880. Eventually, my independent spirit required an intervention by a child psychologist and a sacred tome entitled *Dare to Discipline*, which taught my parents how to teach me to rein it in. A necessity, when one takes into account the expectations of a Mormon life.

I knew when I accepted Alicia's invitation that Illinois wasn't far or particularly exotic. But I'd never been, and it sounded like fun. An adventure. Something spontaneous, for once. And since arriving, I have encountered a series of unexpected turns. On the days I'm not at the ballpark, I work next to Alicia in the windowless basement of Manufacturers' News—a company that publishes an annual nationwide directory of manufacturing companies—stuffing envelopes for minimum wage. Alicia, with her master's degree from Northwestern, and I, with my secondary teaching certification, sit at a long table in a stuffy, dusty, linoleum-tiled room for eight hours at a stretch. The mechanical movements of our bodies simulate the drone of fluorescent bulbs and the white noise of the prehistoric folding machine that bends each "renew your ad" letter into a crisp, perfect trifold.

The job is so awful it's *almost* funny. But despite its depressive, soul-sucking lack of air and energy, I feel like I need to be here. Because standing in the kitchen over a bowl of Raisin Bran a few days after my arrival, I asked Alicia what could have possibly possessed her to take the worst, most depressing job within a twenty-mile radius.

Her shoulders slumped; she sighed heavily. "I don't want to have to talk to anyone." And for the first time since I'd arrived, I really looked at her: my vivacious friend—blue-eyed, brunette, quick to laugh at anything. How had I not noticed her listless body language, her blank-looking eyes?

"Have you heard from Dan?" I asked, referring to the live-in boyfriend of four years, a painter who was away at an artist's colony for the summer. His absence had prompted my arrival; she didn't want to be alone in a place so grim we were already referring to it as Frankenstein's house.

"He called last night," she said, putting her bowl in the sink. And then, after a pause, "He thinks he might be gay." This admission came as no surprise to me. Dan's the kind of guy you don't believe is straight even when he's been dating your best friend for four years. "He said he's not sure he loves me." Alicia's voice dropped nearly to a whisper. "When I asked if I needed an AIDS test, there was *silence* before he said no, of course not."

I didn't say anything. I was too busy searching for the *right* thing. I know she's uncomfortable talking about her relationship with me. She's been skipping over any part of her life that involves sex—to protect my Mormon sensibilities—since she lost her virginity in high school to a guy I couldn't stand, for good reason, it turns out. He pressured her into sex after they'd been together for a year, after he promised he loved her and wanted to be with her forever. Less than a month later, he dumped her for a cheerleader rumored to be easy.

The night of that terrible breakup, I was playing my saxophone in the pep band at a basketball game. Halfway through "The Lion Sleeps Tonight" I had a sinking feeling. I knew something was wrong and walked out in the middle of the first quarter, knowing I'd hear about it the next day from our band teacher, who was prone to fits of rage regarding *participation points*. I drove straight to Alicia's house and found her dangling her feet in her backyard hot tub, devastated. Inconsolable. She kept saying how foolish she felt. How taken. She kept repeating, through tears, "I'm ruined. Who's going to want me now?"

I couldn't believe her virginity meant that much to her—meant that much to *anyone* who wasn't religious. But more than anything, I was shocked to hear her connect virginity to her sense of worth. The idea of *ruin* felt wrong. Untrue. Impossible. I said a silent prayer, asking God to help me comfort my friend, who felt destroyed by this horrible, selfish boy. And guiltily, I also thanked God that I would never have to feel the way she felt then.

I've never been great at flirting, dating, guys. Alicia, on the other hand, has had one boyfriend after another since she and I met in seventh grade. Her relationships, since we were freshmen in high school, have lasted years. So it's no mystery why she shares so little about her and Dan. I'm sure she thinks I won't understand what she's going through—and also, that I'll judge her by my Mormon standards.

Believe me, I tell her, if I weren't LDS, I wouldn't still be a virgin at twenty-four. At least I wouldn't *want* to be. I wouldn't be tortured, either, lying awake nights, sweating in the second-floor bedroom of Frankenstein's house, dreaming of a young Paul Newman. Picturing him pushing me up against a wall in Big Daddy's store. It's sometimes all I can do to keep from moving my hand toward my own body—committing the sin of masturbation, for the first time ever. The urgency and intensity of my desire is increasing steadily, and honestly it's come as a surprise. I've been told my whole life not to *let him*, and bought in to the myth that such desire is singular to boys and men. So I guess both Alicia and I have things we'd rather not talk about.

But as her best friend, it's my job to take care of her. So when she stacked her cereal bowl in the dishwasher, put the box of Raisin Bran back in the cupboard, and pointedly changed the subject from Dan and AIDS tests back to Manufacturers' News, I didn't push it.

"I could get you a job there," she said, getting animated. "Come on. We could hang out together. It's not so bad."

"Sign me up," I told her, thinking I could use our envelope-stuffing time to help her sort out her next move, support her through what I hoped would be her imminent breakup.

Alicia and I live close enough to work to drive home for lunch, but I usually end up eating alone, while Alicia's upstairs on the phone with Dan. Today, she sits down heavily when she emerges from her room.

"What?" I ask.

"I don't know," she says, sounding exhausted. Upset, though dry-eyed. "I don't know if I love him either. Or what to do now."

"Well you can't *stay* with him," I say, my fork suspended in mid-air. I know I'm being bossy, but I can't help it. It's been *weeks* since the "I might be gay I don't know if I love you" conversation, and I can't believe she hasn't already started packing. Or sent *his* stuff back to his mom in Ohio. I'd have done it for her had she asked, or even hinted.

"I just want what *you* have," Alicia admits, picking a crouton from the salad I made for her. "You've always been so happy," she says miserably.

I instantly feel a surge of nervousness. This is my first "missionary opportunity"; I'm supposed to proclaim the Gospel in situations like these. So I take a deep breath, and dive in. "It's the church." I shrug, feigning nonchalance.

Though its members may be flawed, the Gospel allowed me to grow up knowing my family of four is united under God. We are our own country, indivisible. And by living the way I've been taught to live, I've felt loved, purposeful, and connected to what is divine. When I pray, I tell Alicia, I feel a quiet thrumming in my body—a sense of being understood in a way that is complete. Like water flowing, impossibly, in the shape of a circle.

I know that what I feel defies logic. I also know it's real. In the same way it's impossible to talk someone into believing in God, I could never be talked *out* of believing. I know there is insight to be found in the words of scripture. I know that when I go there for answers, I feel more than the human impulse to make meaning. I am guided to certain words, certain verses. I've felt inspiration rushing through me as visceral as rain.

"I've always felt like something's missing," Alicia says. "Like, what's the *point*?"

I'm surprised to hear Alicia say she's looking for a spiritual life. She's come to church with my family to play her cello at sacrament meetings; she's been at my house for a hundred meals at which she's bowed her head while my mom, my dad, my brother, or I said a prayer. She came to church dances when we were in high school, and joined me for service projects. But she's never once asked about my religion. And I'm not one to push—to set down my bowl of Chef Boyardee ravioli during the episode of *Days of Our Lives* we'd skipped sixth period to watch, in order to prophesy about my Lord and Savior Jesus Christ. But here is my friend, asking. Wanting what I've been given, and commanded to share.

"If you're serious," I say, my heart pounding, "I can call the missionaries. They'll ask you to be baptized on the second visit. You don't have to say yes. If you want to learn about the church, it's easy to arrange." In this moment, I feel like one of my divine purposes is being fulfilled.

In the Mormon Church, *every* member is asked to be a missionary. I chose not to serve an official mission. I thought if God wanted me to renounce life as I knew it at age twenty-one and dedicate eighteen months to teaching his Gospel, I'd have a spiritual confirmation of that plan. An impression, a prompting, a whisper of a still small voice. I didn't. Perhaps because this is my mission. Maybe this is how I will do God's work. Maybe my coming here was part of a greater design: the appointed time for me to share with Alicia what I never knew she's always wanted.

If she were baptized, Alicia could create a life like mine if that's what she wants. A family wherein no one drinks, no one cheats, no one lies, and no one leaves. Looking across the table at her, I think of my father, who didn't grow up Mormon. He was baptized when he was in high school. I think of the ways his baptism changed his life.

It removed him from the alcoholic dynamics that governed his family. But more than that, because of his spiritual conversion, he learned to be a husband and father. He learned forgiveness, and trust. He learned to let himself be guided by spirit as much as ambition or denial—and to let go of the anger that trailed him like a ghost from his childhood home.

My dad was in his teens when his parents divorced. And almost immediately after his father left to marry the mistress, his mother's drinking escalated from the 1950s glamour of cocktails in the afternoon to uncontested daily binges. My dad says he'd come home from school most days to find her passed out on the couch. He started spending time with a Mormon family in the neighborhood, whose last name was also Hardy. He ate there, and played basketball on their church league. He still laughs about how they'd trick neighbor kids into putting whole eggs in their mouths—*betcha can't do it*. He describes their short-lived moments of triumph before the quick slap to the underside of their chins, the explosive burst of yolk and white.

The daughter of this surrogate Hardy family was a beautiful girl who invited my dad to learn about the Church of Jesus Christ of Latter-day Saints, as is probably to be expected, given that missionary work is one of the three stated missions of the church. But when I asked my dad about his decision to be baptized, he said, "I'm not a stupid man. I didn't fall for some 'flirt to convert' operation. I'd never have done it if I hadn't felt something real—a confirmation of spiritual truth. Are you kidding? I was a completely unsupervised teenage boy. You think I'd have made that kind of commitment if I didn't truly believe?"

After lunch, on our drive back to work, I'm still thinking about my dad—and my conversation with Alicia. She could have an experience similar to his. Whatever emptiness she's been feeling, for who knows how long, could be filled by the knowledge that she is known and beloved of God. She could give her future children every good thing my family gave me. I feel blessed to have something to offer: hope, possibly faith, maybe the path to a large and lasting happiness.

I'd hoped there would be sister missionaries in Evanston—so Alicia and I could avoid the strangeness inherent in receiving lessons on the prophet Joseph Smith or the plan of salvation from a stuttering, bumbling nineteen-year-old guy we'd otherwise tease until he blushed and laughed. Unfortunately, there aren't, so Alicia's weekly discussions are given by two young men: the socially awkward, thick-glasses-wearing one who stumbles over his words, and his companion, a sweet, boyish, utterly forgettable guy from Idaho.

Our conversations are innocent enough, but tense in intangible ways. There is a tortured energy between us, as if they are too aware that we are girls, too aware they shouldn't notice we're girls, are afraid to relax in the event that flirting might accidentally occur. But Alicia is a good sport; she answers their questions earnestly, does her best to be serious, and spiritual. She does her assigned reading from the Book of Mormon, writes down questions for the missionaries in her neat, round-edged handwriting, and begins to pray every night—for confirmation that God exists, and to know the direction in which her life should go.

The only moments of the missionaries' visits that feel natural come after the closing prayer, when they ask if we need help with anything—because community service is as much a part of their missions as teaching the Gospel. Often we say yes, and the sweet, boyish Idahoan tucks his striped tie between the buttons of his short-sleeved dress shirt and investigates under the hood of Dan's car, which Alicia's been driving.

Recently, it's started overheating in a way that seems dangerous—as if the whole car might burst into flames if we don't pull over. That crisis is quickly averted when the missionary, with no hint of irony, explains what a radiator is, and where to put the water. When he's finished, he shakes our hands and waves good-bye, but not before insisting we take the car for a drive. Let's be sure it's fixed, he says. Call us tomorrow if it's still not running right. The missionaries honk twice as they drive away, and our car is not far behind theirs, pulling into the tree-lined street.

Before Alicia makes her first turn, I guess which way she's going, and why. She takes this route to work, and at the appointed time, she scrunches forward and I lean back so she can see her dream house through the passenger window. It's a small yellow rambler with white trim, sitting daintily at the top of a sloping lawn. There's a knee-high white fence surrounding its tidy yard. There are flower beds. Shutters. A porch swing.

"I've got my camera," I say, opening the glove compartment.

She looks intrigued, then immediately disappointed. "I feel stupid," she says.

"So what?" I say. "Who's going to see?"

"What if they're home?"

"Who cares—what's the worst they'll do?"

She slows down, as usual, in front of the house, then grins widely and slams on the brakes. She runs over the sidewalk and into the yard, leaving her door open for a speedy getaway. I roll down my window and snap her picture a second before she dashes back around to hop in, worried that the owners will emerge, enraged, to kick her off their sweet, suburban grass.

When I get the photo developed, Alicia is so far in the foreground she looks taller than the roof. She is leaning forward with her hands on her knees, smiling broadly. Alicia is poised and ready to dive head-first into *settling down*. She wants a husband—a hot dad, she specifies, holding her breath every time she sees a man in a baseball hat with a baby strapped to his chest, or an unshaven, bed-headed man holding hands with a toddler getting free samples at the local Great Harvest Bread store. She wants babies, a house with a yard, dependable routines, a clear idea of what, when, and with whom her life will happen. She wants someone to take care of her, and I try hard not to be judgmental of that need. Maybe one day I'll have it, too.

I'm not at all surprised by her readiness for the husband, the house, the kids. But the distance by which I've fallen behind becomes clear enough to stun me one afternoon while we're out walking Frankenstein's dog. A young mother pushes a stroller past us. Maybe she waves. Maybe she says hi. I don't give her a second thought. I don't look at the baby. I could not describe either of them if you offered me five million dollars in unmarked bills. I'm thirty yards ahead, still talking to myself before I realize Alicia has stopped to watch them. She keeps watching until they turn the corner at the end of the block.

"What?" I ask, when she finally catches up to me.

"Oh, I can't wait," she sighs. "When I see babies, I feel my uterus clench."

This is the part where my jaw falls open.

Literally.

Because do people *feel* that? Am *I* supposed to be feeling that? Should I be worried? My uterus has never once made its needs known. I get that most women want children; most *people* want children, regardless of their religion, or lack of. For Mormon women, however, motherhood is an *identity*, rather than a role. At twenty-four, should I have envisioned myself as a mother? Should I have picked out names and imagined what my kids will look like?

I've thought about my wedding, sure. It was impossible not to get caught up, in the wedding-hungry atmosphere at BYU, with wondering if it would turn out to be this crush, or that one. But, truthfully, my wedding fantasies have generally been a vehicle to think about my wedding *night:* how it might feel to have a man watch me undress, slowly, in a candlelit room.

What I *have* fantasized about, the way some girls dream of proposals, weddings, and babies, is my hypothetical appearance on *Oprah.* I have spent inordinate amounts of time speculating on what I will *wear* for my appearance on *Oprah*, and how Oprah will *introduce* me, booming in her full-throated voice, over the audience's cued applause, "Ni-*cole* Haaaardyyy!" and how I will walk onstage with grace and confidence and really good hair.

Oprah will hug me and I will put my hands to my face as I sit down, feigning embarrassment at such an effusive welcome. Oprah will cross her legs, lean forward in her chair, and get down to the business of culling my most perceptive insights, my most profound thoughts, via a series of pressing questions about my latest best seller. She will read passages aloud, and she will cry, which will make *me* cry, because Oprah is *crying* over my sentences!

After the show we'll eat cookies in the green room and talk about her feud with David Letterman, and from that day forward we'll be best friends even though I am not a *dog person*. I will fake it, for Oprah; I will stuff my pockets with organic sausage treats for Sophie and Solomon, and maybe even pet them.

Obviously, I can't leave Chicago without having dinner at Oprah's restaurant, the Eccentric. Alicia agrees wholeheartedly and plans our big night out the same day I buy my plane ticket home. She humors me as I take a moment on the sidewalk outside the restaurant, stand still and breathe in the printed affirmations on the restaurant's grand awnings: *art, life, literature,* and *liberté.* With those words in my lungs, I revise my fantasy further, knowing I wouldn't have to fake, even for a second, my heartfelt devotion to each and every one.

Alicia and I follow the hostess through a series of huge rooms decked out with deep leather chairs, beaded chandeliers, and—the best part—a kitchen behind glass, framed by red velvet theater curtains. I'm grateful for the cereal and salads, the sandwiches and Top Ramen Alicia and I have eaten all summer long. Cheap food has availed us the opportunity to drop fifty dollars each on one delectable meal, so artfully presented we've brought our cameras to document our experience, course by course.

Alicia orders a beer, sheepishly—though why would I care? She hasn't decided to be baptized, and I'm not under the impression that drinking is inherently evil. It's just something Mormons don't do: one element of the Word of Wisdom, the health code we live by. Alicia has had only three missionary discussions; she should have a beer if she wants a beer. I toast with sparkling water, and we savor each bite as if it might be our last. Alicia and I offer tastes to each other— swordfish, grilled mushrooms, garlic shrimp—and discuss whether or not we'd *actually* die if Oprah showed up at our table.

After dinner, on our walk to the car in the still-hot night, as we carry our leftovers in glossy white boxes, a man steps onto the side-walk in front of us. "Spare some change?" he asks. He's wearing layers of baggy clothes despite the heat. His beard is overgrown, his hands dirty. The duffel bag on the sidewalk makes it clear he'll be sleeping on the street tonight—and that he has been doing so for some time.

"Sorry," I say, and shake my head. I don't have any cash, and I hate to carry a purse. What do I need, besides a credit card and lip-stick, which I keep in my pocket?

"I can't," says Alicia, apologetically. "I'm poor."

The man takes a step forward, pushes his hat back so we can see his face. "No," he says, raising his voice. "*I'm* poor."

That two-word sentence, the harsh truth of it, takes the air from our lungs. All of our energy—our Oprah-inspired buzz—dissipates into the silence between us as we walk back to the car.

Had this man been born to my mother and father, he would most likely be where I am now, carrying a leftover polenta cake home to eat with an egg in the morning. He'd be wondering where his fledgling career might take him after this first—possibly only—carefree, youth-ful summer. If I had been born into his life, I could easily be where he is now. I don't believe I deserve a situation different from his—that I earned one, or was somehow chosen. I don't believe there was any simple choice: I worked harder, I chose sobriety, I turned my home-work in on time, and that made all the difference. When people say everything happens for a reason, I think of situations like these, and I bristle. Because no, not everything.

I happened into love, opportunity, and good parenting in white, middle-class America. So I feel a certain amount of responsibility, inspired by the book of Matthew: "For I was an hungered, and ye gave me meat: I was thirsty, and ye gave me drink: I was a stranger, and ye took me in . . . Verily I say unto you, Inasmuch as ye have done it unto one of the least of these my brethren, ye have done it unto me."

I'm supposed to be a grown-up now, but there is still so much I don't understand: for instance, how to do the right thing in this situation. And what *is* the right thing, when I have nothing to offer but sympathy and the insult of half-eaten polenta?

There is still a tight knot in my throat when Alicia and I get to the car, an uneasiness in my stomach as we drive. Not of danger. Not of guilt, even. But a sense of shifting. Opening. To make room for the realization that I am connected to the world in a way broader and more complex than I have considered, or allowed myself to consider. A sheltered life subsidized by books was a perfect start. But that can't be everything—that can't continue to define my view of the world, and the people in it.

At home, after we've locked the car, locked the front door, and put our leftovers in the fridge, after I've said good night to Alicia and crawled into bed, I close my eyes as I do every night, and I pray. I thank God for every privilege of my life, every beautiful thing given to me without consequence or condition. For my loving family, and the chance to spend this summer with Alicia. But when the time comes for me to ask God to guide me safely home to Seattle, I feel a dark sense of loss—the sense that I am coming too soon to the end of something just begun.

As if in response, it appears again: a recent memory in which I see myself from the outside, as if I don't know, already, what's about to happen. I'm riding the el on a weekday night, Howard-bound on the red line, still in my uniform after a loss to the Pittsburgh Pirates. It's late enough to be dark enough that the windows reflect inward, like mirrors hung in darkness. In each reflection I am wilted, weary, sweat-slick, and exhausted—a girl alone in a gleaming row of red and orange seats.

The train car is almost empty. Plastic handholds dangle at intervals from the ceiling, swinging in opposition to the train. My throat is ragged, my calves high and tight as baseballs. I lean into the dark press of humidity, the comforting weight of another Midwest night. My body sways in rhythm with the train, and somewhere between Lawrence and Argyle, I doze, despite the starts and stops, the heavy sigh of sliding doors that usher out the few remaining passengers. All but one.

When I open my eyes, I'm already caught in the tunnel of his gaze. Time has decelerated, like in the moment before a crash. So all I see, slowed down and magnified, is a man, looking at me. He is wearing faded blue coveralls, unzipped to the waist. A white tank top, underneath. His hands are blackened with oil or paint, and his arm is a long, dark caress over the seatback beside him. His eyes are a shock of green.

In the movies, this is when the voice in her head tells the girl to get out. Tells her to run, before she is robbed or raped or killed, pressed against a wall with a hand on her throat. Get up now, and look for it—the nearest exit, next stop, or the door to the adjacent car. But what I do instead is stay. I want to know what happens when I refuse to move. When I give as he gives, in the silent, deliberate study of the other.

His eyes, deep and clear as water, are the reassurance. *Doubt not, fear not.* His skin, beautifully marked by viriligo, is like a map—a drift of brown and white continents drawn on the planes of his face. Between us, I feel a sense of recognition—as if he and I could be part of the same whole. As if I could be the whiteness laid into the dark of his skin.

The metallic clatter and shriek of wheels, the jostle of the car on its tracks, the ache of my exhausted legs, all of it has gone missing. In its place are the words of a psalm: "He shall cover thee with his feathers, and under his wings shalt thou trust: his truth shall be thy shield and buckler. Thou shalt not be afraid for the terror by night; nor for the arrow that flieth by day."

It only lasts seconds, this exchange—before I close my eyes again, unable to name what I'm feeling, unable to find a word meaning communion, kindred, revelation, desire. Already I'm wondering if it will happen again, and when: that what I've been conditioned to fear, taught to avoid, will reveal instead the strangest, most inexplicable beauty.

Chapter 4

I strain my heart, I stretch my hands,
And catch at hope.

—CHRISTINA ROSSETTI, "DE PROFUNDIS"

———◆———

I grimace into the rearview mirror, checking for stray lipstick, or remnants of breakfast. I check my bag to be sure I have my ID and Social Security card, as well as my résumé. I'm hopeful there will be paperwork to fill out after this morning's interview. Just across Western Avenue, above Red Robin on Seattle's Pier 55, await the business offices of Argosy Cruises. I cross my fingers as I climb the stairs, because after an entire school year spent living in my parents' house and substitute teaching—a job that feels a lot like hell on earth—I need summer work that's *fun*. "Tour guide" has a lovely ring to it: mostly because it doesn't start before 10:00 AM, and it allows for shorts and a tan. I'm already picturing myself narrating the history, landscape, and attractions of Elliott Bay from the upper deck of a boat—looking cute in my epaulets, and soaking up more than my required daily allowance of vitamin D.

I'm surprised that the guy conducting the interview is my age. I was expecting someone older. But what's more surprising, when he stands to shake my hand, is his *size*. He has to be six foot seven, has to weigh more than three hundred pounds. He looks slightly familiar—and if I knew anything about the WWE, I'd realize what I recognize is a face I've likely seen while flipping channels. My interviewer bears a striking resemblance to a professional wrestler called the Big Boss Man. He introduces himself as Murphy—one name only, like Prince or Elvis—and smiles mischievously as I sit down in the chair facing his desk.

He looks intently at my résumé, then up at me, then back to my résumé. Something like five times. His face tells me he's having a hard time taking himself seriously, and I'm tempted to look for a candid camera. He asks me zero questions about my work experience, except for my three-month stint at Wrigley Field last summer. He wants to know if I ever met Sammy Sosa, and I say no, not really; once I handed him a Pepsi, which he didn't pay for. Not that I'd expect him to have his wallet in the dugout, but still. I took home five bucks less than usual that day, and Sammy Sosa likely made fifty grand.

Murphy nods pensively, as if handing a Pepsi to Sammy Sosa is the *exact* skill he's been looking for in a potential employee.

"What would happen if I called your references?" he asks.

"Right now?"

"Yeah, right now."

"Go for it," I say, as if it's a dare.

Murphy looks at me while talking into the phone. What he doesn't know is the guy on the other end is my dad's business partner, for whom I did admin work during summers through high school and college. That detail only makes the whole thing more entertaining for me.

"So what do you think, should I hire her?" Murphy says into the phone, so loud he's practically shouting. It's the first time I notice his accent—something East Coasty: New York or New Jersey. "She looks like a troublemaker. Like an office-supply stealer." (Pause.) "No, seriously. Did you count the staplers?" (Longer pause.) "What about *paper clips?*"

During the next break in the conversation, Murphy gives me the thumbs down, makes an exaggerated, disappointed face. "Really," he says, incredulously, his voice going comically high. "You don't *say?*" He leans back in his chair, stretching the phone cord to maximum capacity. Then shakes his head, as if to prepare me for terrible news. After Murphy says good-bye, he slams down the phone and points a finger straight at my face, Uncle Sam–style. "You're hired!" he shouts, and holds his arms out wide, as if expecting a hug. I get the impression he's *this close* to giving me a "Come here, you!" and a congratulatory noogie.

Filling out my paperwork in the accountant's cubicle, I'm convinced that everything is about to change. I'll spend the summer giving lakes tours and harbor tours while searching for a full-time teaching job, so I'll never have to sub again. I'll have a salary, and benefits, and an apartment of my own—all of which might take my mind off what's going on with Alicia.

After our summer in Chicago, she didn't get a job either, and joined me in the humiliating (if temporary) situation of moving back home. Worse, she's had to deal with the fallout of her ugly breakup with Dan, as well as her family's objections to her seeing the Mormon missionaries and deciding to be baptized.

Alicia called me the night she arrived back in Seattle to say that when she saw Mount Rainier from twenty thousand feet she felt a surge of energy, like she could feel the life being breathed back into her. She immediately got a new haircut, bought new clothes, and threw herself into the project of repainting her bedroom a lovely French blue. When that small project turned into a need to repaint the entirety of her mother's house, Alicia's mom cornered me in her kitchen. She was angry, suspicious of my part in these sudden changes. "What's *wrong* with her?" she shouted, referring to Alicia, who was standing right next to me. I noticed the ice clinking in her glass. Wondered whether it was, indeed, water.

"Everything's different!" she cried. "What have you done?"

Her concerns were increased exponentially by the speed and intensity with which Alicia fell in love. To a Mormon guy I'd introduced her to. Alicia and I went to high school with Brandon, but we ran in different circles: he was cool and we weren't, so the two of them never met. Brandon and I were church friends, however, and became real friends at BYU, where he enrolled after a few years of rebellion at a state school. Turns out he hated Provo, and college in general, so he ended up back at home, too, after being offered a high-paying sales position that promised rapid promotion and didn't require a degree.

The three of us only had to hang out once or twice before it became clear they'd rather be alone. At first, I wouldn't have predicted that she'd be turned on by precisely what turns me off about Brandon. Then again, we've always liked opposite types. She finds it sexy—his stereotypical masculinity. His uncompromising, arrogant opinions. His pretending-to-be-kidding brand of chauvinism. I'd never date him—and I'm sure that feeling goes both ways. But as a friend, Brandon has been my favorite. Hilarious, and generous, and fun. My junior and senior years of college, he was my platonic boyfriend. The man in my life. And now he hardly notices me. He and Alicia have begun communicating in a way that excludes me. Looking at each other in a way no one's ever looked at me. A way that says they wish I'd leave the room already.

I'm happy that they're in love, but it's terrible to feel jealous of my friends. Terrible to be frightened that I'll be left out, or left behind. I'm embarrassed by my selfishness. My pettiness. And by how much it hurts to be maligned by Alicia's family. Her mother obviously thinks I've brainwashed Alicia—that I had some grand plan to *pounce* when she was emotionally weak. It's like she's forgotten she's known me since I was twelve—and *loved* the fact that her daughter was best friends with a Mormon girl. Alicia benefited from the influence of my goody-two-shoes—which her parents appreciated. Until now.

So I'm more than ready for something wonderful to happen. Something to be excited about, lacking undercurrents of sadness, jealousy, or resentment. I'm twenty-five and Mormon, which means what everyone's expecting is marriage. All six of my best college friends are married. My brother is married. Every Mormon girl in my high school class, and probably the two or three below me, is married. Alicia and Brandon are talking about marriage.

I'm not expecting a proposal anytime soon, though I wouldn't mind an invitation to dinner followed by a good-night makeout on the couch. It's been three years since I even *kissed* anyone. My current concern, however, is figuring out how to secure a bowline on a three-story boat without losing a foot or hand. It's my first day of training, and Murphy is making an example of me in front of the other new hires. Eight of us are standing on the dock, receiving instruction on knots that are more complicated than they appear. And it's scary to be the one in charge of not crashing a boat that can hold four hundred people. But the water's calm near the pier. The boat isn't going anywhere, so Murphy keeps making me tie and retie the same line, all the while telling me about a company event— a Mariners game, I should come, and meet the rest of the employees. He'll meet me in front of the building tomorrow, say five o'clock?

What Murphy doesn't say is it's an event for the management, hosted by the owners of the company. During the first two innings, he sits unfazed while his co-workers entertain themselves by pelting us with popcorn and pretending to make out with themselves.

"Is this a *date*?" I ask, embarrassed that it took me so long to catch up. "Are we on a date right now?"

"Well, that all depends," he says, taking a long, thoughtful sip of his soda. "On whether or not you feel *harassed*."

"I might not sue," I say. I'm intrigued. And flattered. It's just a summer job, something to tide me over until the school year, so why not date my boss, who's hilarious, and obviously likes me?

I raise my hand to get the attention of the peanut vendor, and when he points to the oversize button on his jersey that says three dollars, I point at Murphy, who makes a big show of reaching for his wallet. "Oh, *great*," he jokes. "I can already see how *this* is going to play out."

And so can I. I can't count how many times since Alicia's baptism I've heard the scripture from the Book of Mormon, regarding missionary work. The promise to those who "bring, save it be one soul unto me, how great shall be your joy with him in the kingdom of my Father!" I'm wondering if Murphy could be the reward, if falling in love could be the joy I've been promised. Maybe I won't have to feel hurt or lonely anymore when Brandon and Alicia squeeze me out. Maybe my mother's prediction was just a couple years off. Maybe *this* is the year I'll meet my future husband.

A week after that Mariners game I agree to meet Murphy at his house—a run-down mint-green rental in Seattle's University District—a cooler, if sketchier, neighborhood than mine. We'll do dinner and a movie, he says: a proper *date* date, to make up for the bamboozlement of the first.

Murphy's roommate answers my knock and lets me in, only to open a door off the kitchen and point to a flight of creaky wooden steps leading into the dank, creepy basement. Murphy lives in said basement, ironically dubbed The Love Dungeon.

His is one of two rooms across from the washer and dryer, but I don't know which. I walk slowly, accosted by the smell of mildew. Why didn't he answer the door? Did I get the day wrong, or did he forget about me? It occurs to me that Murphy could have a *collection* of women in his freezer for all I know. And if I end up dismembered in a deep freeze, my mother will never forgive me. What was

I doing skulking around in a strange man's basement? she'll demand. And I'll be forced to admit—since I'm dead—that she makes a valid point.

I call out, and no one answers. I consider a quick getaway out the back—but I've driven all this way. And one of the doors—the one missing its knob—is slightly ajar. I push lightly, and stand back as it swings into the room. Murphy is sleeping—or pretending, in the style of the Big Bad Wolf.

I stand in his doorway, feeling tense and unsure. A man in a bed. I have no idea what to do with that. Even in college, the BYU honor code prohibited boys and girls from entering each other's bedrooms. People had to rent racquetball courts and climb into playground equipment in order to make out. So no, I've never been in bed with a man. And I feel a little like throwing up when Murphy says a sleepy-eyed hello and opens the covers to invite me in. He pats the mattress next to him, and I sit down, tentatively.

But beyond that, I can't move. Because in my head I'm twelve years old, sitting in Sister Jepson's Sunday school class. I'm looking intently at a line graph that ends, tragically, at "intercourse." I'm embarrassed that at my age I still feel like a novice when it comes to dating and men. Sister Jepson would be proud that I've still never gone past "necking." But the fact that I haven't is making this situation triply awkward. Perched on the edge of Murphy's bed, I'm not sure whether to get in or get out, what signals I'd be giving if I accepted his invitation.

When Murphy reaches for me, I hold my breath, and let him pull me under. But not before squeezing my eyes shut, and uttering a fervent mental prayer: *Pleasebewearingpants. Pleasebewearingpants. Pleasebewearingpants.* When he moves his hand from my stomach to my hip, the only thing I can think to say I blurt shrilly at the ceiling. "I'm a virgin and I have to stay that way!"

Murphy doesn't flinch. Doesn't laugh, or condescend. He simply pulls me closer, and buries his face in my hair. "Don't worry," he whispers. "I've got you."

I can't say anything in response. My eyes have filled, unexpectedly, with tears. I never imagined I could lie next to a man and know, immediately, to trust him. That I could feel safe enough to let all my defenses go. Or that if I laid still and listened, I could hear my pulse adjust to the rhythm of his.

I say a prayer of thanks that Murphy can't see my face. How could I explain the silent, relentless flood of tears—the rush of relief and gratitude I feel, for the simple grace of being touched. For knowing, finally, what it feels like to be enveloped by the body of another.

I've felt envious, watching couples on weekend mornings, and in springtime: leaning into one another as they walk, lying against each other on the grass, looking at one another as if no one else exists in the world. I've wanted it for myself: the casual twining of limbs, the effortless, intimate ways people touch.

But I've always known to be careful about love. I overheard, as a kid, enough of my mother's hushed conversations about LDS women whose husbands up and left, or were, on the rare occasion, abusive, addicted, closeted, philandering. I promised myself I'd never be the woman who would leave if she could—who should leave, but can't. Even my parents, who have always loved each other, hit a rough patch when I was a kid. There were fights so frightening I hid in my playroom closet, praying God would make me disappear. There was a trial separation, which ended when my father gave up his bachelor pad with the spiral staircase and came back to us. But that doesn't mean I wasn't always aware of where the money came from, and what might happen if he left for good. After that, I nursed a thick, sweaty apprehension whenever I heard my parents argue.

I've always known I wouldn't be one of those Mormon girls who married at eighteen, nineteen, twenty, had kids right away, had no marketable skills and a habit of financial dependence. But now I'm old enough. I've done enough for myself, not to have to be afraid.

"When's the movie?" I ask quietly, rolling over to look at Murphy. I hope there aren't tearstains on my face, or the giveaway of runny mascara.

"Half hour ago," he says, and pulls me back into his chest. We stay in bed until the early hours of morning. We stay in our clothes as well. And my fears are further assuaged when Murphy tells me he's Catholic, and appreciates my religious commitments. We'll wait as long as I want to, he assures me. He's a patient man.

Murphy is at my apartment two months later when I receive Alicia and Brandon's wedding invitation. Holding it in my hand, I can't help but think this is the end, in certain ways. Brandon will become Alicia's confidant. He will be her best friend, her first priority. She'll get pregnant right away, if all goes well, and we'll see each other even less after that.

Last week, at the Woodland Park Zoo, somewhere on the winding path between the elephants and orangutans, a toddler ran by holding a balloon. As soon as his mother was out of earshot, Alicia, still four weeks before her marriage, grabbed Brandon's arm and scream-whispered, "Impregnate me!" All three of us knew she was only half kidding.

Already, we talk so much less. We see each other so rarely, in comparison to how things used to be. Turns out three actually *is* a crowd. I sigh and hand the invitation to Murphy. He looks at me, rather than it.

"Hey," he says, in his quiet voice. "What's wrong?"

"I'm just sad." I shrug. "Her family hates me. And I miss my friend."

Murphy puts his arms around me and says, "Poor you," in a way that somehow doesn't feel condescending. "Don't cry," he says, kissing the top of my head. "You always have me."

"You're not the same," I say miserably, my face buried in his sweatshirt.

"I know," he says. Then shouts, without warning, "I'm *better!*"

I can't help but burst out laughing, thinking *this* is the man I love: a loud, foulmouthed, finger-pointing New Jersey transplant who has the spectacular quality of truly believing all my worst traits are endearing. He tells everyone that when I'm in a terrible mood it's only because I'm hungry, chilly, sleepy, or I have to go number two. For the first time in his life, he says, he *understands* a woman. He points at me, shouting, "Best girlfriend ever!" while I cringe at the fact that everyone we know now knows how I act when I have to poo.

Though I'm happy, too, to be falling in love as quickly, sweetly, and chastely as I fell into his bed on our second date. I've never been so adored, and Murphy can't believe he's so lucky to have a girl like me. He says it to everyone. His friends, my friends, my family. Ours is a dynamic I've learned well, via the example of my parents: one that speaks of lasting love, and the way things ought to be.

In their relationship, too, my mother is the catch. My father—particularly in his younger days—the lovable jackass. When they were dating, my dad borrowed another woman's car to take my mother camping. He gave my mom a hickey at the dinner table the first time he met her parents. My mother swears, despite his emphatic denial, that my dad gave *her* the engagement ring he bought for the girl with the car—known always and forever as Big Boob Jan.

If I ever forget to admire him enough, Murphy reminds me, "You'd be *unemployed* if it weren't for me." Which is partly true. Murphy came to my rescue like the heroes of yore, at the tail end of summer. I saw a job for a full-time English teacher posted online only three hours before the application period closed, but I was short one letter of recommendation. Conflict of interest be damned, Murphy wrote a letter singing my praises, and had it waiting when I arrived at his office half an hour later. I ended up getting the job—based heavily on my teaching demonstrations—but Murphy still takes full credit. I don't mind. It was the sweetest, most romantic thing anyone had ever done for me.

Until early this morning, when a freak early November storm blew in and incapacitated the city, closed every school in two counties, and made the hilly, unplowed roads of Seattle virtually impassable. Murphy called as soon as he woke up to see if I had power, and to ask if he'd left his coat in my car. He can't find it anywhere, and got tired of looking.

"My first snow day," I say wistfully into the phone. School will be canceled for days, if the weather report can be trusted. I've already put my book bag full of midterm essays in the closet—as if to make all my responsibilities disappear. I'm curled in a blanket in front of the fireplace, watching the thick flakes fall outside—pretending the greenbelt between me and the freeway is an acre of forest. Given the absence of traffic and the towering, snow-covered cedar trees, it's like someone's shaken a snow globe with me inside it.

"I wish we were snowed in *together*," I say, picturing Murphy freezing in his basement on the opposite side of Lake Washington. "We could make a snowman, and drink hot chocolate, and read books by the fire."

Two hours later, I'm snapped from my reverie by a muffled knock on the door. I can't imagine who it could be, and I look cautiously through the peephole: in it, I see a supersize Santa shaking snow from his hat.

Murphy shouts, "Ho ho ho!" when I swing the door open. "I didn't even put my *thumb* out," he says, stomping his feet. "People just kept pulling over, yelling *Hey Santa, hop in*! I could have been a *serial* killer."

He unbuckles his gigantic patent leather belt and shrugs out of his fur-trimmed jacket. "What?" he says, in response to my baffled look. "Where else can I find a coat that fits?" He'd raided the storage closet at work, borrowed the Santa suit he wears every year at the company party.

Murphy and I snuggle on the couch, drink hot chocolate, and read books by the fire. Outside, some kids are building a snowman. They're bundled into puffy pants and parkas, moon boots and colorful hats. We watch them carefully roll three snowballs, working in pairs to make the base, body, and head. They assemble the snowman at the top of a small hill, adding sticks for arms, charcoal for eyes, a carrot for the nose. When they're done, they stand at the bottom of the hill, admiring their work. Until one of them lets out a scream like William Wallace on the warpath against the English, and suddenly it is a pig pile of destruction: a punching, kicking, barehanded snowman massacre.

"When we have kids," says Murphy, "they'll build *two* snowmen. One to keep, and one to kick the crap out of."

"When we have kids?" I repeat, my mug poised in midair.

"Sure." He walks to the kitchen to make us some popcorn. "They'll be smart like you, and good-lookin' like me," he says, snapping his thick, black suspenders.

My heart is a hammer in my chest. I look at Murphy, in my kitchen, making us snacks. He *hitchhiked* through a snowstorm—made half the trip on the back of a snowmobile—just to spend the day with me.

My eyes instinctively gravitate to the framed print of *The Lady of Shalott* above the fireplace. Again, I look to her unreadable expression, as if the answer might lie there. If only she could talk, like a mirror, mirror on the wall. Tell me: Is she joyful or regretful? Singing or suffocating?

I've prayed so often that I'll find love. I know marriage is a sacred, necessary ordinance, required to reach the celestial kingdom. And more temporally, I want love, and partnership, and sex. I've prayed for a man who could erase my doubts, inspire me to want what our prophets have taught is "life's greatest career—that of homemaker, wife, and mother." But every time I get close, there's something. Just last Sunday, I was handed a flyer reminding me about the ward's monthly Enrichment meeting, encouraging me to "consider meaningful topics such as these":

Meal planning
Nutrition
Food preparation
Home storage
Emergency preparedness
Cleaning
Organizing
Beautifying the home
Sewing
Gardening

Of course Enrichment meetings aren't required, and Enrichment is only one of many programs sponsored by the Relief Society—the church's women's organization—but that list reads to me like a list of punishments. I can't imagine chores enriching my life. Neither can I imagine making them a large measure of my life's work.

"Ask, and ye shall receive," say the scriptures, "that your joy may be full." So I have prayed, every night, that all I've been promised will come to pass. That I'll be drawn to what I'm supposed to want. And here is what I've asked for. A sweet, charming man, wearing velveteen Santa pants. Planning our future. Saying "when we have kids." He's here, wanting me, saying when.

Chapter 5

———◆———

Valentine's Day rolls around eight months into Murphy's and my relationship. In the month leading up to it, I became obsessed with the quest to find the thing he's never had and always wanted: a leather jacket. For even the most intrepid, finding a fashionable XXXLT is a challenge. But the only store that carries Murphy's size is Big and Tall Casual Male, whose sartorial choices vacillate between poly-blend Cosby sweaters and nylon sports jerseys the size of bed sheets.

Last week, however, in a sweeping Valentine miracle, I found a leather jacket that neither featured an elastic waistband nor looked like it was previously owned by Andrew Dice Clay. I figured out a way to afford it on my first-year teacher's salary, and it was all I could do not to spoil the surprise before tonight.

I hand the gigantic, carefully wrapped box to Murphy at Seattle's swank Dahlia Lounge, where we've just ordered a dinner neither of us could afford were it not for the promotions Murphy often receives from vendors—something to do with the Downtown Seattle Association. Murphy is in thrall to his new jacket. Keeps smelling it, and petting it, and saying it's perfect. In return, he gives me a sweet, hilarious, handmade Valentine. And a book about the Holocaust.

"Oh, please be kidding," I say, covering my mouth. I unveil the cover further, which features a black-and-white photograph of Hitler's youth army: one boy, in the forefront, is holding a flag adorned with a swastika the size of a Volkswagen Beetle. I rewrap the book quickly, and shove it into my lap—before anyone can think *I* think the Holocaust is a symbol of romance and affection. I pitch forward in slow motion, groaning, until my forehead hits the table, audibly.

"What's the matter, Stinky?" Murphy asks, moving the candle away from my hair.

"Murphy," I say, into the tablecloth, "there's nothing about genocide that says I love you. Not one thing." I can't stop laughing. "It's the worst Valentine gift *ever*. Like *award-winningly* bad."

"Noooo," he says. "It's a *great* gift. I was being thoughtful."

I sit up, and lean toward him. "This book," I say, in a stage whisper, pointing to my lap with both hands, "chronicles the starvation, torture, and death of six million people."

"Yeah," he says, waving away that detail. "But remember? We went to that bookstore in Fremont last month. And you picked up this book. And *you* said, 'Hey, this would be good for school.' Because *you teach the Holocaust*. I remembered what it was and where it was, and I went back and got it." He puts his finger in the air, as if to indicate Exhibit A. "See, *thought*ful."

"So listen," I say, holding his hand. "Remember how you told me on our first date that you're a big giant jackass? That it just happens, no matter how much you try to fight it?"

"Yes."

"Like when you told your co-worker Tina how you made up this supercute nickname for me, and she said, 'You ass-hat, don't you know "stinky lovemuffin" is a synonym for smelly vagina?'"

"Yes."

"And now every time I see Tina, I have a crisis, like I should defend my lady parts."

Murphy nods, as if to say, "Yep, you got me there."

"If I *tried* to think of a worse Valentine gift, I couldn't do it."

"That bad?" he asks. "Really?" He is truly incredulous.

"Genocide," is all I say. I look at him deliberately, to let that word sink in.

"But I was so *thought*ful," he says. And now *he* can't stop laughing.

"So, listen. I'm giving you a do-over. You and I are going to pretend *this*," I say, pointing to the book again, "*never happened.*"

"Sure, Stinky. But quit pointing to your crotch already."

I fall forward again, in horrified slow motion, until my head plunks down on the table.

"And I'm keeping my leather jacket!"

When I groan into the tablecloth, Murphy pets my hair like Lennie—that sweet, unwitting rabbit killer in *Of Mice and Men*. "Pre-tty," Murphy says, in a creepy, affected voice.

This is what's happening when the waiter approaches with our salads. He leans down to ask, in a whisper, if everything is all right.

"Everything's *great*," Murphy shouts, and I snap to attention, feeling like I've just been busted. "Best girlfriend ever!" he declares, as the waiter sets down our hearts of palm.

The night before Alicia's wedding rehearsal, Murphy calls from the hospital. "Hey, Stinky!" he yells into the phone. "I just got hit by a car! I rolled half a block downhill and I'm not even *bleeding*. That jacket you gave me is the best!"

"Oh yeah?" I say. "Well that *book* you gave me still sucks ass." Murphy laughs so hard he drops the phone and hangs up on me. It takes a while for us to reconnect, for him to assure me he really is fine, doesn't need a ride home, and will still be my plus-one to the rehearsal, which starts in less than twenty-four hours.

Ten minutes into the wedding rehearsal, Murphy's taken over the whole thing—bossing everyone around, telling who to stand where in the country club ballroom and clarifying the details of what should happen when. "You Mormons don't know *anything* about weddings," he keeps yelling, in mock exasperation, which reduces everyone to giggles. Because it's pretty much true.

Most LDS marriages take place in temples or the chapels where we meet on Sundays rather than country club ballrooms. Temple marriages, also called sealings, usually include no more than eight to ten people. They're absent of the walk down the aisle, the photographers, the flower girls, the bridesmaids and groomsmen—nearly everything associated with traditional weddings.

No one may enter an LDS temple who's not an active member of the church in possession of a temple recommend—verification that said person is spiritually worthy to enter the most sacred place on earth. But most times—since the ceremonies are so small—even for LDS people, "going to a wedding" means going to a reception or open house where there is often little more than a gift table, a receiving line, punch, and cake.

It's common for Mormons not to attend the temple weddings of their friends and family members: I didn't attend my brother's last summer, though I flew to Oakland for the reception and to have my photo taken with the rest of the wedding party. Missing the ceremony wasn't the least bit weird to me—though I get that the exclusion of loved ones from a marriage is inconceivable (if not offensive) to nonmembers. To others, it sounds crazy to ask family and friends to wait in the lobby or on the temple grounds for the bride and groom to emerge *after* they've been sealed for time and eternity. For us, it's just the way it's done.

But Alicia and Brandon's case is an exception. New members

must wait a year before entering the temple, so they'll be married by an LDS bishop in a civil ceremony, till death do they part, until their temple sealing next year, which will bind them—and their children— eternally. The one-year delay is a welcome blessing for Alicia. Obviously, she wants her family, none of whom are Mormon, to see her get married. Even if they think this is another in a series of mistakes: marrying so soon after her breakup with Dan, getting baptized so soon after meeting her Mormon fiancé, after only a few months of studying the Gospel. It's no wonder they're confused and terrified. So I try not to take their resentment personally, try not to feel hurt that I'm getting the cold shoulder, from Alicia's mother in particular. She'll eventually see that Alicia is happy, that none of these are mistakes.

Across the room, Murphy is doing an impersonation of the absent bridesmaids. He's perfected a comically dainty stride, towering over the groomsmen on their walk down the makeshift aisle. The bishop, seeing his opportunity, approaches to ask if he and I can talk. He's been in my parents' ward for years; I consider him a family friend and trust his advice, though I'm not expecting to receive any today.

He guides me toward the windows on the far side of the room, which overlook expanses of manicured grass, sidewalks lined with daffodils, and a driving range carved from a thick forest of pine trees. What it takes me too long to realize is that the bishop wants to talk to me about Murphy. About the dangers inherent in marrying outside the church—even though I assure him Murphy and I aren't talking seriously about marriage.

"*Yet*," he says. "Murphy's a great guy," the bishop insists. "No one's ever going to argue with that. He obviously loves you. But be careful. Imagine yourself doing this alone. Going to church with your kids every Sunday, while he's at home watching football.

"You won't have the priesthood in your home. He won't be able to perform fathers' blessings, or baptize your kids. Your marriage will end when one of you dies. You'll be reminded every day, in some way or another, that you made a gamble. That it might not pay off."

I focus on one of the small white flags on the putting green, and try my best to imagine it. Try to picture myself married to Murphy. Try to picture the kids we'd have together. But the images aren't forming.

"You'll always be wishing Murphy were *with you*," says the bishop. "You want your husband to share the spiritual part of your life, the *most important* part of your life. Imagine a man coming home to you every night who doesn't understand what means most to you."

I look over at Murphy, who's entertaining both groom and best man with some anecdote or another. To my horror, the subject of *dwarf tossing* comes up now and again—and I pray he's not telling stories about Little T, a friend of his from Jersey, who looks like Mr. T, but tiny. He *wants* to be tossed; it's good work, when he can get it.

The bishop clears his throat, and I snap back to attention— to the question—which is: does Murphy know what means most to me?

The bishop is looking at me. He is waiting for a response. He wants to know: could I marry a man who doesn't understand my spiritual beliefs, or share them?

"What is it that you want, for your future?" he asks.

"I want what everyone wants. Love. Passion. A sense of purpose."

"The Gospel is the key to all of those things," the bishop assures me.

I don't doubt that assertion. So I promise to consider asking Murphy to see the missionaries. It's not that I couldn't marry Murphy if he remained Catholic. There are always a few "part-member families" in the ward; it's not that uncommon. But we couldn't be sealed in the temple for eternity. And it would be easier, if we shared our religious beliefs. We would be closer; our love would be stronger, more complete. And maybe our religious differences *are* the source of my trepidation. Why would I not at least ask? I *want* my mother's dream to be my dream. I want to brim with joy when Murphy says "when we get married," "when we have kids." I've purposely kept a space open for a maternal desire to set in. I've been waiting for a spiritual confirmation that I am what God has created me to be, according to the doctrine of my faith. And I'll keep living a faithful LDS life, regardless of what Murphy decides. Because I know what exists outside of the church, and that it's not the life I want.

I've overheard enough stories: the man who lived next door when I was a kid, who traveled all the time and kept giving his wife the clap. I didn't know what that word meant, but I knew two things: it wasn't good, and they weren't Mormon. The teenager down the street, who got caught with two younger kids and a pile of dirty magazines: not Mormon. Neither was the lady at the grocery store, who talked through a hole in her throat. Or the dad at the company picnic, who drank too many beers, yelled and swore at his kids, and fell into a sleep so deep he didn't flinch when his kids set off firecrackers next to his head. They laughed, but I said a prayer, thanking God that my dad would never let us die in a fire because he couldn't wake up when things turned scary.

Truthfully, though, my own family history—its pieced-together stories, its hazy, far-off memories—has provided the only cautionary tale I've needed. The perfect example of what not to do.

In the living room of the second of the three houses I lived in growing up, my paternal grandfather and I once played an uneventful game of This Little Piggy. I remember feeling awed and slightly uncomfortable: a man I'd never met, who looked like my dad. "This is your Grandpa," someone must have said. That's my only memory of him.

He was so absent from my father's life—and mine—that my parents literally forgot to tell me when he died. A few months ago, I stopped by my parents' house to pick up some books from my old room. I stayed for a few minutes to chat with my mom, who was looking through a mail-order catalog. While we talked, I did her the favor of finishing off a pint of Cherry Garcia. Suddenly, she looked up. "Oh!" she said. "Did we tell you? Your grandfather died."

"*When?*" I asked, swallowing too quickly, feeling a cold burn in my throat. "And which one?"

"Your dad's dad. It was a few weeks ago." In response to my blank look, she shrugged and said, "Oops." She rummaged through her small kitchen desk, came up with a newspaper article. "Here," she said, handing it over.

My grandfather's obituary took up a quarter page of the *New York Times*. It included a large photograph, credited to the Associated Press. "The *New York TIMES?*" I exclaimed, completely mystified.

My mother didn't answer. She was engrossed, or pretending to be, in her catalog. Everything I learned from the obituary was news to me: Evidently, my father's father worked in the Army Intelligence Corps in WWII. He was assistant military attaché at the US embassy in London. He was employed by the Ford Foundation in New York City, and awarded the Order of Merit by the Peruvian government, which could explain the beautiful set of bone china plates I inherited from my father's mother, of whom I have no memory. They're patterned with an intricate Incan-looking design, in turquoise and gold.

But the following paragraph contained the real shocker: my grandfather was appointed commissioner of the Federal Housing Administration by President John F. Kennedy.

"John F. *Kennedy?!*"

My mother shrugged. "That didn't make him a good person," she said. "Didn't make him a good father. That's for sure."

"I know, but JFK!" I was drawn immediately into an imagining of my grandfather. I pictured him in the afterlife, wearing a tuxedo, slow dancing with Marilyn Monroe. But the tension in my mother's voice reminded me: that as brilliant as he was at the rise of his career, my grandfather was a magnificent failure to his family.

He was so occupied with his work, his alcoholism, and his mistress, so uninterested in his three children, the story goes, that he refused to let them call him Dad. He insisted they use his first name instead. He'd warned his wife, when she brought up the subject of children: he'd pay for them, but he would do nothing more.

"I thought you knew that part," my mother said, referring to JFK. But who would have told me? Not my dad, who only talks about his past in elliptical asides. Not my mother, who wrote her in-laws off from the beginning, knowing they'd never accept her. When my father first brought her home—a girl descended from Arkansas ridge runners who worked at a cereal factory to put herself through college—they were unimpressed. They corrected her grammar. Said, she's the girl you fool around with, not the one you marry—a comment that has yet to be forgiven.

The cause of my grandfather's death was conspicuously absent from his obituary. "Did Dad go to the funeral?" I asked my mom. But he wouldn't have left town without telling me, without asking me to check in on my mother, who as a result of her own past, still doesn't like to be alone after dark.

"He only found out afterward. When Sallee called to ask for money," my mother said, with a dismissive eye roll. Sallee is the infamous mistress, though I suppose she would now be my step-grandmother. She'd been married to Neal for thirty-eight years by the time he died, and everything I know firsthand about her stems from another faded, jagged-edged memory. She wet herself on Uncle John and Aunt Joyce's furniture, the first and only time our families had Thanksgiving together. On purpose, for some unfathomable reason.

My grandfather's obituary made things clear, if one read between the lines. By the end, I had a picture of his life. A cartoon line drawing of a man in a bow tie hiking quickly up the side of a mountain. At the summit, he sits, legs crossed, admiring the view. Until the highball glass in his hand shifts his weight just enough to send him tumbling, ass first and backward, down the opposite side. His glasses fly off along the way. He lands flat, battered, and lifeless—a stick figure with X's for eyes.

My grandfather is not the only one of my father's relatives to come to an unhappy, alcoholic end: my grandmother Dorothy—my father's mother—drank herself to death in 1977. Aunt Margaret, my father's sister, followed, though decades later. She left her jewelry to me, including a spectacular topaz ring and necklace that must be ten carats apiece. Though of Margaret, as well, I have only one memory. She and I folded laundry together in my parents' living room. I remember thinking how glamorous her job sounded, working in publishing in New York City. But Margaret looked fragile rather than glamorous. Her skin and hair were brittle, slightly yellow. She was shy, or reluctant to talk. Her hands kept shaking. Even so, she taught me how to fold a fitted sheet, though the afternoon we did it together was the one and only time I've gotten it right.

Sometimes I imagine Margaret as a girl: the youngest child, like me. Except her father ran off with another woman. Her mother was incapacitated by addiction. Her brothers left home the minute they were old enough: John to IBM and NYU, my dad to BYU. So Margaret's debilitating loneliness, her alcoholism, and her series of suicide attempts aren't difficult to understand. I have everything she spent her life trying, and failing, to find.

I don't expect Murphy to convert, I tell him. I just want him to know what I believe. But secretly, I hope he'll convert. I remember watching Alicia rise, joyful and dripping, from the baptismal font. Dressed in white, moved to tears by the spirit of God and the promise of a fresh start, clean slate, new life. Not to mention a marriage built on a sure, shared spiritual foundation.

In return, I agree to learn about Catholicism, a project that began and ended on Easter Sunday. We decided to celebrate the Resurrection of Christ first at Murphy's church, and later, at mine. Mormons don't believe in original sin; children are baptized at age eight—the age of accountability. Before that time, they're innocent, allowed to ascend straight to the celestial kingdom, the highest of the three levels of exaltation, if they die. So I'm horrified when the priest, after baptizing a baby, says, "You are no longer a child of darkness."

"*Darkness?*" I hiss at Murphy, trying to conceal the fact that his religion is seriously freaking me out. The incense, the chanting, the robes, the standing and kneeling. But most of all, the infant baptism. "*Child* of *dark*ness?!" I repeat, at once stunned and repelled.

Murphy lasts longer, taking the LDS missionary discussions once a week for a month before he refuses to continue. He cannot spend his whole life, or even one more week, he announces, listening to the predictable, excruciating *speech patterns* of every prayer and address from the pulpit.

We don't talk much about these failed attempts. We pick the needle off the record that's skipping, and start it in a fresh groove. But I've begun to wonder: when people envy our comedic timing, our easy affection, the fact that Murphy and I never argue, the sweet things he does for me, what I never offer up in response is that in the year we've been dating, I can count exactly two times I've been tempted to tear my clothes off and commit the sin of fornication. And shouldn't we at least *want* to?

How many times have I been told that the happiest people are those who marry their best friends? Passion fades. All that may be true, but I'm worried about a marriage lacking passion from the get-go. I need to know, at least for a season, what that kind of love looks like. Smells like, sounds like, feels like. I know it exists—can exist in conjunction with friendship, partnership, spiritual communion. The woman I share a classroom with—my assigned mentor, age sixty—insisted her doctor change one of her medications because it hinders her sex drive. When I raised my eyebrows, she laughed. The clitoris doesn't stop working after menopause, she assured me. So it seems a frightening risk to hope I'll never need more than comfortable, dependable, and sweet. Marriage, after all, is for eternity.

Then again, what do I know about erotic love? Maybe it develops over time, once sex is actually sanctioned. Maybe when Murphy's allowed to touch my erogenous zones, I'll feel . . . erogenous. Maybe our platonic sleepovers will morph into unbridled, riotous sexcapades, given a notarized certificate of marriage.

Murphy has saved up his yearly vacation time so he can join me on a late-summer road trip to Utah. He's never been, and I'd rather not drive fifteen hours alone to visit my former college roommate, Krista. After a day in the car gorging on processed mini-mart food, Murphy and I arrive in Provo. Krista and I are catching up with news of the past two years, eating pizza, and watching, enthralled, as her two-year-old daughter ferries random objects across the living room to Murphy. He's patiently building a Jenga tower of toys and books and cookware beside his chair, to be put back in their rightful places after she's tucked into bed.

I can't get my head around the fact that Krista's married and has a daughter old enough walk and (sort of) talk. The whole scene seems surreal, as if any minute we'll be transported back to our shared apartment, angling for the bathroom or rushing out the door, can't be late again, to biology lab.

The phone rings just as Krista holds up one of my boots: brown suede with a three-inch platform heel. "If there was *ever* a pair of shoes that did not fit my lifestyle," she says, reaching for the receiver. But we stop laughing when she raises a hand to shush us. When she rushes to turn on the television.

We first see the drawn face of the network anchorman. His eyes are downcast, and he's holding a hand to his earpiece, as if to hear more clearly. He looks straight into the camera to announce, "In a statement released earlier tonight from Buckingham Palace, Diana, Princess of Wales, has been pronounced dead." The screen flips to coverage of her brutally mangled Mercedes-Benz, a close-up on the deployed airbags. The Mercedes suspended in the claws of a crane, unrecognizable as a car when viewed from the front or the right. Back to the anchorman again, who repeats: "Dodi Al-Fayed, dead. Princess Diana, dead, at age thirty-six." The words are a blur on every channel: high-speed collision . . . paparazzi . . . two-lane tunnel . . . no barrier . . . head trauma . . . cardiac arrest.

"I remember waking up in the middle of the night to see the wedding," Krista says. "I kept arranging my yellow blanket into a gown. I dragged it behind me—like a train—for days afterward."

"Did you see that Barbara Walters special?" I ask. "When Diana talked about how she was never allowed to be anything but that eighteen-year-old girl everyone fell in love with. She could never escape peoples' idea of her. The family, the public—they resented her evolution."

We sit transfixed by the newsfeed, as if its repetition will offer some insight beyond what we already suspect: there must be some relief in escaping such a life. The hounding paparazzi, the cruel tabloid stories, the unrelenting pressure to be something to so many people, most of whom were strangers. I look over at Murphy, and can't help but wonder if the two of us are also speeding toward something immovable and catastrophic.

Two days later, it's time to head home. Murphy suggests the long way; he wants me to see the Big Sky valley. I have a week until my teaching contract says I have to be back. So why not drive a thousand miles out of our way to see something amazing?

We're sixty miles past the Montana state line when Murphy looks over at me. "How fast do you think the car can go?"

"You mean *my* car?" I feel myself stiffen under the semantics, though I know my reaction doesn't make sense. He washes my car. He puts gas in my car. He drives when I don't feel like it—has driven the vast majority of this trip so I can appropriate the stereo, enjoy my snacks, and fully appreciate the landscape of the American West. So why am I irritated by the grammatical union of his and mine?

"On *your* car," Murphy says, drawing out the vowels, teasing me, "the speedometer goes to one-forty."

We've just passed another sign indicating there is no speed limit beyond what we decide is safe and reasonable. "So let's see," I say, smiling an apology. I open a short can of Pringles and put my feet on the dash.

Murphy hits the gas and launches into a story about one of his co-workers. I watch the speedometer climb steadily to 80, 90, 95. I hear him talking, but I have my eye on a telephone pole ahead of me; it is halfway to the horizon, and before I can blink twice it is whizzing past my head. I can't help but flash to images from the news: the Mercedes crushed against a pillar in the Pont de l'Alma road tunnel. The twenty-five-foot train of Princess Diana's wedding gown, the white perfection of it, easing slightly to the left of the red carpet, sliding slowly toward the black-and-white marble parquet floor.

At 110, the car starts to shudder. I watch the RPM needle climb steadily toward the red line. I picture the grainy close-up of a stretcher, unfolding. At 115 Murphy looks over at me, points his finger in the air, and says, "So Huffy McPuffy says to me, *right* before he falls down the stairs—"

"Murphy."

"Yes, my love."

"If you're going to drive my car at a hundred twenty miles per hour, could you put both hands on the wheel? Look at the road, maybe?"

"Sure, Stinky!" he shouts over the rising engine noise. At 125, he glances over at me, eyes wide. "Holy crap, we'd be killed in a *second* if we hit a pothole."

Half an hour later, well after we've returned to normal speed, Murphy declares, "Brown sign!" and takes us on a thirty-mile jaunt to a ghost town. He cannot resist a brown highway sign marking a tourist destination, and I don't have any complaints. These detours have provided a range of amusing disappointments—buttes and battlefields, the smallest of this, the biggest of that.

As soon as we arrive in the ghost town, I can see why everyone else left. There is not a tree, not a shrub, not a stray dog or a drop of water. Nothing but a row of shacks keeling on a sea of dust. The main road is a narrow dirt lane lined with buildings erected hastily, as if people knew they'd desert them after the first flash of gold, drop of oil, herd of buffalo: whatever it was that brought them here.

Murphy is off from the start, poking his head into windows, wandering in and out of buildings. Fifty yards away in the flat, straight distance, he turns to face me with his feet apart, his hand on a make-believe holster. I imagine tumbleweeds, a low, faraway whistle.

"Hey Stinky, I'm the sheriff!" he shouts, twirling imaginary guns.

I wave and walk into the one-room schoolhouse. A dozen iron desks sit bolted in perfect rows, facing the front of the room. I'm preparing to read *To Kill a Mockingbird* with my students in a few weeks, just like last year: two sections a day both semesters. I can't help but think of Burris Ewell, the cootie-covered bully who showed up, like his brothers and sisters, every year for the first day of school—to be entered into the registry—then never again, until the first day of the following year.

His petulant voice rings in my ears: "Ain't no snot-nosed slut of a schoolteacher ever born c'n make me do nothin'! You ain't makin' me go nowhere, missus. You just remember that, you ain't makin' me go nowhere!"

But this town was built years before Burris Ewell would have lived—at the turn of the century, no doubt. I imagine myself teaching in this school, following the list of Rules for Teachers, ca. 1910, currently posted as a joke in my faculty room. I'd be required to remain unmarried, in that scenario. I'd be banned from keeping company with men and leaving the city limits without permission. I'd not be allowed to dress in bright colors, dye my hair, smoke cigarettes, ride in an automobile with any man who was not a relative, or wear dresses any shorter than two inches above the ankle. I'd be required to be home every night by 8:00 and to wear at least two petticoats. Not to mention the scrubbing of the schoolroom floors.

I see myself with my hair pinned up tidily, in a bun. I'm wearing a floor-length calico dress adorned with a swarm of buttons. Buttons clutching my wrists and my neck, buttons running the length of my sweat-drenched back, and climbing the sides of my boots. Just thinking about it, I feel so claustrophobic I'd unzip my skin if I could.

Itching to get out of the room, I turn for the door, thinking a prayer of gratitude: for air-conditioning, windowpanes, women's suffrage, dry erase boards, my current passport, women's liberation, custodial crews, the civil rights movement, and Rid shampoo. But before I reach the porch, Murphy clomps up the schoolroom stairs. He's walking as if he is wearing spurs and/or mysteriously, heinously injured. He holsters his make-believe gun and glances around, resting his hands on either side of the doorframe.

"Oooh, you could be the schoolmarm," he says, waggling his eyebrows. "*If you know what I mean.*"

It takes me only a second to register why I feel affronted. Not only at church but at work, and not only at work but in our relationship, and not only in our relationship but *in his sexual fantasy* of our relationship, I am required to be pristine. I *am* the schoolmarm. I have *always been* the fucking schoolmarm. And in this moment—in this fantasy at least—I want access to my body. I want to own my sexuality, for once in my life. I want to be the opposite of every adjective my church leaders use to describe women—the antonym of good, tender, merciful, and kind. Graceful, delicate, divine. Radiant, sensitive, selfless. Dignified. Quietly strong. Charming, peaceful, refined. Virtuous and loving. Deserving of reverence. Above all, possessing the nature to nurture.

With this list of adjectives roiling in my head, and the "when we get married," and *the* car, I feel the blur of a tunnel closing in, a concrete barrier approaching at a deadly speed. I duck under one of Murphy's arms and make a run for it—down the steps, across the road, through the swinging doors of what would have been the saloon. In the desiccated mirror above the bar, I see myself reflected in a different imagination. Here, I'm a woman whose hair gleams a rich henna red. My dress is cobalt blue, silk, with a neckline certain to inspire thoughts deliciously impure. A guy named Slim plays vaudeville songs on the piano, while a line of thirsty men watches my every move.

In real life, I step behind the bar, trailing a finger through the dust. And in my fantasy, I pour whiskey. I tell stories, joke with men who stay longer than they should, put off the short walk home for dinner or back to the mine. I wink and say, "This one's on me, Sugar," sliding a glass down the length of the bar. My persona is a perfect marriage of brash and coy: "Damn right I own the place. Better treat me right if you want your whistle wet." Over the din of music and laughter, I turn my attention to the business at hand—and the pleasure of knowing there's a fat stash of hundreds in my bustier, a pearl-handled Derringer strapped to my thigh.

I look up to see Murphy backlit in the doorway. "There you are," he says. "I thought I'd lost you." He holds out his hand, says it's time we got back on the road. And though we try our best, I never do get to see the Big Sky valley; a storm rolls in at sunset, just as we do. In minutes, the sky turns the color of charcoal, spits out deafening, apocalyptic stones of hail. We pull to the side of the highway and watch all color leach from the plains, like a TV suddenly flipped to black-and-white.

But it's not until two weeks later that what's been bottled up between us bursts out in a similar torrent. "I love you *because* you're Mormon," Murphy says emphatically. "It's who you are. Our kids can be Mormon; *you* can be Mormon. I wouldn't want to change that!" His voice rises in frustration; it's too loud, right in my ear. I pull away from where I've been lying against him. "But every time I go to church with you, I feel like everyone's trying to trap me in a room and convert me." Which, in truth, they are. "I want you, and your family, to love me for who *I* am," he shouts, "To let me be who I am."

"I do love you," I say. "I promise I do."

But I let Murphy break things off. The next morning, when he calls to say he didn't sleep all night, maybe we made a mistake, I say, no; you were right. I let him be the one who decided. I let him believe our religious differences are the insurmountable problem. Why would I admit the awful, unnecessary truth—that I'd marry him regardless, if when I left his house last night, just beneath the weight of my sadness, I didn't feel a wash of relief. I'd marry him tomorrow if I didn't feel myself hesitate every time he says, "You're the love of my life; I'll never need anything but you." How could I bring myself to say I want more than the everything Murphy is offering.

Chapter 6

If music be the food of love, play on.
Give me excess of it.

—WILLIAM SHAKESPEARE

———————◆———————

The clacking Cuban rhythm of *la clave* drifts from the third-floor windows of the OddFellows Building on Tenth and East Pine. I'm standing on the sidewalk outside, letting the syncopated pulse, the tropical cacophony of bongos, congas, and timbales wash over me. This is the soundtrack, and upstairs the velvet-curtained Century Ballroom is the setting of my secret life. By night, I'm a salsa dancer.

I dance three, four, sometimes five nights a week, needing it like other people need medicine, or street drugs. I've been addicted since my first lesson two years ago, and I follow the salsa schedule as if Moses himself brought it down from the mount: Tuesdays at Misty's, Thursdays and Saturdays at Century Ballroom, Fridays at China Harbor, Wednesdays at Vito's, Sundays at the Last Supper Club, where I've never gone, except for once on my birthday, because nightclubs and the Sabbath don't mix.

Inside, I walk the edge of the three-thousand-square-foot hardwood floor, dodging dancers dressed to the nines and slick with sweat. I hurry to the balcony to change my shoes and stash my bag under a long, velvet-covered bench. And from my vantage point at the railing, I watch the crowd: a kaleidoscope of color and sound, turning and weaving, spinning in chaotic though predictable patterns.

"Hola, Mami," says a voice behind me. I turn to see Miguel Martinez giving me the up-and-down: appraising my rhinestone-studded dance shoes, and my dress, which bares one of my shoulders, shows a few inches of leg above the knee. My mouth I've painted scarlet red. I am set and ready to give my body to a man—any man—to lead.

Miguel has a jaw so big he is like a caricature of himself. He sports a pompadour, a black button-down shirt, and a light-colored suit. He teaches the occasional dance class, and, if the rumors are true, he will move into your house and spend every one of your dollars if you give him the chance.

I kiss him hello, grab his hand, and practically run downstairs to the dance floor. In his arms, I am a tornado of hair and sequins: skirt flaring, eyes flashing. He leads me through a never-ending store of intricate moves, every one of our steps riffing off the basic quick-quick-slow, quick-quick-slow. And when our dance is over, I make my way to the fan near the stage, to cool off and catch my breath—all the while thanking God in heaven the floor was too crowded for Miguel to have pulled out his signature move: flamboyant, embarrassing James Brown splits.

Minutes later, I'm dancing with the dark and delicious Oris, thinking of nothing but the pleasure of moving in rhythm with his body. He is taller than I—a rare thing, given my heels. His shoulder and bicep under my left hand are a testament to the glory and goodness of God. Since the semester I taught a world myth survey, I can't help but think of him as Osiris, the mythological Egyptian king who ruled through kindness and persuasion, who was sometimes called the lord of love and silence. I bask in the music, and the thrill of knowing it doesn't matter if my neckline is low, if my dress is tight.

Here, I am not a Mormon, not a virgin, not a schoolteacher. I am only a woman here, only my body moving in response to the pressure of someone else's hands.

Toward the end of the night, when the crowd is starting to thin, I stand near the stage, resting my burning feet. A thrilling blast of horns introduces the first measures of a favorite song, and I look up to see James walking toward me, dressed entirely in black. The cocktail tables at the edges of the room blur out of focus, like a scene from a made-for-TV movie. Our eyes lock as the sea of dancers parts in front of us.

In slow motion.

Backed by a high-powered wind machine.

The mysterious, elusive James is the man I am always hoping to see. He is a former US Marine who briefly worked as a journalist and a drummer before joining the police force and making detective as fast as his department allowed. A tough guy with great rhythm, he's also a stickler for the subjunctive mood.

There isn't much about James that doesn't turn me on. He's the fantasy, the if-only. He's the Rockettes' sequined sparkle-pants, the dusk rose '57 Thunderbird with white leather interior. He's the villa on the French Riviera, the date to Cannes with George Clooney. James is what other people, living other lives, get to have. So I settle for the way he looks at me without looking away, his dangerous-feeling flirtation, the breathtaking closeness of him, certain times we dance.

He rests a hand on my hip and leans in to kiss me hello, which makes me feel tingly *down there*. I'm embarrassed by my reaction to James: how I blush when he's near me, how I have to work not to sigh over the vowels in his name. "James," I say, though in my head it's a purr. "What's with the sideburns?"

Required to look tough for his job, his facial hair often does the work of creating personae. He puts his hand to his face, shakes his head, and without saying a word, guides me ahead of him, to the dance floor.

"You know," I say, looking over my shoulder, "if Luke Perry was—"

"If Luke Perry *were*," James corrects, smiling wryly. His deep, boyish dimples work in contrast to his square chin, the perpetual shadow of his beard.

"You've got to stop doing that."

"I will, when you get it right." He turns to face me, puts his right hand under my shoulder blade, and stands close enough to make me nervous. His body is dense and muscular, a thick, magnetic force.

"Stop," I say, laughing.

"What am I doing?" He's teasing me on purpose. Inching closer, murmuring in my ear. Rather than respond, I blush more deeply. "Tell me," he says, but all I can think about is the heat of his breath on my skin, the millimeters of fabric separating his thigh from mine. We're standing too still, too close in the crush of dancers swirling around us, but the man is the one who leads. He isn't moving so I can't either. He knows what he's doing.

James knows I'm Mormon, can tell I'm attracted to him, and that it unnerves me. He's probably inside my head right now, where I'm picturing myself in leather pants and five-inch heels, sliding a leg behind both of his, knocking him flat on his back, *Charlie's Angels*-style. In that scenario, I *pounce*.

But in reality, the most I can do is allow myself to be tortured by wanting him closer and needing him to step away, let me breathe. Just when I think I can't take it, in the second before I cut and run, leave him stranded on the dance floor, James steps forward on the one—my cue to dance. Soon I am sweating, spinning, laughing, flushed with pheromones and joy. "Do that thing that makes me scream," I call over the music. There's a move he does, a series of dizzying, complicated turns, ending in a deep, ridiculous dip.

"Yes, love," he says, spinning me into his chest. "For you—anything."

Moments like these are the Band-Aid I've come to depend on.

The overnight cure for the profound asexuality of my life. Though
James is my favorite, it doesn't matter who I dance with; what matters
is being held in the arms of one man after another, moving my hips
in the figure of an eight until sweat runs the length of my back. Human contact is what matters. A sliver of physical intimacy, a promise
of what might one day come.

These moments are the antidote to dating in the LDS community, as well, which continues to provide none of the above. Leila—an
exotically beautiful, single LDS schoolteacher who slid into the role
of best friend after Alicia had a baby, went silent, and moved away—
convinced me two years ago to sign up for LDSSingles.com. I worried that online dating speaks to desperation, and cited—among a
slew of examples—the guy who took her on a brutal, high-elevation
hike and kept shouting, when she fell behind, "Come *on*! You *do*
work out, don't you?" Leila trumped that argument by pointing out
that he introduced her to salsa dancing at least—a blessed alternative to our other available dance venues: awkward, demoralizing
singles dances held in church gyms, or nightclubs teeming with
creepers set and ready to rub up against us when our backs are
turned.

Leila also pointed out that we already know every age-appropriate
single Mormon man in the greater Seattle/Tacoma area. "It's time for
broader horizons," she insisted, and sat down at her computer to sign
me up, under the username longcoolwoman, for a free thirty-day
trial. "If you want to marry in the church, geography cannot be an
issue," Leila declared, checking "nationwide" under the search crite-
ria. And she's not wrong: the Mormon dating pool, small to begin
with, is shrinking exponentially with every passing year. I played
along, spent the next two hours searching for Mormon men who are
attractive, employed, educated, no more than two inches shorter than
I, no more than ten years older, who lack overt commitment phobia,
porn addiction, obvious misogynistic or homosexual tendencies,

and the immediate need for a new mommy for their four-plus children.

Over the next month, in the pursuit of love in the LDS kingdom of God, I flirted impressively online—so clever, so attentive; I rushed home after work and woke up early, breathless as Meg Ryan, to see if *I Had Mail.* It wasn't long before I put on a fabulous outfit, and, with a prayer in my heart, flew to LA to meet an up-and-coming indie filmmaker. I love California, and movies, and writers. I imagined us living near the beach, wearing sunglasses all year round. Collaborating on projects, talking about *craft* over Niçoise salads at outdoor cafés. It may have worked out, if we'd had even an ounce of chemistry.

My one-month trial turned into a one-year subscription when I noticed the profile of a delightfully brainy Boston MBA. We met in person for the first time at a mutual friend's party in New York, where he started every conversation by inhaling deeply, and throwing out some snooty gambit along the lines of "for those of you who don't already *subscribe* to the *New Yorker* . . ." or "what you *don't* know about the Ivy League . . ."

Upon my return to Seattle, I met a sci-fi aficionado who declared at dinner, between two excruciating pauses, "You sure eat a lot."

It's been two years since then, and not much has changed. The most important and difficult thing, at twenty-nine, is not to get discouraged. I've known for ten years at least that if the kind of man I want exists within the Church of Jesus Christ of Latter-day Saints, he is rare, not unlike the endangered red panda of the Himalayas. Show me an LDS man who's wickedly funny, politically liberal, brighter than the average bear, and uncommitted to 1950s gender roles, and I will show you the shaggy tail and waddling gait of the *Ailurus fulgens,* its mischievous mouth rife with bamboo.

Leila is on the hunt for her own red panda: one who could also be forgiving of the years she was less than devout. She and I circle around the same conversation nearly every time we meet. "There have to be men out there like us: committed to the Gospel, if not the culture of the church," she says. I nod in agreement. "Mormon, but normal. Two Normons in a sea of Boremons and Whoremons."

Tonight, like every night at the salsa club, there is a rush for the door during the last song. Stay ten minutes too long, and the harrowing reality lights will break every romantic spell, call attention to smeared makeup, wilted hair, sweat-soaked clothes. Outside, the night air is a welcome relief, and I stop to pull my hair back, needing the breeze on my neck. I hear footsteps close behind me and turn to see Miguel, who offers to walk me down the long stretch of parking on Eleventh Avenue.

Seconds later, he cuts to the chase. "Take me home with you," he murmurs, in his thick Cuban accent, with a hand on the small of my back. Before I can respond, he says, inches from my ear. "*Corazón.* Don't say no."

"Miguel," I say in my firm but kind schoolteacher tone. "There is zero percent chance of that happening. But thank you."

He holds up his hands, as if I've misunderstood. "*Mira.* I just want to sleep next to you. Nothing else, I promise. You break my heart you're so beautiful. I just want to be close." His brow is furrowed, his eyes beseeching. He is like a character from a telenovela.

I laugh out loud. "Do women *fall* for that?"

He grins, and pulls me close to him. "*Ay*, you are so mean. I *like* it." I laugh harder when he nuzzles into my neck.

"Come on, now; let's go, *nena*," says Miguel, but I keep walking.

"Maybe try Tracey?" I suggest, pointing to a slightly trashy-looking brunette walking ahead of us. I notice James as well, holding his car door open for a beautiful girl named Chloe. I know nothing about her, except that her hair is like a Pantene commercial, and she somehow manages never to sweat. I'd heard they were seeing each other, but still. I wish it were me, sitting next to him in the dark of his car, wondering whether he'll take me straight home, or invite me back to his place.

"Oh, that girl, she hates me," says Miguel, dismissively, not noticing my gaze still lingering on James. "I am already a bad boy, for her."

"This is me," I say, stopping to fish for my keys. "Thanks for walking me."

"Okay, okay," he capitulates, but steps closer. "I know, you're a nice girl. But sometimes," he puts his hands on my waist, "even nice girls, they like to kiss?"

I roll my eyes, feigning more irritation than I actually feel. I'm mildly charmed. "You've got two minutes," I say, leaning into Miguel. "And keep your hands off my ass."

In the same way I've learned to cull every sensation from the four-minute flirtations I have on the dance floor, I sustain myself on the occasional interlude like this, my back pressed up against a car door, a man's mouth on mine. I hone in on the details—the scratch of his beard against my neck, the grip of his hand in my hair, some scent, some shiver of memory to turn over in my mouth, to savor during the long drive home to my empty bed.

Since Murphy and I broke up three years ago, life hasn't exactly been what I expected: it's become less rather than more adventurous. I've done well at my job, earned a master of education and a continuing teaching certificate, bought a car, and a house in a slightly unsavory, soon-to-be-gentrified neighborhood. An investment. Someplace I won't be reluctant to leave when I get married. Because in the LDS world, the man's job takes priority: he'll be the breadwinner. We'll live where he works, whoever he'll turn out to be. The other side of that compromise is the timeshare I bought two years ago—with points to cash in at destinations worldwide. Now, my hypothetical Mormon husband will never be able to say it's impractical to travel. "Too late now," I'll trill. "It's paid for," as I click on the link for Sayulita.

Those worries, however, remain entirely unfounded—I've had no romantic prospects, unless you count the short-lived relationship with a beautiful East African man, who, on what turned out to be our last date said, "I feel like I might freak out and rape you." He was probably exaggerating, probably just didn't think about how to appropriately express his frustration with my uncompromising virginity. I wasn't about to stick around and find out.

Otherwise, life has settled into a series of predictable patterns, dictated mostly by work: Monday through Friday I'm up at 6:00, at work by 7:10, though my contract says 7:00. I spend my workdays like Pavlov's dog, living my life in response to bells: seventeen minutes for this, nine minutes for that, five to walk, twenty to eat. Sprinkle in a few nights out dancing, then my workweek ends Saturday afternoon, after I supervise weekend detention—why not, I'd be grading papers at home anyway, for free.

Sundays I go to church at a singles ward, where the entire congregation is made up of unmarried Mormons between eighteen and thirty—our leaders' plan to help us meet and marry. Sunday dinner with my parents is followed by a short detour to my dad's office, where I log in to LDSSingles.com, hoping for a sighting of the illusory red panda.

There are four exceptions per year, when I skip the singles ward and join my parents' congregation: Christmas, Easter, Father's Day, and Mother's Day, which is this week. I arrive early, knowing my mom will be late, as usual. I spent half my childhood sitting on a curb, last to be picked up from summer camp and field trips, soccer practice and sleepovers. By age ten I'd trained my ears to distinguish the sound of a Volvo from half a mile away. I never doubted she'd show up eventually, but I also never failed to be infuriated.

Today is *her* day, however, so I am practicing my patience. I save her seat on the end of the padded wooden pew with a bouquet of waxy, deep-purple tulips. It's a color both she and I love, theatrically called Queen of the Night. I catch my father's eye, and wave. He's sitting at the front of the chapel, in the first row of seats, near the grand piano. He's currently serving as the second counselor in the bishopric, meaning he's one of the three spiritual and administrative leaders of the ward—all of them middle-aged men in dark suits and white shirts. My dad's tie, however, is a daring shade of pink, in contrast to the conservative stripes of the others. I recognize it right away: last year's Father's Day gift, from yours truly. I nod to the empty seat beside me, and lift my eyebrows. My dad raises his hands in defeat, and I can almost hear him say it: "Rather than fight it, kiddo, I prefer to stay married."

"Welcome brothers and sisters, on this beautiful Sabbath morning," the bishop says, approaching the wooden pulpit after the opening prayer and hymn. He's a stockbroker by day, called to be bishop the year before, a duty that generally lasts five years before another worthy priesthood holder is asked to take over.

"As you know, today is the day we celebrate the mothers of our ward," he says, adjusting the microphone and looking down at his notes. "The prophet Gordon B. Hinckley said, 'God planted within women something divine that expresses itself in quiet strength, in refinement, in peace, in goodness, in virtue, in truth, in love. And all of these remarkable qualities find their truest and most satisfying expression in motherhood.'" He looks out to the congregation and says, "So let us all have a prayer in our hearts today as we thank the Lord for our kind and loving mothers."

My mother sits down in the middle of the bishop's welcome— followed, as usual, by a wave of expensive perfume. "Yeah, *right*," she whispers, picking a stray hair from my sweater and setting the tulips on her lap. "I'm not thanking anyone for *my* mother."

Every year on this day, she listens as two adults and a youth speaker each talk for ten minutes on the assigned topic of "mothers." Rainbows and butterflies spill from their mouths, float heavenward beside charming anecdotes of family outings and homemade pie. And every year, my mother's eyes well with tears as the real-life nightmares of her childhood surface from the place she keeps them buried.

Her mother, my maternal grandmother, was the convert on that side of the family, so my mother was baptized at age eight, like most members are. But despite her conversion, my grandmother was violent and manipulative, a pedophile who terrorized my mother, and invited others into her house—and her bed—to do the same. My maternal grandfather, a long-haul trucker, was kind and loving. But he was gone much of the time, and pretended not to know what was happening to his daughter at the hands of his wife.

Because both her parents failed her so profoundly, and because I believe the spirit is eternal, I sometimes imagine I was with my mother, then. I am grown, in this imagining—a spirit version of my current self. My mother is the child walking beside me, down a bleak, dusty road after school. It's 1955, early September in Battle Creek, Michigan, and the temperature is nearing ninety. The air buzzes around our ears, and with each step toward her house, my mother is moving farther and farther from safety. I can't stop what is about to happen, can't keep her from putting her hand on the knob, opening the door to greet her abuser.

But I imagine she can sense me next to her. That she can feel my hand on her shoulder, like a swirl of cool air against her thin cotton dress. I imagine my words are stronger than the waves of despair and self-hatred rising like heat from her skin. "You will survive this," I say to the girl who became my mother. "You are a warrior."

Sitting beside me, holding the bouquet of purple tulips I've brought, my mother is in her fifties. Still beautiful: silver-haired, and indomitable. The one time I asked how she reconciles her faith with her mother's hypocrisy and abuse, her answer was simple: "I didn't think about it," she said. "I don't think about it."

My mother's relationship with God has been unfailing. The Gospel kept her sane, kept her from killing herself when she felt she might. Her spiritual life kept her from continuing to believe, as her mother insisted, that she was worthless. God has promised my mother that she will one day live with him, and be glorified. Her temple marriage seals her, eternally, to the family she created. She will be with my father, my brother, and me, forever in joy—as long as all of us remain worthy.

My mother reaches to hold my hand. I know what to do, what comes next. She's already said the first line of the drama we've invented to exorcise the spirits of her past: "I'm not thanking anyone for *my* mother." And now it's my job to set up the joke, to say the awful thing.

"Isn't she dead yet?" I whisper.

"She's so mean, even God doesn't want her," my mother responds, holding in a smile.

I squeeze her hand, and she blesses my cheek with an imprint of her red lips. She keeps her hand in mine until the organ's last chord fades over the echo of the sacrament hymn, the signal that we should close our eyes, bow our heads, and wait for the resounding voice of a teenage boy. He asks us to eat the bread he's broken in remembrance of the body of God's son, to take his name upon us, to keep the commandments we've been given, that we will always have his spirit to be with us.

A hush settles over the room as he prays. It settles within me, as well. Each time I exhale, I imagine Jesus rebuking the wind, saying unto the sea, "Peace, be still." During the sacrament service, in its singular, blessed silence, I am a daughter of God—nothing else, nothing less. It's during this time that I often think of verses from the book of Luke. "But even the very hairs of your head are all numbered."

I eat the bread that's been broken for me, and I drink the water that has likewise been blessed. "Fear not," he said. "Ye are of more value than many sparrows."

I promise, as I do every Sunday, to always remember him; and I pray that God will also remember me.

Near the end of the meeting, the bishop stands again, clears his throat into the microphone. He thanks the choir, the speakers, and the young men who blessed and passed the sacrament.

"At this time," he says, "we would like to ask all women over the age of eighteen to stand, so the youth of our ward can present a gift of appreciation to you as mothers."

There's always a gift—some small token, often handmade. This is the first time I can remember being asked to receive it, though the request isn't that strange; the LDS Gospel assures every woman she'll bear children in the hereafter if she is denied that blessing on earth. Motherhood is every woman's spiritual birthright.

The bishop cues the organist, and the children's hymn "Love at Home" resounds as teenagers swarm both aisles, holding grocery bags teeming with carnations. They hand beribboned corsages down the padded wooden pews. Like peanuts at a baseball game, they're passed from husband to child, to older brother, to toddler, to younger sister, to older sister, and, finally, to mother or grandmother, cousin or aunt—whichever stands closest, waiting to receive.

My mother pokes me in the ribs when I make no move to stand.

"No way," I whisper. "It's *Mother's* Day."

"But look," she motions across the aisle at a college-aged girl, standing tall.

"Mom. Sister Bingham is married, and plans to have one million babies. She already looks pregnant."

"That might just be her dress. Well, then, what about Janice?" She looks ahead to a woman my age who's been trying for ten years to conceive and/or adopt.

"Why are you making this a big deal?" I whisper, irritated.

"You're making it a big deal. They're just being nice."

"I'm not wearing a *corsage* all day, pretending I feel something I don't."

"Well, I don't want to wear that ugly thing either," my mother whispers, pinching the inside of my arm, like she did when I was a kid, misbehaving. "But I'm being *polite*."

She stands as the carnations approach. I watch them marching forward and sideways down the rows, and my heart is a drum in my ears. I feel the flowers encroaching like a delicate, pink tsunami. My jaw locks against it. My teeth grind, as a surge of panic rushes through me. My mind flashes, without warning, to an image from a short story I often read with my students: the flushed, sweating face of Mathilda, a fierce, beautiful child, who, when her doctor violently, ecstatically, pushes a wooden tongue depressor into her mouth to save her from diphtheria, reduces it to splinters, leaving her own mouth cut and bloody.

I step quickly into the aisle, though I shouldn't, in the middle of the service. But I'm seeing only the door, needing its weight between me and the voice that calls after: "Like Eve, your motherhood began before you were born . . . It is the essence of who you are as women. It defines your very identity, your divine stature and nature, and the unique traits your Father gave you."

My throat closes against the words I can't swallow, not one more time. Because it's not *true*, what they're telling me—what they've been telling me since I was a child. There cannot be only one way to be a woman. My identity cannot be something I've never felt.

I try to steady myself with a hand on the wall, but these subversive thoughts only serve to increase my panic. I'm bent at the waist, nearly crippled by the possibility that what I've been taught is a lie. *I* have to be wrong, rather than the church, the Gospel, the prophet. I must be misunderstanding God's will, or his plan for me. I need to feel what I'm supposed to, *be* what I'm supposed to. I've been taught that the LDS gospel is absolute truth; if one lie is revealed, what then? How could I allow it? Let my entire belief system collapse like a house of cards.

Leaning against the wall separating me from the rest of the congregation, I do as I have always done. I turn to God. Through the rush of blood in my ears, I ask him to help me breathe through this. Dilute the thick, liquid-feeling fear, strong as a fist around my lungs. Help me return to my place in the pew beside my mother, sit still, act normal, pretend all I needed was a drink of water.

Chapter 7

And the day came when the risk to remain tight in a bud was more painful than the risk it took to blossom.

—ANAÏS NIN

———— ◆ ————

I awake, with a start, to a noise at the door. I sit up, frightened, realizing I've been asleep in a bed in what I thought was my house, but the real owners are at the door. Rattling their keys, opening the lock. They have arrived without warning. They are coming inside, and I can't be discovered. I have only seconds to erase all evidence of myself. I rush frantically, shoving clothes and books inside the closet, pushing papers and books under the bed. I sweep my arm across the dresser, dumping jewelry and photographs haphazardly into drawers.

I usually awake in the middle of this nightmare sleepwalk, disoriented, chagrined to find myself doing it, again. Sometimes it's not until morning that I see the evidence: once I woke to find I'd taken down all the pictures in my bedroom and set them neatly against the walls, facing inward, to reveal nothing but blank brown paper, hooks, and wire.

I've always assumed it was a stress dream, prompted by grad school, or work, or both. Until last night, halfway through a reading by the poet Jane Hirshfield. She looked up from her book of poems to address the small crowd gathered in the event space at the Elliott Bay Book Company. "You know the dream everyone has?" she said, her long, graying hair backlit by the lamp at the side of the stage, lending her the air of a clairvoyant. "Where you're in your house and one room leads to another room, which leads to another, all of which are unfinished?"

I've never had the dream she's describing, so I waited to hear where the story would take her, how it would inform the poem she would read next. She went on with a wave of her hand. "Obviously, the house represents soul and self. You all know that." She said it in a throwaway tone, an apologetic aside. "Jungian psychology."

All I could hear after that was my heartbeat in my ears. All I could feel was the chill running through me, the hair standing up on my arms. How long have I been having the dream, now—a year, two years? How long have my brain and body been trying to tell me: *I don't live in my house.*

I can't shake last night's experience—my recurring dream—and what it might mean, though I'm doing my best to focus on work. It's a professional development day, and I'm one of ten teachers sitting in a circle of desks in a windowless classroom adjacent to the library. We're as ready as we'll ever be to learn the art of the Socratic seminar. Our instructor is a dapper, gray-haired consultant in a charcoal suit and crimson tie. It's clear from his clothes that he is better paid than we. He's crush-worthy, though, which brightens my mood. Also, he's made the epic mistake of telling us we should "model student behavior."

"Hey, Mr. Peterson," I call to the chemistry teacher. "Can you teach me how to make *E*?"

Ms. Daniels, a young, green-eyed English teacher raises her hand. "Um, *excuse* me? I need to go to the *day*care? So I can *breast*feed? It's been like three *hours*, and I'm—"

"Whatever, *Deanna*," interrupts Ms. Duncan, my assigned mentor. "There's only one of us allowed out at a time, and I have to *smoke*."

Mr. Walters, a history teacher, is graffiti-ing his desk with a mechanical pencil. Writing the numbers 420 in every shape, size, and font he can imagine—a symbol of the culturally appointed time for kids across America to get good and high.

I'm disappointed when the silver fox asks us to settle down, class, and pay attention before I can do my impression of Clay, the tenth-grade boy too lazy to walk to the trash, who put his aluminum gum wrapper in the electrical outlet, which popped like a gunshot. Sparks flew. Clay ended up in the nurse's office with a free round of electroshock therapy and first-degree burns on his hand. Or maybe I would've done my impression of Billy, who came to school one morning wearing his mother's contact lenses. Not realizing the problem, he'd politely raised his hand for permission to go throw up.

The consultant, having regained our attention, asks us to read from the text he's handed out. He indicates to me, and I look down at the photocopy of *Salvador Late or Early* by Sandra Cisneros.

"Salvador with eyes the color of caterpillar," I begin. "Salvador of the crooked hair and crooked teeth, Salvador whose name the teacher cannot remember, is a boy who is no one's friend, runs along somewhere in that vague direction where homes are the color of bad weather . . ." My voice melts into the too-long sentence, savoring the rhythms that conjure the boy so clearly I can almost feel him in the room.

Ms. Daniels takes up where I leave off, but I'm back again at the beginning, feeling every syllable in my mouth and picturing Salvador—his crooked teeth, his crooked hair. Watching as he combs his brothers' hair with water, feeds them from a cup made of tin.

Soon, it is Mr. Walters reading, "that forty-pound body of boy with its geography of scars, its history of hurt, limbs stuffed with feathers and rags, in what part of the eyes, in what part of the heart, in that cage of the chest where something throbs with both fists and knows only what Salvador knows," a sentence that inspires a sudden rush of tears. The now-familiar collapse of my lungs under a merciless hand, squeezing.

The sentence is an echo inside me, a call to the throbbing fists of my own heart, and the answer comes without warning. Everything I've pushed down, locked away, begged to stay silent rushes to the surface of my consciousness. My throat is a pulse, contracted and burning with the effort to remain silent. My vision is a frightened blur, and I put my forehead in my hands, let my hair fall forward to hide this visceral, disproportionate reaction.

My colleagues feel far away from me; their voices have a tinny, distant sound—Mr. Walters saying, "the color of caterpillar. What a phrase. And *the boy* was inside the throat that must apologize."

"Homes the color of bad weather," says Ms. Duncan. "In a vague direction, no one even knows where."

In front of me is the story, certain words raised and rippled inside perfect, circular teardrops. These words, blurred and magnified, will serve as evidence. Watermarks to remind me, in case I try to forget Salvador, disappearing. Like a memory of kites. Like me, disappearing. Allowing myself to disappear. Living according to the "they say" and the "you should." Allowing the should and the they to determine my choices, dictate my life, what am I *doing* living in Kent, wearing sweater sets and sensible shoes, driving a fucking *Corolla*? Whose life am I living?

This is the moment, I think, still hiding behind my hair, still looking at the tearstained photocopy on my desk, remembering an interview Toni Morrison gave. She talked about struggling as a single mother, working as an editor at a publishing house. Working late one night, unsure of what to do next, she wrote down the only two things that mattered: "Mother my children. Write books." After that, she said, everything was clear. Not easier, but clear. Regardless of what my colleagues are learning, what I'm supposed to be learning, prompted by a handsome man in a suit and tie, the only thing I can do is write the numbers one and two in the margin of *Salvador Late or Early.* "Write books," I print in capitals, by the number one. "See the world" is number two. But I add a third: "Decide."

When I get home from work, I change into flannel pants and crawl into my sleigh bed. It's the first piece of real furniture I ever bought, and serves as my office: it's where I read, plan lessons, grade papers, write letters, pay bills, make calls. On the pillow next to me is a collection of stories lying facedown, open to the page where I last left off. *Reasons to Live* by Amy Hempel.

She gave a reading one afternoon, at BYU; I'd never heard of her at the time, had never even been to a reading before. She had a quiet, intense presence, a glamour reminiscent of Julie Christie's. Her prose was hypnotic, as if her words hung in the air long after she released them. I bought her book and read it twice, every word, from beginning to end. Krista saw it lying on our couch, and snatched it up. She brought it to me, held in two fingers, as if it might be made of plastic explosives.

"Reasons to *live?*" she said, visibly upset. She asked if I were *looking for some.* We laughed for weeks about that misunderstanding, but after what happened today at work, I'm thinking maybe Krista wasn't so far off.

Amy Hempel teaches at Bennington College, according to the back of her book. And the website for Bennington College says there is a master of fine arts program for creative writing, which admits nine to ten students per genre twice per year. I decide to be one of them.

I make calls to Ms. Daniels, Ms. Duncan, and one other colleague to propose a writer's group that will meet once a month. I figure I'll need deadlines and feedback to help me prepare my writing sample. I decide to study poetry, though I've never written poetry beyond the angsty teenage variety. But it seems easier to produce fifteen pages of poetry than fifty pages of prose before August, when applications are due. I look online for classes to take, because I'll need letters of recommendation, and who better to write them than teachers?

Seven months later, when I drop my application into a blue metal mailbox on the side of the road, I know I may not get in; I probably won't, given the odds. I also know it doesn't matter. I've taken the first of however many steps will be required to set myself on the path to writing. I've sent, in that manila envelope, the biggest, most beautiful fuck-you to the "they say" and the "you should." To every naysaying voice—including my own—telling me writing isn't wise, isn't practical, isn't possible or responsible, for a girl like me.

The week before my birthday, on a blustery, rain-smelling autumn day, I get the news I've been waiting for. "I'm calling with what I hope will be good news," says the voice on the phone, which belongs to Liam Rector, director of the Bennington Writing Seminars. "I'd like to offer you a spot in the Writing Seminars program, beginning in January."

"Really?" I say, in the voice you'd use if it were George Clooney on the phone, asking you to be his date to Cannes. "Holy crap, thank you. Thank you. All I've been wanting is a reason to quit my job."

The four administrators in my building have divided into two warring factions, and my work environment has become unbearable. My principal is on the opposite of the side that champions me, and despite my stellar teaching evaluations, she seems bent on calling me into her office for disciplinary lectures, which I generally disregard. It's hard to have respect for a boss with a penchant for getting drunk at faculty parties, flaunting her very obvious breast augmentation, and (rumor has it) sleeping with teachers. Not to mention she's a liar who throws her teachers under the bus.

The first of these lectures dealt with my wardrobe. She accused me of dressing inappropriately for work. I looked down at my boat-neck sweater, knee-length skirt, and boots. "You tell me," I said, glancing pointedly at her blouse, straining against its buttons, her skirt so short the control top of her pantyhose showed when she crossed her legs.

Most recently, she accused me of coming to school hungover, and telling my students how I "love to party." I stared out the window of her office, counting my rage slowly down from ten. The effort to stay professional fought valiantly against my righteous-feeling anger. "You know I'm Mormon, right?" I asked, and she responded with a chilly silence. "Which means I don't *party*. I've never had a drink in my life. I look tired in the mornings because I'm *tired*. I'm late sometimes because of *traffic*."

A bell rang then, and I left, despite having not been excused. I would have slammed the door were it not for the hydraulic arm, likely installed to prevent exactly that kind of dramatic exit.

"Don't do anything rash," Liam interjects. "The benefit of the low-residency program is you can *keep* your job. Remember, you'll only be in Vermont twice per year, for ten days at a time. Give it some thought."

"Sure. Of course. Yes, I'll be there. I'm saying yes!" I hang up before my voice has a chance to break, and I lie back on the couch, devolving into a tearful, joyful, ecstatic mess. I keep the news to myself—at least for tonight. As soon as I share it, my excitement will be diluted, almost immediately: by my boss's objections, my parents' worries. Why would I quit my job, give up my salary, benefits, and retirement plan in favor of an unnecessary degree that will put me significantly into debt and not further my career? I have a mortgage to think about. Why not just take a class on the weekends or in the summer, if I want to write poems? They won't understand why I'd risk anything, everything, for this chance.

When I talk to my principal, I tell her a lie: "I'd like to stay on full-time, take unpaid leave during my residencies," I say from my usual seat in her office. "Unfortunately, those twenty days per year don't line up with summer or winter break, so I'll need a sub. But I hope we can work it out." I know she'll say no. She'll say no to letting me work half-time, too; it's more expensive to pay two half-time teachers than one full-time, though I'm fuzzy on exactly why. No surprise, she does exactly what I expect her to: tells me I'll need to defer my acceptance and finish the contract I signed in September.

"You can leave at the end of the year," she says, untangling her earring from a strand of her oversprayed, overprocessed hair.

"That's not an option," I say, which is true. If I don't go in January, I'll have to reapply. And I was waitlisted this time—only got my spot because another student forfeited hers. Who knows if I'd even be accepted again. "I'll finish this semester," I concede. "But I'll still need a sub for ten days in January. I have plenty of sick leave."

"That's not how sick leave works."

"I might suddenly take ill in January, then." Our conversation has clearly devolved into a battle of wills, and I'm not about to back down.

"If that's your decision, don't come back after Christmas," she says, though she and I both know that's the worst thing for my students. They'll have to finish the last month of the term with whatever sub can be scrounged up, who may or may not know anything about world mythology, poetry, or speech and debate. "There could be legal action," she warns, "if we can't fill your spot."

"I'll take my chances," I say, standing up to leave. She's bluffing. It's expensive to sue, and there are always teachers looking for jobs. I walk out feeling the most glorious collage of relief, excitement, hope, happiness, and pride that I did not tell her to kiss my ass. I'd have done it, maybe, if it weren't for the fact that I'm already gone.

When I hung up after that call from Liam, I lay on my couch, thinking *this is how it begins*. I slowly let out the breath I wasn't aware I'd been holding. Lying there, cradling the phone to my chest, what I felt washing over me was something akin to forgiveness. Like I'd made a vital reparation to myself. *Here I go*, I thought. *Here. I. go.*

I'll be thirty next week, which will bring a bigger change even than Bennington. After my birthday, I'll be considered a single adult, rather than a *young* single adult. Ironic that I feel young, look young, *am* young everywhere else in the world. But at church, I'll no longer lay claim to that adjective. And since single adults aren't allowed to attend wards designed for *young* single adults, I'll be evicted from my congregation.

Leila, who's younger than I am, will stay, and I'll begin attending the family ward whose boundaries include my address. Ward boundaries, worldwide, work like school districts. Depending on where we live, members are assigned a specific time and place to worship: this way it's easy for people to build close communities, and to help each other when needed. It also means that the ward where my membership records will be transferred is made up entirely of strangers. I'll likely be the only adult in the congregation who's never been married.

The separation of young single adults from (plain old) single adults is supposedly a precaution against older men courting girls as young as eighteen. I'm not sure why said girls can't be taught to simply say no to men they're not interested in dating. Truthfully, I'm not sure it's a good idea to separate singles at all. Because we're absent from regular congregations, we singles—and our concerns—aren't often considered. Our absence reinforces the fact that a single life cannot be respected the way a married life can; it certainly can't be admired—unless as an example of how to bear a trial.

Singlehood is a problem to be solved. Even the bishops in singles wards are impatient with us, frustrated with the amount of time they spend away from their families, dealing with violations of the law of chastity. There's an easy solution, we're often reminded. "Just *choose* one," said one bishop to a male friend of mine, and indicated, like a game show host, the array of available women before him.

Men, in particular, are often faulted for their singlehood. Our leaders will stand at the pulpit and say, "If you are a young man of appropriate age and are not married, don't waste time in idle pursuits. Get on with life and focus on getting married . . . make your highest priority finding a worthy, eternal companion." The implication is always the same: *life* is married life, when you're LDS.

Single women, rather than being chastised, are reassured that since we're not at fault for not having been chosen, we'll be rewarded after death with marriage and children. Every time someone offers up this platitude, I bristle. I wonder if it helps anyone—the earnest assurance that everything will be better, once we're dead.

Singles wards often feel less like a place of worship than a three-hour speed date, or an up-close example of Darwin's theory of sexual selection—wherein individuals of the same sex ostracize or kill their rivals in order to excite or charm potential mates. Any given Sunday, I could lose an eye to one of the fifty or so sweet-seeming, cutthroat girls who will *trample* one another, bash each other over the heads with the trays of freshly baked cookies they've made, the care packages they've assembled, the coolers packed full of snacks for the guys, for the big game. These women will take out the kneecaps of their sisters in Christ, do anything to get access to the gene pool of the ward's two or three most eligible bachelors.

Even so, singles wards have at least provided tangible evidence that I am not alone in the strange and difficult quest for love in the Mormon world. But my time is up: having failed to marry out of the ward, I've aged out, instead. I can leave quietly, or wait until the ward secretary notices my change in church-appointed status—at which point I'll be politely asked to leave.

My plan is to begin attending church with my parents, rather than the assigned family ward near my house. I eat dinner with my parents every week anyway, and in the ward where I grew up, there are still people who have known me since childhood, who treat me as if I belong. It's less likely there than at other wards that I'll be asked week after week if I'm visiting, is my husband with me, where do my kids go to school, how many do I have, and what are their ages.

But even at my parents' ward, going to church has required, for some time, a dedicated ritual of defense. Every time I visit, I'm asked (by five, ten, fifteen well-intentioned family friends or acquaintances) if I'm dating, who I'm dating, is it serious, am I worried. It's common to overhear conversations about other single women: "Well it's no *wonder* she's not married. You've seen how she's let herself go." "It's no *wonder* she's not married; all she does is work." I can always count on a rash of unsolicited advice: perhaps if I didn't focus so much on my *career*, people suggest. Maybe I'm just too picky? Things would be easier, wouldn't they, if I weren't so *tall*?

So the Sunday after my thirtieth birthday, I dress painstakingly, like the Book of Mormon's Captain Moroni preparing for battle. Just as he fastened on his head plate, his breastplate and shields, and girded his armor about his loins, I gird mine with pantyhose and a pencil skirt, high heels and a cashmere sweater. I apply my mascara, and wish, with each delicate stroke, for a pair of Wonder Woman's golden bangles: forget her killer rack and star-spangled panties; I'd walk the Mojave Desert for a set of bullet-deflecting bracelets.

It turns out I don't need them. People are welcoming and kind, they're so happy to have me, I look beautiful, and who does my hair? Congratulations on my acceptance to graduate school, they say, and are proud of me for following my heart. The talks and lessons are inspiring, and I breathe a sigh of relief, walking out of Relief Society— the last hour, when the women and men meet separately. I didn't need to feel defensive. It could be okay here, I think, just as a toddler careens around the corner, bouncing off me onto the floor.

The voice telling him not to run in church is one I recognize, and I turn to see a girl I knew in high school. She reaches down to scoop up her son.

"Sasha," I say, smiling. "Look at you."

She shifts the baby on her hip, and laughs. "Oh, I'm an old married lady," she says. "This is Adam. My youngest. He's driving Mommy crazy. Aren't you, Mister?"

Adam grabs a handful of her hair, leans toward me.

"Sweet baby," I say, holding his hand, which he tries to put in his mouth.

"They say it because it's true. You don't even know what love *is* until you become a mother. You'll see," she says, squeezing my arm. "One day."

"That's what they tell me," I say, forcing a smile. But what I wish I had the courage to say is I would gladly, gratefully take what doesn't even register for her, as love. What I wouldn't give for a good-night phone call. An emergency contact. Someone who sleeps better when I'm there, who cares if the plane lands safely. Someone to call me sweetheart, bring soup when I'm sick, sunblock my back, forget to buy milk. What I wouldn't give for a man's body keeping me up at night, continually interrupting my sleep.

If I were brave, I'd tell her: I can't count the number of prayers I've said thanking God that I don't crave children. Because how could I bear the weight of wanting more?

My first day at Bennington, I'm given a set of keys and shown to a room in a house that must be a hundred years old. It's haunted, says my undergraduate guide, ominously. She shows me how to work the radiator, warns me about the noises it'll make in the middle of the night. Afterward, I trudge through the snow with the rest of the new students to a small, tiered classroom for our welcome speech.

Liam Rector is standing in the front of the room. He has thick, dark hair with a widow's peak, a beard with a white stripe on the chin. He looks like Wolfman Jack would look, if Wolfman Jack were a poet wearing a lavender tweed three-piece suit. He welcomes us "to the tribe" in a way that seems slightly dramatic. He loses me with a short lecture on "the vortex," then to end our meeting, he shows the profane, disturbing "always be closing" scene from *Glengarry Glenn Ross*.

On the screen in front of us, Alec Baldwin looks at one of the pasty, weak real-estate salesmen and commands, "*Put. That coff*ee. down. *Coffee*," he insists, drawing out the syllables, "is for closers only." In response to Jack Lemmon's incredulous face, he asks, "You think I'm fucking with you? I am *not* fucking with you."

I saw this movie in college, and didn't get it. Wondered if everyone who *said* they got it was just acting cool.

Alec Baldwin is now brandishing a set of brass balls, now showing off his Rolex. "*Get* them to *sign* on the *line* that is dotted. You *hear* me, you fuckin' faggots?"

I'm sure there's a metaphor here, but I'm hard-pressed to see it in the context of "Welcome to Bennington!" I'm not the only one, it turns out: a girl in the back of the room politely says when it's over—not at all under her breath—"What. The. Fuck." During the collective laugh that follows, that welcome release of tension, it hits home that I am not at BYU anymore. Even in the University of Washington's master of education program, people waited until *after* class to drop the f-bomb.

During lunch, I sit with three strangers at a round cafeteria table, not knowing they're about to become some of my best friends. Over our veggie lasagna and kale, we share what brought us here: Kim's crumbling marriage, Sariah's career undercut by a sense of stagnancy. All of us except Sue—who despite the demands of work, marriage, and baby managed to finish a novel—have mainly been dreaming of writing. Sariah and Kim both nod when I say I woke up one day wondering, *Whose life is this, and how did I end up living it?*

At the bar each night, after hours of workshops and lectures and readings, I learn more about the lives of the other MFA students. The average age in our program is forty, meaning that for most of us this is the beginning of a do-over, a second something: career, marriage, graduate degree. And much of what I learn about my new friends' lives, by an LDS standard, is scandalous. There is drinking, smoking, sex, and drugs. There is talk of depression, abuse, alcoholism, infidelity, divorce, mental illness, and abortion. I am shocked at the openness with which people reveal their secrets and personal failures. Until I realize: not everyone has been raised to believe silence should accompany doubt. Not everyone has been raised in a culture of perfection; they don't see a benefit to the shellac required to keep up appearances.

Among my classmates, there are tattoos and piercings and extreme hairstyles. There is homosexuality and promiscuity and distrust of religion. There is activism, atheism, skepticism. And what I feel in their company is acceptance. Is empathy. Is belonging, in a way I have never felt it. The things that set me so apart in my Mormon life mean nothing here. My singleness, my childlessness, my virginity are utterly inconsequential—though the latter is of interest, obviously. But the frame for their curiosity is new: my new friends—all writers—are drawn, above all, to story. Over the next ten days, we feed ours to each other in decadent pieces. We relish them the way women in TV commercials eat chocolate, or wash their hair.

I live and study and eat with my classmates for days, sometimes a week, before I find out whether they're married, whether or not they have kids. We have other, more pressing things to talk about—and for that, I literally thank heaven. Every conversation is about what we've read, where we've studied, traveled, and worked; what we're writing, what we *wish* we were writing, whether workshops were brutal, and what inspiration has struck since we saw each other last. We talk about what we want to go back to, after our residency, and what we're dreading. And at the end of almost every day, my new friends talk and drink and smoke at the campus bar. I go with them, for the talking and the laughing. I order a cranberry and soda and dance with utter abandon in the company of people who—despite all outward evidence—are indeed my tribe.

These are my people, I think, making fresh tracks through deep snow on the last night of my first residency. I look up at the stars, and watch my breath billow into the freezing air. I close my eyes and stand there, breathing. Thanking God I've finally found them. That he led me to them. And I pray that this change will be enough. That this is all I will need to make my life feel right.

Chapter 8

The question is not what you look at, but what you see.

—HENRY DAVID THOREAU

———— ◆ ————

P icture yourself on the most thrilling roller coaster of your life," says Tim.

We're sitting in a hot tub on the sundeck of a Carnival Cruise ship, sipping virgin daiquiris. Beside us, in the pool, there's a flirty, drunken game of volleyball under way. Reggae covers of Cyndi Lauper and Eric Clapton blast from the ship's speakers; the smell of pepperoni wafts from the snack bar.

Leila is chatting with Tim's friend Derek on the other side of the hot tub about how much she loves Costco. For real, that's what she's talking about. Tim leans closer to me, takes a conspiratorial tone. "Imagine the adrenaline; imagine the most boundless joy rushing toward you at speeds up to ninety-five miles per hour. There's a sharp bank of a corner, one that throws you to the side. It bruises your ribs, but you're still laughing. Then the car slams on the brakes, and you start climbing to the crest of the hill."

"Okay," I say, starting in on my pineapple garnish.

"You've ridden the Millennium Force, right?"

"No. Where is it?"

He ignores the question. "It's something like three hundred feet tall; you can see Lake Erie from up there. You can see *Canada*. So you're at the top of this hill, and suddenly you're zooming down a ramp so steep it feels like a cliff, and out of nowhere, you're attacked by a swarm of bees. *Killer* bees." He pauses for effect, puts his empty glass on the deck beside us.

There's a round of shrieks and high fives from the pool. I look down to be sure the Jacuzzi jets have not done anything untoward to my swimsuit top. After three decades of swimsuit wedgies, I've decided I'm simply too tall for one-piece swimsuits. Modesty be damned, I'm done caring whether other Mormons will be offended by the sight of my midriff.

"So the bees *attack*," Tim says. "They sting you until you think you might die. But you're strapped in, and there's nothing to do but sit there and slap yourself in the face to try to keep from being stung, and stung, and stung. And just when you think it might be worth it to jump—"

"And kill yourself," I say, nodding.

"Right. You're thinking about it. But then, there's a burst of speed. You hit another corner, and the car tilts toward a sky that's blue and bright, and it's so fun you can't even *remember* the swarm."

"Okay?" I'm waiting for the punch line.

"That was my marriage," he says. "Roller coaster. Bees."

We're on the second day of a four-day cruise to Ensenada, fifty spots reserved for members of LDSSingles.com hoping to find their eternal companions, or at the very least, a PG-rated cruise fling. Leila begged me to come, insisting we'd find men who like to travel. I couldn't convince her that Ensenada isn't a place where people who like to travel *like to go*. Besides, cruising isn't really traveling; it's being trapped in an overpriced, floating hotel with thirty thousand drunken tourists. To make matters worse, between the time we booked our reservations and the ship's departure, she met someone online. She's about to be engaged, is only here because her ticket is nonrefundable.

I'm here because I can't give up hope. Regardless of the fact that I've rarely made it to the second date with an LDS man I've met online, and never once to the third, I've convinced myself I just have to keep at it. My dates, over the past few years, have begun to feel fraught. Brittle with the joint hope that this could be the night when everything changes. With both of us thinking into our water glasses, *Please, God, let it be you.* Both of us knowing how badly, and how soon, we need it to happen—we can't be celibate forever, and neither can we consider the alternative. I look at Tim, who's laughing at a joke Derek just made, and there it is, right below the surface, that familiar *let it be you.*

Tim is outgoing, isn't shy about calling bullshit fairly openly on much of the judgment and posturing of certain other LDS singles onboard. He sometimes breaks into goofy songs: a shorter, more hawkish Danny Kaye. Derek is his opposite: introverted, soft-spoken, easily flustered. The four of us were unaware we'd be causing a stir by deciding to sit in the hot tub on Sunday. I *still* don't know why that was a big deal, why the hot tub—as opposed to shuffleboard, minigolf, or karaoke—constituted breaking the Sabbath.

Either way, we are openly criticized and given a wide berth at dinner, which we hardly notice. Leila and I are caught up in the fun of wearing cocktail dresses and comparing horror stories with Tim and Derek of recent dates gone bad. Tim tells us about his first post-divorce date: a casual dinner with an old friend, not Mormon. She threw a rotary phone at his head when he refused to sleep with her. "Women," he says, shaking his head, "don't like to be refused."

I turn to Leila, "Tell the one about the Handsome Mormon Pharmacist."

She groans, loudly enough that people look over, pointedly. "He showed up to my apartment in clothes *sopping wet*," she says. "He'd taken them *straight* from the washing machine."

"He didn't," Derek insists, already anticipating the punch line.

"*Yes*," she says, getting animated. "He said *all* his clothes were dirty. He complained of *chafing* all night, and then wanted to cuddle."

"Remember the guy who showed up with his best friend in the car, and made you ride in the backseat?" I say.

Leila bursts out laughing, having forgotten that guy. She makes me tell about my date with the AT&T exec who used the tableside olive oil as moisturizer. He worked it into his arms, exclaiming, "Gee, this is potent stuff. I can't get it to rub in!" Later, he stood up in the aisle of the restaurant and grabbed his ass, citing a "wicked butt cramp." He stuck me with the bill, claiming he'd forgotten his wallet. He recited an original poem, which went on for what felt like ten minutes, and began:

Dear Lord, you have blessed me with a mama
who is bright and strong, and true
she always tells me what to do
she is good, through and through.

Our peals of laughter soon drift into silence, then something darker, more real. We seem expected to put up with bad manners and bizarre behavior from LDS men, I say. Things we'd *never* subject ourselves to on dates with nonmembers—simply because of their LDS-ness. My theory is that many LDS men have never learned how to treat women properly because they've always been the supply to an unrelenting demand. Leila continues, saying there are plenty of smart, successful, well-mannered men outside the church who want to date us, but with them we're pressured to lower *other* standards.

"Same for guys," Tim points out. "Except we get telephones thrown at us when *we* don't put out."

After dinner, Leila and I take the elevator to the uppermost deck of the ship, which at this hour is virtually empty. We kick off our sandals and lie on lounge chairs under the moon. The sky and sea are like mirrors, one for the shimmering abyss of the other. We are silent for a long time, wishing on the stars.

"Any word from Mr. Football?" Leila asks. She's still hoping he'll turn up again, though it's been nearly a year.

I sigh heavily, remembering. *This man could be a contender,* I thought, the first time I clicked on his profile—a pro athlete turned broadcaster, handsome, well-read, ambitious. And my heart sang the weekend he came through Seattle on business; we talked books and made eyes at each other over curried goat and cornbread at my favorite divey Caribbean place. When he flew home to Virginia after a doorstep kiss that left me dizzy, I concocted a magical, hypothetical romance in my head—a fantasy to fill in the three thousand miles between us: he'd travel during the NFL season, which would be perfect. I'd spend those cold, rainy months writing, wearing one of his old T-shirts; I'd spend time with my friends, and fly to wherever whenever whatever game was being played when either he or I felt lonely for the other.

He'd work every room until he got a fat network job, just like he'd planned, and after our temple marriage, he'd charm my pants literally off. He'd have free time in the off-season, which I pictured as an uninterrupted stretch of lazy mornings, all omelets and sex and newspapers spread the length of the table.

Though what really happened when I dropped Mr. Football at his hotel at the end of our second date was something even I couldn't have imagined. Things looked promising, at first. He invited me upstairs. He dimmed the lights. Pushed me playfully backward onto the bed, and pinned my hands above my head. But before we could even get properly started on a PG-rated makeout, his entire body went limp on top of me. At first I thought he was kidding—but when he didn't move for several consecutive seconds, I blanched. *He has died of a heart attack*, I thought. *Like old men do with call girls in the movies.*

But he wasn't a septuagenarian, and I'm about as far from a hooker as a girl can get. Also, I could hear him breathing in my ear. Turns out he'd simply fallen asleep.

Not knowing what else to do, I squirmed from beneath the three hundred pounds of that uniquely demoralizing rejection, gathered my shoes and coat, and snuck quietly from the room. As if it would be rude to wake him.

Still, I was unwilling to give up the dream. He travels a lot, I told myself. He works hard. He's *tired*. Over the next two months I let myself build on my initial fantasy, which Mr. Football fueled with encouraging spurts of attention: two- or three-day stretches spent flirting via e-mail, phone, and text. Inevitably, though, they were followed by weeks of radio silence. We went through that cycle three or four times before I lost patience with the program, four years before Greg Behrendt had a platform to tell me what I already knew: he just wasn't that into me.

"I'd be shocked if I heard from him again," I tell Leila, closing my eyes against the stars. I've never told her about the conversation I suspect was the deal breaker. The one that palpably shifted the energy between me and Mr. Football. I was saying, over the phone, how strange it is sometimes—that many of the teenagers in my classroom are having decidedly adult experiences. That even though I'm the adult, I'm more innocent than many of them. It's strange how many kids have had emotional and physical experiences far beyond mine— a situation made *more* bizarre when they come to me to ask if what they've heard or read about sex is true.

I'm not embarrassed to answer their questions, I tell Mr. Football. But there are things I have to work hard not to be horrified by: like my student Jennifer, who got married at seventeen—forced into that union by her parents, when she admitted she was pregnant. If that's not bad enough, she's having an affair with the boy who sits next to her in third period—a fact I can swear to under oath, given the graphic note I found on the floor between their desks last week.

I try not to blanch, I tell Mr. Football, when in the middle of a lesson on the symbolism of Piggy's broken glasses, a student calls out that she needs to check on her son in the campus day care. I'm glad she's still in school, but could she learn not to interrupt, at least? She still has a child's lack of impulse control, and she is *raising a child*. It's just weird sometimes, my prolonged state of innocence, and the absence of theirs.

"Do you ever get that feeling?" I asked. "That you're stuck in a strange in-between?"

"Not really," he said. "I'm proud of the ways I'm different."

"I'm not saying I'm ashamed. I'm saying it's surreal."

"So what do you tell them about sex, anyway?"

"Nothing specific. I generally just confirm or deny the veracity of their information. I tell them there's no hurry. That it's not ideal to end up with a child in the school day care—obviously, that makes life harder. Unnecessarily complicated."

"So you say 'don't do it, but if you do, use protection'?"

"I think you're oversimplifying. But I don't have a problem with sex education. Kids need information in order to make good decisions. Not everyone gets it at home. Some get silence; some get propaganda. Few kids are religiously committed to abstinence; that much I know. And if they're going to have sex—if they're *already* having sex—they should know how to stay healthy, how not to have unwanted pregnancies."

"It sounds like your ethics are really situational."

"Because it's naïve to think everyone's in the same situation. If I had a teacher who was a vegetarian for religious reasons, it wouldn't affect *my* behavior, even if he insisted it's the way God, or Buddha, or Allah wanted me to live. I'd think it's great that *he's* a vegetarian: it's a mindful, healthy way to live. But my values wouldn't change because he said to change them."

"I just don't think you can give kids permission to have premarital sex."

"I'm not; I'd get fired, for one thing. Sure, I'd rather they stay virgins until marriage, or at least adulthood; but that's not always a realistic expectation. So for those who don't plan to wait—who have no *reason* to wait—I'd rather they have condoms than HIV; I'd rather they take a pill than have an abortion. Still, when I talk to them, all I do is answer their questions about periods and pregnancy and STDs. I just dispel myths."

"What if you taught kids at church?"

"I'd give them the reasons for abstinence. I'm *doing* it; obviously I believe it's the right decision. But if they asked me about birth control, I'd talk to them."

"I don't see how you can say, 'don't do it, but here's what to do if you do.' You sound like those parents who think it's okay to buy kids alcohol because at least they know when and where they're drinking."

"I don't think it's the same at all. I wouldn't *buy* birth control for them. I wouldn't host a party at my house, dim the lights, and blast Marvin Gaye."

There was a long silence on the other end of the phone, during which I wondered if Mr. Football and I would agree to disagree, or if this conversation would mark the end of our fantasy future together.

Leila waves her hand, as if to snap me out of my reverie. "You can do better," she says, dismissing him outright. "I mean look at you. Who falls asleep on *that*?" I laugh, and she reaches over her armrest to grab my wrist. "Wait! You still haven't told me about that guy in LA. The director?"

"Producer." A family friend set us up this past month, insisting—when I expressed concern about the nineteen-year age gap—he's a *really young* forty-nine. "So he picks me up at LAX, and immediately shushes me when I get in the car."

"Excuse me?"

"Yeah. He turns up the stereo so he can listen more closely to the *drum solo* in Phil Collins's 'In the Air Tonight.'"

"Stop!" Her laughter is inappropriately loud. A couple on a romantic stroll looks over at us to make it clear we're killing their mood. "It's true. He *shushes* me, and then he whispers, with his eyes closed, 'I *love* Phil Collins.' Later, he randomly brings up the subject of peanut butter. We're walking on the Santa Monica Pier, and he says, 'Marie *loves* peanut butter. You know—Marie Osmond? We dated in college. She was into it, but I just couldn't handle being *Mister* Marie Osmond.'"

Leila can't stop laughing. But as entertaining as it is to tell these stories, to implicate the men, what I don't say is it's my fault, too. I fall just as short of their ideal, regardless of my Mormonness. I don't tell her about the inevitable moment on every first date, when the LDS man asks how many children I want—and the silence that hangs above our heads, ticking like a bomb, while I try to decide whether or not to tell the truth: I don't think I want any. I suppose it's possible I could change my mind. But I'm doubtful. That loaded silence between my date and me makes everything clear: before things even get started, they are always already finished.

Leila wouldn't understand that part; she has a number in her head, like every other Mormon woman I know. Names picked out, and a picture of what they'll be like.

In a show of solidarity, she says, "One day this will all be hilarious. In a less depressing kind of way." I smile, hoping she's right. But I'm thinking that's easy for her to say, with the boyfriend in the wings, the long talks they've already had about what kind of diamond she likes best.

The next morning, I further besmirch my reputation with the LDS singles by inciting a bus-wide scandal on our way home from a market in Ensenada—which turns out to be nothing more than a ramshackle row of shacks stuffed with blankets and shot glasses, shell necklaces and macramé, baby-size maracas and sombreros: novelty items perfect for cruise shippers on a three-hour stop before the ship sets sail again.

I've recently bought a round, glass-topped dining room table, so I linger in front of a display of lace tablecloths. I suspect they may have been made in China, but they're pretty, regardless. In particular, one with a border of calla lilies. The vendor is kind-faced. Eager without being aggressive. He holds the tablecloth up so I can see the design.

He peeks from behind it and says, "Treinta pesos!"

I step farther into his stall to escape the blazing sun. The tablecloth really is pretty. And I do need one. "*Veinte* pesos," I say, struggling to recall every lingering shred of my high school Spanish. "Con un beso." I smile and offer my cheek.

The vendor grins and slaps himself on the leg. His friend runs for a step stool, which the tablecloth man stands on so he can reach my face. He kisses me lightly, hops down, and wraps my purchase in a cheap, blue plastic bag.

"*Mi amor*," he says with his hand on his heart. I hand him the twenty pesos, and back on the bus I recount the story to another woman who paid the full treinta for the same tablecloth. She gasps and announces, in a voice that travels far and wide, "That sounds like *prostitution* to me!"

The rumor of my whoredom spreads like wildfire, and needless to say my dance card remains conspicuously empty for the rest of day three and all of day four. A situation most likely exacerbated by the fact that Tim and I, in the same way people add "in bed" to the end of every fortune cookie fortune, can't stop with the punch line: "that sounds like *prostitution* to me!"

At the end of our cruise, Tim purposely misses his flight home in order to spend a few extra hours with me at LAX—a surprising gesture. I wasn't sure he'd considered me more than a friend. And late that night, when he calls to see if I made it home safely, we lie in our separate beds, talking for hours, telling our secrets. It turns out he's been divorced not once, but twice. Which makes him feel, as a Mormon man, like a two-time loser. In return, I reveal what I've learned since coming home, unemployed, from my first Bennington residency: I like being a waitress more than I liked being a teacher. Even so, my ego gets involved sometimes. When you're a teacher, people assume you're smart, dedicated, engaged in a noble cause. The assumptions about waitresses are often the opposite.

Clinging to our anecdotes, our jokes and revelations, is the un-spoken hope we both feel: that we'll find an end to our loneliness in the other. He wants to come visit, Tim says, next time he can get time off when his ex has custody of his son. It won't be until Christmas, which is still five months away—but if I'm not seeing anyone by then, and he isn't either . . .

We talk every night, sometimes for hours. We send hundreds of e-mails into the ether. Each of us is obviously trying on the idea of the other—the idea of marriage to the other, a family with the other. The more I get to know him, I realize how different we are; but difference is the spice of life, no? I've never pictured myself with someone who supports the NRA, who has a hundred-pound Great Dane, who loves living in a small midwestern town, who didn't finish college, who is shorter and weighs less than I, who doesn't read voraciously for pleasure. But Tim's a good father. And he doesn't want more children. I'm attracted to his sense of humor, as well as his tendency to tell it like it is. He's bright, and witty. And I've known short men who found my height a turn-on. He's not uptight, or uncompromising. He cooks, and cleans, and does his own laundry. He and his second ex-wife had a good sex life, which I find reassuring.

So I'm nervous, waiting for him at the airport just before Christmas. I keep checking my hair. Keep hoping I chose the right outfit to make the right impression, after six months apart. I'm anticipating being alone with him—answering the questions we didn't get to on the cruise: Are we physically attracted? Should we keep hoping, making silent concessions in our heads, putting our carts miles ahead of their horses, posing questions to one another that begin, "if we got married . . ."

He is there, suddenly, right beside me. He's come up behind me, and looks different than I remember, having recently bleached the ends of his hair in an unflattering, too-old-to-be-in-a-boy-band kind of way. But hair grows, and I'm happy to see him. We hug, and drive home, both of us talking too much, nervous, given everything that's at stake.

I show him to my guest room, give him a tour of the spare bath and the kitchen, and say good night. It isn't long before I hear him knocking softly at my bedroom door. I'm awake still. I left my door ajar, just in case. I didn't expect we'd sleep in the same bed, but maybe he'd want to talk, which might lead to making out a little, because he's only here for two days, and isn't that why he's flown here?

He climbs onto my bed, and straddles me—on top of the covers. It's a move I didn't expect, one that makes me nervous, though I'm intrigued. "Couldn't sleep," he says, softly. And then, with a smile, "Let's get this thing over with."

The kiss is nice—nothing spectacular, no skyrockets in flight. But nice enough I'd keep going, to see if it got better. But he pulls away after a few seconds. "Okay," he whispers. "Good night again." He crosses the hall again, back to the guest room.

The next morning I wake up late and find him downstairs, eating toast and flipping through a Victoria's Secret catalog.

"I see you've found the Mormon porn." I pour myself a glass of juice. "Want some yogurt? Banana? That's pretty much all I have."

"So about the kiss," he says, closing the magazine. "It's not like it was *bad*."

I nearly choke on my orange juice, wondering how long he's been up, practicing this speech.

"I'm not saying you're a *bad kisser*. Just that it felt a lot like kissing my sister."

"Wow," I say. "That's a lot for nine AM." I put my glass in the sink. "So what are you saying? Do you even want to stay? Should I take you to the airport?"

I wish I'd changed out of my pajamas, brushed my teeth, at least, before being told I don't have a shred of sex appeal. I feel too vulnerable, with my hair a mess and my mouth like a fuzzy mothball.

"No," he says, taking a huge bite of toast. "That seems stupid, right? I mean we're friends; we *like* each other. I'm just a mess over my divorce, still. I shouldn't be, but I am. I feel like you're the girl I should have waited for. I just didn't know you'd show up. I'll get there." His voice and his look are sincere. "I will. Just not this weekend. I want to love you," he says. "To fall in love with you. I do." That final sentence nearly erases the one about the kiss. It's the one I want to hear. I want to be hopeful, and I want to be loved.

I dropped Tim at the airport this morning, and I'm distracted, working my lunch shift at Circa—where I started working after taking a cue from the movies. Onscreen, artists, writers, and actors are always waiting tables. Thinking they must know something I didn't, I answered an ad on a whim: "Waitress needed: call Chris." Within a week I realized I could live on what I make working twenty-five to thirty hours a week—easily, when factoring in the small scholarship I received from the Van and Ardith Hardy Foundation. To my surprise, my parents called just before I went to Vermont last January.

"If this is what you're going to do," said my mom, "you can't do it halfway."

My dad, on the extension in his office, said, "We want you to work as hard as you can, on your studies, for these two years." Two days later, a check for three hundred dollars turned up in my mailbox, with a note saying the same amount will arrive promptly on the first of every month, until graduation. *Be brilliant.* Love, Mom and Dad.

It didn't take long to figure out I'll never go back to teaching public high school. Why would I, when I can make virtually the same money waiting tables, have no stress, and work half the hours? When I can give away or trade my shifts if I need time to write or study. When I'll never have to wake up early, take my work home, or talk to anyone's parents—unless it's in regard to the nightly specials, the Spanish grenache that pairs beautifully with our house-made mole sauce.

I'm thinking about Tim, the will we or won't we, wondering what the likelihood is of us becoming one of those couples who were just friends until one day, poof! The switch flipped. So it takes me a while to notice the man at the bar. Notice him noticing me.

Two hours later, he's still there. Sitting at the bar, sipping iced tea and watching me work—not even pretending to read. I have to keep refilling his glass, and feel myself blush every time I enter his personal space. He's good-looking, but not necessarily my type: he's got dreadlocks halfway down his back, wears jewelry in his hair.

When the lunch rush finally dies down I find out he's a metal sculptor. He finds a way to mention he wears leather chaps, sometimes, welding in his studio, and I try not to picture sparks, and sweat, and leather.

"Let me take you to dinner," he says.

"No thank you," I say, taking a load of clean glasses from the dishwasher, conscious of my neckline every time I bend down. "I find you incredibly attractive; don't get me wrong. But you don't want to go out with me. I promise."

"See, *that's* where you've got it wrong," he says, laughing.

"I'm telling you I'd love to, but it's a bad idea."

"What, are you married?"

"I'm religious."

"How religious?"

I lean against the bar, give him a look.

"Muslim?" he asks.

I shake my head. "Mormon."

He reaches for his wallet. "This is my card," he says, sliding it across the bar. "I'm just asking you to dinner. We'll eat; we'll talk. It'll be fun."

"Jomo." I read his name out loud, and my expression asks the question.

"My parents were hippies. It means 'burning spear' in Swahili."

"Of course it does," I say, sliding his card into the pocket of my apron. He laughs, and I can't help but blush at the entendre. "I appreciate the invitation. But I know how this goes."

"You know how this goes?" He raises an eyebrow.

"Yes. You'll take me to dinner. There'll be candlelight; it'll be *very* romantic. We'll flirt, and we'll laugh. You'll walk me to the door, and before you know it, you're inside." He nods, as if he expects as much. "And then, we're on the couch. There's music."

"What kind of music?"

"Use your imagination. We look deeply into each other's eyes. You move closer." I'm entertaining myself by now. "You take me *gently in your arms*."

"Do I?" he says, laughing.

"And then we're kissing."

"Oh yeah?"

"Yes. We're kissing. And it's good. So I *respond*. And you think something is going to happen." I slap my hands on the bar, abruptly. "But I say, 'No. I can't. I told you.' I don't *want* you to stop. But I tell you to. The signals are confusing."

He nods in agreement.

"Right? So on our second or third or fourth date, frustration leads to irritation, and you say, 'Why are we even *doing* this, when neither of us can compromise?' You can't keep pretending sex isn't a crucial part of an adult relationship. And I say in a tired voice, 'I know.'"

Jomo leans back in his chair. "Maybe you don't know *everything*," he suggests.

"I know enough." I'm thinking of my friend Patrick, whom I first met dancing a year ago. We became friends, and then friends who make out occasionally, and from there to my first-ever foray into second base, and third, which is *well* past the line I promised Sister Jepson, and God, I'd never cross before marriage. That series of events made one thing crystal clear: the slope is slippery.

I can't keep dating men who aren't also committed to abstinence. I need an LDS boyfriend, because it's no longer amateur hour outside the church. Men my age—like Jomo, for instance—have generally spent the last ten to fifteen years having active sex lives. Developing persuasive moves. Honing their skills. Any date beyond the first has become nearly impossible. Not because they don't respect my boundaries, but because I am solely responsible to set them, and to enforce them, and never to falter, even for a minute, definitely not for an hour; because to falter would mean to jeopardize my eternal salvation—and that is a lot to take on when a man's breath is on your neck and his hand is tracing the curve of your lower back, underneath your shirt, and all you want in life is to wrap a leg around his waist and climb him like a tree.

I flip the switch on the bar dishwasher, starting another load of glasses, and put on a false, wistful smile. "But wasn't it fun, while it lasted?"

"Damn, girl," says Jomo. "You can play hard to get."

"Unfortunately for both of us," I say, softening, "I'm not playing."

A month later, I'm on the phone with Tim, talking about laws of attraction. "It might not hurt if you grew your hair longer," he says. "Guys love long hair."

"What is that, anyway?"

He ignores the question. "And you could stand to lose ten pounds."

My first instinct is to tell him to bite me. Either that, or grow four inches and put on thirty pounds of muscle. Maybe get a nose job, and *stop* already with the pleated khakis. But I have put on a few pounds since I started working at the restaurant. I miss my skinny jeans. And I like my hair long, too. It's only short because a recent attempt at going platinum went terribly awry and required a six-inch amputation. These truths allow me to pretend I don't know what Tim is really saying: Why can't I be a five foot four, emotionally abusive brunette? He could love me, if only I were more like his ex.

"I want you to meet my parents," Tim says, in the next breath. They don't live far from me, just an hour south of Seattle. "I've told them so much about you," he says. "And I trust their judgment more than mine right now. They really want to meet you."

In my head, I realize it's crazy to be talking like this—but in the Mormon world, marriage is always the elephant in the room. Given our ages, how we met, and the fact that I don't want to be a virgin forever, it's not *that* crazy. Sure, we only met six months ago, we live six states away from each other, and have only kissed once—an experience that was mediocre at best. But I know what my options are. How few they are, and how urgent my needs. So I agree to meet Tim Sr. and Helen.

I bring flowers, I compliment Helen's lasagna, and I listen intently when she goes on about how no matter how many times she tells her husband how the dishtowels should be folded, she has to open the drawer and refold them when he isn't looking. She looks at me conspiratorially, urging me toward a shared nod of the head, an exasperated look in regard to *men*.

Tim Sr. shrugs happily, as if to say, "I may be incompetent, but I sure do try." I shrug along with him, and admit to Helen I've never folded a dishtowel the same way twice in my life. But what's probably more correct is I don't wash my dishtowels because I don't use my dishtowels, because I don't cook. Like, ever.

When I had my kitchen remodeled—for purely aesthetic reasons— the contractor who installed my stove left me a desperate note—weeks later—begging me to boil something, bake something, roast something. Shit, he'll *buy* me a freaking frozen pizza. He just needs to know if everything works right. So, no. Dishtowels aren't on my list of priorities. I eat popcorn for dinner three nights a week. If you open my refrigerator, all you'll find is four kinds of mustard, a six-month-old shallot, a withered lemon, and a stack of Christmas plates that have been there since 1997. It seems as good a place as any to store them.

It's not just cooking I avoid. It's pretty much every household task. I live in a condo so other people will do the planting, pruning, and weeding. Last week—all week—I washed my underwear in the shower because I didn't feel like doing laundry. Two pairs of my pants are hemmed with blue painters' tape. The house gets cleaned when I'm expecting company, because *I* don't care if there are dishes in the living room, or if my clothes are strewn on the floor. Growing up, when other girls wanted to play house, I flat-out refused. I would only play school, or *Solid Gold* dancer.

I've never been one to put stock in astrology, but when a Circa regular offered to read my chart, I played along—out of curiosity, and so as not to jeopardize my tip. She asked the time and date of my birthday, and returned with a wealth of information. The first thing she said was, "You are not domestic." It was enough to make me think twice about the position of the sun and moon the night I came shrieking into the world.

Tim's parents seem to adore me, despite my glaring shortcomings in the arena of dishtowels. And all that will change, Helen assures me, in a trilling voice, once I get married. On the drive back to my house, I ask myself what I'm doing, and why. The answer is simple: I have to give this a chance, because at least Tim, who is LDS, *wants* to want me. It's the closest I've come, with a Mormon man, to love. So I put the red flags aside: the fact that we don't like each other's politics, or taste in books or movies, or fashion sense. Because at least he is not emasculated by my personality—like the man, who, in the lobby of church one Sunday, approached to tell me what my problem is: I don't need a man.

"Mormon men are raised to be providers," he said. "You already have everything we're supposed to provide—car, house, clothes, food. What's left to give you?" I mentioned love, sex, intimacy, partnership— the things I *actually* need someone for. He just shrugged.

I know my life has become, over the past decade, more and more "male" by LDS measures. So I considered for a few minutes what that guy was saying. Maybe no LDS man wants to date another LDS man, no matter how pretty she is. Maybe I *am* emasculating. "Intimidat-ing" is the word of choice among my mother and her friends. But what I chose to believe instead, is that that guy was full of crap. So what if he doesn't want a woman like me, or if most LDS men don't. I only need one. I refuse to believe there isn't one LDS man who doesn't equate need with love. Who wouldn't be willing to *wait and see* what our married life would be like, rather than needing to plan and con-trol it before the end of the first date. Maybe Tim could be that guy.

I'm cleaning out my car when I come across Jomo's card in the pocket of an apron I haven't worn in months. Don't ask me why, against my better judgment, I call. Most likely it's vanity. Tim is still in Michi-gan, and we're both still waiting for something to change, something to click between us. I'm worried that if it doesn't work with Tim, it'll never work with an LDS guy, and I'll die an old, lonely, shriveled-up virgin. Which is maybe why I call Jomo: to be reminded that not everyone thinks kissing me is like kissing his sister. That some men can't take their eyes off the ten pounds Tim would rather I lost.

Jomo suggests an afternoon picnic, and a walk at Lincoln Park. *Perfect.* On an afternoon date, there will be no darkness, no candlelight, none of the physical expectations sunset inspires. But as soon as we sit down on a bench overlooking the rocky beach, there is a palpable energy between us—as if someone has replaced our cheese and crackers with figs and honey, a dozen oysters, shark fin soup, and the powdered horn of a rhinoceros. Jomo doesn't touch me all day, except with his *relentless, piercing gaze.* He keeps a respectful distance, until I open the door to my house. He puts a hand flat against my ribcage, and pushes me against the doorframe.

His other hand is on my neck, riding the line between a caress and something darker. He makes me wait for the kiss that leaves us breathless, tangled on the floor of my entryway with the door still open. Fifteen seconds later, we're tearing into each other in a scene from a movie it would be against my religion to watch. And when his hands skip all pleasantries and go straight to the buttons of my jeans, I want everything that is about to happen. *I could let myself have this, feel this; for once I could,* I think, dizzy under the weight of his body.

I'm undone by the smell of him, like fresh earth and vetiver. By the thick ropes of his hair in my hands and the heat of his hands on my skin. By his mouth teasing, asking, pushing until my breath goes jagged. Until all I can think about is letting go. Letting him. Opening my clothes and my body to skin and sweat, to the sweet, pungent fragrance building between us.

He pulls away, kneeling between my legs to unbuckle his belt, and it's now. Now or never, and there is nothing I can do when he leans toward me but block him with a stiff arm to his chest. Shake my head no. Curl into myself, push him away saying *go, please, I can't.* I close my eyes and turn my head, hoping he'll be gone before my frustration erupts in the torrent of tears I feel building.

Alone in the open doorway, I'm holding myself around the ribs. Curling into the fetal position, kicking the door shut behind Jomo, who left without a word. I lay there, keening, sobbing for what feels like hours. I let my nose run unchecked, let tears run into my ears and mouth. *How can I teach myself?* says the voice in my head. *Not to feel what my body feels, not to need it?*

I'm telling this story to my Bennington friends who have gathered for a midterm visit in San Francisco. It is the supporting evidence I use to explain the trip I've decided to take, in two weeks, with Tim. Sue and Sariah are sitting on opposite sides of Kim's green velveteen couch. Kim walks in from the kitchen with a plate of cheese when I announce, "*Jomo* is the reason I said yes when Tim invited me on vacation."

"*Tim?*" says Kim. She puts a hand over her mouth, takes it away to say, theatrically, "Mr. *I'm Not Attracted to You*? Mr. *Why Don't You Lose Ten Pounds*? Why would you do that to yourself?"

"Did you not hear the story about Jomo?" I say emphatically, swirling the ice in my water glass.

"I heard it," Sue says, drily. "I'd go on a trip with *him*. Though I doubt my husband would approve."

"*Jomo* is the reason I can't see Jomo again. If I want to be Mormon, I can't keep going out with men who aren't."

Sue and Sariah exchange a look I can't quite read. "Are you sure you want to *be* that?" says Kim gently. "With all due respect. It's not working for you."

"I can't just *not* be Mormon," I say, feeling a sudden flash of anger. "I can't just give up because it's hard." Even after all this time, my friends don't get it. They think my belief system can be fluid. Can be edited, revised, or altered to fit.

"No one's saying to do that," Sariah assures me. "It just doesn't feel like they get you. They don't appreciate you."

I don't say anything. I'm trying not to be offended that they seem to think the only reason I've been devout for so long is because it's been convenient.

"I'm worried," says Sue, getting practical. "You're undatable in your church because you don't want kids; you're undatable outside your church because what heterosexual man is going to date a woman for months or years and not pursue sex?"

"Right," I say.

"So how long can a person live in a problem without a solution?" Kim asks. "Realistically?"

"I'm expected to do it forever. To find solace in friendship and service to others."

"I love you," says Sue, taking a sip of her wine. "I do. But our friendship couldn't take the place of what I feel when I get in bed with Peter."

"I don't *want* to be celibate my whole life," I say. "But I can't have sex outside of marriage, especially accidentally, with some random. I have to get married. I have to date Mormons. *That's* why I'm going on vacation with Tim!"

I feel the same frustration in this conversation as I do when the church ladies tell me the stories of their husbands, or their friends, or their sisters, who were nonmembers when they met. "There are good people outside the church, don't forget." And in hushed voices, "Don't worry; if he *really* loves you, he'll wait."

What would they say if I told them the truth? That for years I've been having orgasms in my sleep, or when I drive down a particularly bumpy road, or if I cross my legs while wearing tight pants, or ninety seconds into a good-night kiss if his knee ends up in the right place. *I* crave sex. *I* may not be able to wait. And "if he loves me"? How would they respond if I said no man stays long enough to fall in love. Why would they, in the face of such glaring incompatibility?

"All I can do is not date," I say, reaching for a feta-stuffed olive. "Or hope that chemistry will magically appear between Tim and me." My friends' expressions remain skeptical—a mirror of my own feelings, if I were being honest.

Tim and I will be at sea for a week this time, with Tim's sister and her husband, their two kids, and Tim's ten-year-old son. It's clearly a tryout. I wish I were cool enough to say, like Crash Davis in *Bull Durham*, "After twelve years in the minor leagues, I don't try out." Instead, I try out. I play the role of stepmother, slathering sunblock on Tim's son every couple hours, scarred by memories of my own raised and blistered burns. I carry all the towels and sunscreen and water bottles and books and room keys and dry clothes everywhere we go, regardless of the fact that mine is not the only set of arms that works.

Every day, Tim finds time to say the same thing he's been saying all along. His voice is a record, skipping: I'm not attracted, not attracted, attracted to you. But I *want*, I *wish* I could be.

"Please wait," he says, one night in our cabin, into the pitch of darkness that separates our bunks. Quietly, so as not to wake his sleeping son. "I *should* love you."

Pretending to be asleep, I imagine his words in the air between us, shrinking, with each repetition, into nothing: *I should should should should.*

I'm so caught up in my own longing, it's impossible to know if what I feel has anything to do with him. I can't possibly love him, either. So why does it hurt so much to hear him say he doesn't love me?

The third day of our trip finds me hiding behind a lifeboat on the promenade deck, wishing my appendix would burst. Oh, to be airlifted to an unsanitary, third-rate surgical clinic. Anything but to be trapped here, pretending. The fourth day finds me weeping, silently, facedown in my towel on the lido deck, skipping lunch in favor of this private, necessary release.

But the fifth day—on the bow of a thirty-foot cabin cruiser off the island of Grand Cayman—is where and when I fall in love. The rest of Tim's family is still snorkeling at Coral Gardens, the second destination on Captain Marvin's two-stop, five-hour excursion. Tim and I are alone on the boat, lounging in the breeze. The salt and sun dry my hair into waves I didn't know were in its repertoire. Cuban and Caribbean music drifts from the stereo, and I sense, somehow, a homecoming. I feel it on a cellular level—as if the Caribbean Sea, through some trick of osmosis, perfectly replicates the saline of my body. Despite the fact that these tropical waters are a thirteen-hour flight from my Seattle home and a continent away from my Dutch and English ancestors, despite the fact that the sun is a proven enemy to my fair lady skin, I imagine myself belonging to this place. I imagine drinking the sky through a straw, sinking into the rustle of palm fronds, sleeping in the long, bright path the moon lays down when the sea and sky go dark.

"Why don't I live here?" I sigh.

"Seriously," Tim says, between swigs from his water bottle. "Why don't you?"

I fix my gaze on the stunning, impossible blue of the sea, and blink hard behind my sunglasses. The answer to his question lands hard inside me, like a sucker punch to the stomach: *Because I've been waiting for you. For a life I don't even want.*

And because I feel trapped in the terrifying loop of the if-then: If I want sex and love, then I need to get married. If I want to attain the highest level of exaltation, then I need to get married in the temple. If I want to get married in the temple, then I need to find an LDS man, and be worthy of a temple marriage. If I want to be worthy, then I need to keep the law of chastity. If I am going to be able to keep the law of chastity, then I need to get married *soon*.

But looking at Tim, I realize it's true, what I've always said: I'd rather be lonely by myself than lonely in a marriage. I'd rather be single my whole life than marry for the wrong reasons. I feel something like a coin dropping, and I know I have finally, praise God, decided. Tim can't be, won't be what I end up with. My decision is confirmed by a voice from above, not two days later.

Sitting on the floor of the Tom Bradley International Terminal at LAX, I choose to see it as a sign when the gate agent's announcement booms from a speaker above my head. "American Airlines flight 284 serving passengers traveling from Los Angeles to Seattle, our flight is currently oversold. Any passenger willing to take a later flight will receive a travel voucher to any of American's 176 destinations worldwide."

I literally jump and run to the customer service desk, dragging my carry-on bag behind me. Five minutes later, I have in my hand a one-way ticket that will take me back to the island of Grand Cayman to live. Because there's no reason not to.

Turns out, it only takes three phone calls to disassemble my life. The first call is to the Mormon temple in Seattle to find the contact information for the bishop of the Church of Jesus Christ of Latter-day Saints on Grand Cayman. The bishop answers on the first ring, and gives me the number of a woman in the Georgetown ward who rents out the two studio apartments above her house. She has an opening in July, if I'd like to come then, and will I need a ride from the airport? Lastly, I call my Realtor, who sells my house two weeks later, for the full asking price. After I hang up with her, I get online and book a flight, using my American Airlines travel voucher. I give notice at my job, sell my car to a friend, put my nice furniture in storage, and set out for something, anything, different from this.

Chapter 9

Give me this water, that I thirst not.

—JOHN 4:15

———◆———

There are axioms Mormons love to repeat, whether or not they have anything to do with the Gospel of Jesus Christ as revealed to the prophet Joseph Smith. A favorite is, "When something is right, everything will just fall into place." If I believed all of God's intentions were made known via the path of least resistance, I'd say that since my house sold immediately, since my boss told me my job would be waiting when and if I returned, since I found an apartment without even trying, since I got my flight for free, since the day after I arrived, the concierge at the Hyatt Regency offered me her job, her car, and a full set of dive gear for six hundred American dollars, the only logical conclusion would be that God wants me to live in the Cayman Islands.

And I can see why. There is something dreamlike, something otherworldly infused in the cerulean hues of the Caribbean Sea—the ranging shades of turquoise, more fitting to one of my better dreams; the rhythm of waves, prompting a slowing, and a soothing of my heart; the heavy salt air seeping into my lungs, my skin, my hair. The rhythm and the breeze, the waves and the color of the sea—all of them whisper *stay*.

I move into a studio apartment surrounded by palm and mango trees. I unpack my one suitcase, set my laptop on a table that overlooks a laundry line and tile-rimmed swimming pool, and it doesn't occur to me to miss my thirteen-hundred-square-foot suburban townhouse, my attached garage, my guest bedroom, or my extra one and a half baths. The first time I hang a load of laundry to dry in my front yard, I step on a hill of fire ants while wearing flip-flops. My car is a rusted-out, sand-filled Chevy Celebrity wagon, in which I can see the pavement rushing underneath my feet, Fred Flintstone–style. Still, I don't miss my manicured yard, my Kenmore washer and dryer, or my practical, predictable Toyota Corolla. The grocery store reeks of fish and buzzes with flies; the meat department is rife with goat and oxtail. Yet I don't yearn for the pristine aisles of my neighborhood QFC. The fruit bats that screech outside my window at night, the roosters that call at dawn: neither make me feel I am far from home.

On the island, I don't use my bachelor's degree, my teaching certificate, my master of education, what I've learned so far in my MFA, or any of the job skills listed on my résumé. Instead, I work for ten dollars per hour in a chain of retail shops owned by the largest dive company on the island. I sell swimsuits and rum cake, sunblock, disposable waterproof cameras, shell jewelry, postcards, T-shirts, and refrigerator magnets. I check passengers in for sunset sails and snorkeling trips on the company's small fleet of sixty-five-foot catamarans, and I answer the phone, usually to tell people what time we open or close.

Occasionally, I have brief conversations with celebrities. Once I sold a newspaper to Bill Paxton. I helped a skeletal Kate Bosworth try on bikinis—all of which she hated—and said hello to Orlando Bloom when he came to pick her up. Dr. Phil and I once waved hello on my lunchtime beach walk. But what trumps even celebrity sightings is what happens every workday afternoon. Four o'clock is the hour I anticipate from the moment I arrive: the appointed time to dress the mannequins in the Westin boutique. I'm in thrall to the three men made in the image of men made in the image of a god. They're molded from black-painted fiberglass, absent of heads and arms: nothing but torso, suspended from the ceiling by square metal hooks.

Occasionally, people pause in the hotel's gleaming marble hall to watch me attend to the mannequins. Couples never stop, nor groups. But singly they linger, staring through the picture window.

People turn their backs on the seductive jewelry store displays across the hall: the shimmering tanzanite, mined in the foothills of Kilimanjaro, the Rolexes arranged in concentric rows of silver and gold. They stand motionless as voyeurs on the other side of the plate glass, but I hardly notice their eyes on me. I'm captivated, as well—by the intimate rituals of button and buckle. The way a shirt comes to life sliding the sleek black line from shoulder to hip. By the rapture of silk in the break of a trouser leg, and the cascade of linen falling effortlessly to the floor.

Sometimes the flat of my hand lingers too long against a rippled abdomen. My cheekbone rests against the plane of a shoulder blade, or a breast finds home in the muscled valley of a backbone groove. These times, it's not hard to imagine what drove Pygmalion, the mythical sculptor who fell in love with the statue he carved. Even a manufactured body can provide some comfort.

When I write to Sariah, I tell the story like a comedy sketch. I ask, as if I'm joking: Do normal people feel like this? So removed from humanity they find solace in the plastic body of half a male mannequin?

What helps—with loneliness, and longing what puts things into perspective is the blue island air. The steady, calming rhythm of the ocean urging me inside. The very first time I scuba dived, I was on vacation in Mexico with Leila. We did the "resort certification"—a few hours of training in the hotel pool followed by a short, shallow dive under the watchful eye of a dive master. Even then, under those stressful conditions, I felt it: the return to some embryonic memory, a state both spiritual and primal. Comfort, like the lull of a warm, weightless amniotic sea. So my first project on the island was to become certified to dive. I spent nearly every day in the seven weeks between my hire date and my visa clearance in the company of barracuda and angelfish, coral reefs and the magnified thrum of my heart.

On days I feel too alone, I immerse myself in the sea. I let diving become my church. Underwater, in the blue silence, where no human voice can be heard, where nothing exists except my own breath, rising, where my body is unencumbered by the pull of the earth, I listen. Held against the gentle pressure of water, submerged in a world so foreign, so marvelous it could be heaven, I hear the echo of a psalm. *Be still.* I breathe in, and I breathe out. *Be still, and know that I am God.*

Six months after arriving on the island, I board a flight to Albany, the closest airport to Bennington, where my final MFA residency starts in the morning. I've claimed two blankets and the window seat, and between sips of ginger ale and halfhearted attempts at the crossword in the in-flight magazine, I'm wondering how—or if—I'll ever manage to repay the thirty thousand dollars I've taken in student loans. I'll never earn an income from writing poems; my parents were right about that. But a glance at the immaculate, feathered clouds below is all I need to reassure me. Taking this risk is the best decision I've ever made. I know that much already. There are many ways to pay the bills.

Last January, already a year ago now, I stood next to a famous poet at the frozen yogurt machine in the campus cafeteria. He asked me some question, I don't remember what, and my answer began "when I become a writer"—meaning when I get published, when I am validated from the outside. He turned his attention from the graduated swirls of soft serve to look me in the eye. "You *are* a writer," he said. "You've always been."

I want to believe him; I'm trying to believe him—but what already feels essential, what I do know is that the community I've met at Bennington feels like a rescue: this room full of people who'd never question that I could be fulfilled as an underpaid hourly employee who writes poems. It makes sense to them that I would choose that, without ambivalence, or regret.

When I deplane in Albany, there's a drop in temperature of seventy degrees. I burrow into my coat on the shuttle to campus, anxious to turn in my creative thesis—a collection of poems—attend my last days of readings and lectures, reunite with friends, and dance in the pub for the final time. But it's not until I'm sitting with my graduating class in a wood-paneled room that I realize I've done it. I am wearing a cap and gown, waiting for Liam to call my name. Waiting to walk across the stage and claim my diploma.

Our faculty are decked out in extravagant gowns and hoods—tams, some of them. I'm saving a place in my mind for where Jason Shinder should be. My most beloved teacher, recently diagnosed with non-Hodgkin's lymphoma. He's taken this semester off for medical leave, and it's impossible not to wonder, now, if I've already seen him for the last time.

Last winter, we sat together for our final meeting of the term. The window beside us overlooked a snowy expanse of campus. It was like a postcard photo: heavy white boughs in the distance, and in the forefront, one solitary wooden bench.

"Your poems are good," Jason said, in his thick New York accent. "They're inquisitive, disarming, and deeply felt." He paused. "But the true poems will come when you're able to write what you fear. I feel you getting close and pulling back. Changing the subject. Cracking a joke."

"I know."

"So say what it is. Stand in the middle of it, and name it. See what happens then."

"I can't," I said. I looked out the window again, not wanting him to see how easily tears can come, when the right nerve is exposed. Not wanting him to know how fragile I feel some days; like if someone touched me without warning, I'd shatter like glass. I *can't* name my fears while clamoring to cover them up, to patch the cracks in my life's foundation before it breaks wide open beneath my feet.

"I'm proud to have been part of your journey," Jason said, standing up. "I expect more and greater work and life from you. I do." When he hugged me, I could feel his ribs under my hands. I teased him about jogging too much, and not eating—not yet aware of his diagnosis. When he left, I stayed by the window for a long time, staring into the fields of whiteness. Telling myself to ignore his advice. Telling myself he doesn't understand what he's asking.

Liam's hand is warm, shaking mine onstage, and when all thirty of us have officially graduated, I make sure my cap flies highest in the exultant toss of mortarboards in the air. During the long series of hugs that follow, Sariah, Kim, Sue, and I promise to write. To write. To write. To write.

My next flight is a straight line across the nation for a short visit with my family and a night out dancing before my return to Grand Cayman. Climbing the long, wide hotel staircase to the nightclub on the second floor of the Bellevue Red Lion, I feel the music before I can hear it distinctly. My heart beats quickly, in response to percussion and horns. Or perhaps the unexpected appearance of James, who's standing beside the coat-check window.

"Where have you been?" he says, kissing me hello. My hand on his arm inspires a list of mortifying adjectives: Sinewed. Virile. Strapping.

"I live on Grand Cayman," I say, blushing at the words in my head.

"What do you mean, you *live* on Grand Cayman?"

"I live there. I dive and work in a store in a hotel."

"What are you talking about?"

"What are *you* talking about?"

"How did I not know you dive? *I* dive."

"I learned there. How did I not know *you* dive?"

"Are you just repeating what I say?"

I laugh, and before I know what's coming out of my mouth, I say, "You should come visit. You dive. I dive. We could dive. Together. On Grand Cayman. Where I live."

"What do you *mean*, I should come visit?" He's squinting at me, as if suspicious. As if I might be perpetrating some sort of ruse.

"I mean you should visit. I have an apartment, and a car. I work for a dive company."

"You work in a store."

I feel he's about to shine a bright light in my eyes, ask me where I was on the night of. "A store owned by a dive company," I clarify. I can't figure out what he's doing with the who's on first bit. I live in one of the world's best dive locations—why wouldn't I invite James, who dives, to visit?

But my stomach drops when I open an e-mail a month later, from James. Saying he really is coming to visit, how about April? My friends all want to know what I was thinking, inviting a single, dev-astatingly sexy man to visit me on a tropical island. "It just came out," I say. Or else, "he knows I'm Mormon," as if that settles every-thing.

In my mind, it does. Obviously, we won't be *sleeping* together, even though we'll obviously be sleeping together. I only have one bed, and the floor is *tile*. I'm envisioning platonic sleepovers, like the ones I had with Murphy. My friends insist—unable to control their laughter—that he's envisioning something more like a late-night movie on Cinemax.

So my anxiety increases steadily in the weeks before his arrival. I can't figure out a way to bring up the topic of his sexual expectations without sounding like I think I'm irresistible. Who am I to presume he's even considered me that way? He's never gone further than flirting, has never asked me out, or made any kind of move. I'm sure he thinks of me as a dance partner, a friend, a dive buddy. He knows I'm Mormon, is what I keep going back to. And with women like Chloe around, I doubt he's spent any time fantasizing about me.

Standing beside him in my studio apartment, though, it's obvious I should have found a way to broach the subject. Because *James* is standing beside me, in my studio apartment. With a suitcase, and a bag of dive gear. I've never been alone in a room with him, and even in a crowd, I can hardly be near him without getting sidetracked by the unrelenting urge to wrestle him to the ground. And he must be thinking that any minute now I will wrestle him to the ground. Because *why else would I have invited him here?*

These kinds of late-occurring epiphanies are what remind me most of my virginity. It's like I'm afflicted with a form of arrested development—made obvious by my obliviousness to certain social cues, or, say, the implications of inviting a grown man to share my bed in a tropical paradise.

Suddenly, I'm mortified. He's staying for ten days, and I don't know him, really. At thirty-two, I've never spent a week alone with a man—nowhere near. I picture us diving together, eating together, waking up together, brushing our teeth together. He is looking at the bed, waiting for me to say something. We have not discussed sleeping arrangements, and that question is sitting squarely, like an elephant, in my apartment. I picture the elephant wearing sequins, and a fez. I feel my voice going high, my sentences speeding up as I show him around, standing in one spot, pivoting. "There's the kitchen," I say, pointing to the stove. "Bathroom there. Warm water lasts about ten minutes." I indicate the bed, three inches from my right knee. "Bedroom here, closet beside it. Hangers if you need them."

"Are you nervous? You seem nervous," he says. He does not seem nervous. He is trying not to laugh.

"*Yes*," I say. "*Thank* you. It's *weird*, having you here. I mean, you're *you*. And you're *here*. And it's *weird*."

I can't stop thinking how stupid I've been. I don't know anything about James's dating life. When we dance, he acts like there's no one but me—and that fantasy is all I've cared about In the ten to twenty minutes we've spent together, a few times a month over the past two years. But now I see I should have asked more questions. I should have thought things through. Listened to my friends.

"So let's get out of here," says James. He grabs his wallet and holds the door open for me. "I'm starving."

When I wake the next morning, James's body is curled behind mine, and for the first time in my life I understand those women who can't sleep alone. He's forgotten where he is, I suspect, and who I am, and I'm wishing his state of amnesia will last until the second coming of Christ. I'm wishing I'd woken sooner—had more time to savor the warm weight of his chest against my back, his arm keeping by body pressed close. But it's less than a minute before the shrill beep of my alarm, which sends James *leaping* from the bed.

He's disoriented and slightly crouched, as if ready to attack. I wave to him sleepily and pad to the bathroom. We pack quickly—groggily in James's case, since I didn't think to buy coffee for him—and drive half a mile to the airport, where we board a plane the size of a minivan, which takes us to the tiny island of Cayman Brac. For the next four days James and I dive together twice every morning, and afterward eat ceviche under an umbrella made of palm fronds and bamboo. Afternoons, he goes out again, while I read a book in a hammock.

I couldn't help but feel a misplaced, silly sort of pride the first time James and I dove together. I realized right away that he knows what I know: that we're privy, through a miracle of modern technology, to witness what no human was intended by God to see. That there is no place on earth as glorious as the world underwater.

I felt an immediate wash of relief when I saw that James is an expert diver. He gives me my space, underwater. He's never on top of me, never too close, but every time I look to find him, he's looking back at me. He keeps me within a safe distance. I'm grateful to be paired up with James, grateful for his calm, his skill, and his breath control. During our dives, I try not to be judgmental of the two tentative, frightened honeymoon divers clutching the vests of their new husbands. Some people find diving stressful and claustrophobic, I know. Leila, after that first dive we did together in Mexico, literally threw up. The honeymooners in our group have no intention of diving ever again; they've suffered through their certification only for this trip to please their new husbands. They may have love, I think to myself, but I have this weightless, secret world. And James, for now, to share it with.

Evenings, James and I spend hours talking at a bar built on an old wooden dock. We stay up late under the stars, listening to the sea beneath us. Our bodies are sated, heavy feeling, after hours of sea and salt and sun. Sometimes, his forearm brushes mine, and I feel his energy reverberate through my body. We dance in flip-flops on weathered boards open to the night sky. James drinks Havana Club, and his breath, sweet with expensive rum, makes me forget to listen. I'm caught up, imagining his rum-drenched words traveling deep and golden, from his mouth to mine. I imagine easing them into my lungs like Audrey Hepburn drawing smoke through her black lacquered cigarette holder.

"So what happened with you and Chloe?" I ask, sipping my cranberry and soda, remembering her silky, jet-black hair—the kind men love, according to Tim. James signals again to the bartender. He finishes his drink with one swift movement, trades his empty for another generous pour.

"I'm a cop," he says, darkly.

"I don't know what that means."

"It means she was the girl. She was the one and I loved her. I *love* her, and I fucked it up. She's not coming back." There is a long silence. I'm wondering if that's all he's going to say. "Mornings," he continues, "I wake up and there are these few seconds before I remember. Then it hits me, and I swear to God some days I want to put my gun in my mouth." He takes a long swallow and leans back in his chair. He puts the first two fingers of his right hand between his teeth and pretends to pull a trigger.

I am thinking that's a bit *dramatic*, right? He's exaggerating. No one actually wants to blow their brains out over a breakup. You sleep too much, or drink too much (if you're not Mormon), you bathe too little, and sit alone in dark, empty rooms. You have disappointing casual sex and avoid the phone, and your friends, and every song on the radio for months on end. At least according to the movies. And then, there comes a day when you don't think about that person. A whole day, and that's progress. From there, it gets better. Except *how would I know*? What do I know about a breakup that doesn't feel, on some level, like a reprieve? So I shut up and listen while he talks about Chloe who is not coming back, talks and keeps talking until the rum is drained from his glass, is filled and drained again, again, again.

It is the next night or the one after that when James comes to our room after I've gone to sleep. He's been out for a night dive, and then to the bar with newfound friends. I wake to feel him standing at the foot of the bed, silent, unmoving, looking at me. Every cell of my body is shot through with adrenaline. Because James is climbing onto the bed. Crawling, with one leg on either side of me. He finds my hands, and laces his fingers through mine, holding them out from my shoulders. He hasn't said a word, and I'm nervous, turned on, and wondering if he is sober enough to know what he is doing, because there has been no preamble.

Before I can decide whether or not to be afraid, James is kissing me. Purposefully. His kiss is a question I feel thrumming in my head and heart and between my legs and he is waiting for the answer he must already know—that yes is everything I can imagine wanting. Yes is my mouth reaching for his, my fingers tightening, and my hips shifting underneath him. Yes is every waiting day leading up to this moment. Every fantasy I've played out in my head made real by the burn of his beard against my neck and the arch of my body beneath him.

Quickly, before I lose my courage, I turn my head and blurt hopelessly, "I'm so *Mormon.*" I know better than to let my guard down with James, even for a moment. I won't stop, won't want to, won't care until it's too late and the consequences crash down like anvils from the sky.

He collapses next to me, is quiet for a long time. "What do you do?" he asks, finally.

"I do nothing," I say, with an arm over my face, so frustrated I'm on the verge of tears. "*This* is what I do."

But that's not entirely true. Because the more deliberately I've tried to disconnect from my body—shove desire down and lock it in like a clown in a tin box—the more forcefully it jumps out in a sudden, terrifying blast. Right on cue, yet every time the surprise of it stops my heart. Once or twice a year, without fail, what I have shoved down, tried to close off leaps out, without thought or even much provocation.

Most recently, it happened with Colin, one of the dive boat captains. He received a call at work a few months ago. From his father, in Ireland, saying he'd been diagnosed with cancer. I offered Colin a lift home, and he asked if I'd stay for a bit. "I don't want to be alone," he said, taking a long pull from the beer he'd grabbed from the fridge.

He opened the sliding door of his kitchen and led me down a sidewalk snaking from his back patio, into the ocean.

We were just two co-workers talking about a shit situation, both of us still wearing our red polo shirts and blue shorts, sweating into the humid night. We sat on one of the steps on the sidewalk, built in at wide intervals. The surf was a comforting, cool rush over our feet and calves in contrast to the heat radiating from the concrete walk. There was nothing to indicate that the sky was about to break open with a deafening crack, that sheets of rain would pour over us, soaking our clothes and hair. Or that under the initial deluge, steam would rise off the limestone rocks beside us.

Colin and I fell backward, welcoming the rain and the urgent, searching mouth of the other. When the concrete turned cold beneath us, we ran to my car, raced to my house, left our dripping clothes in a heavy pile on the tile floor. That night, we forayed well into what was physically forbidden, though we stayed far this side of sex. I was Mormon; Colin was engaged. That night felt medicinal as much as pleasurable—a necessary dose of physical contact, and release.

I am still waiting to feel the guilt I've been told I should feel, having delved into the forbidden realm of heavy petting: "productive guilt," as it's described at church, prompted by spirit to identify sin and inspire repentance. But the only thing I feel guilty about is the girl who lives in Texas, who's counting the days until Colin's contract ends and she'll walk toward him down the aisle of a church, a dusting of rose petals beneath her feet.

"I wish I were good enough for you," Colin said from my balcony the next morning, in the shade of a mango tree. He was shirtless, had a cigarette in his hand. "I'm just another drunken bastard," he said, like an apology, watching the thin stream of smoke rise into the morning air.

I didn't respond. Because the night before was about nothing but the weather, and our shared, though separate sadness.

"I think I love you," he said, flicking his ash into a mango tree. "What if I love you?" His question didn't surprise me, though it came out of nowhere. We hadn't flirted. We'd never been alone in a room together, before the night before. If he'd been yearning from afar, I knew nothing of it.

"It's the virgin curse," I said. It wasn't the first time a man declared his love, or wondered if that's what he was feeling, immediately after *not* having sex. "It wears off," I assured Colin, and handed him his still-damp shirt. I dressed in my uniform and dropped him at the marina before heading into the boutique—a not-so-subtle move seen by several of our co-workers. His fiancée's former co-workers. Her friends. Colin's indiscretion was assumed to be the worst kind, and that assumption traveled minutes later into the ear of the woman who loved the man who spent last night in my bed.

Is it better or worse that it meant nothing? That the thing that could have cost Colin his marriage was simply the unbidden—though predictable—annual eruption, like a geyser on a timetable, of a need too long suppressed. I can no longer pretend it's not danger-ous, this attempted stifling of my sexuality, and its inevitable out-burst. I can't pretend I'm not hurting people, or that given the wrong man on the wrong night, I couldn't easily be hurt. I am not ignorant of the risk. All of it makes a compelling case for settling down early, like most Mormons do. Before anyone is subject to the danger inher-ent in a midsummer storm.

For the remainder of his vacation, James and I sleep platonically. We talk and entertain each other with our stories: James is a gifted mimic. He does accents, comic bits about his co-workers, and crimi-nals he's arrested, including one who produced an inflatable sex doll when James asked if he was holding. Evenings, James drinks rum and talks about Chloe. It's a relief that his heart aches for her. It makes things easier for me, and familiar. I know what to do, as long as he remains out of reach. As long as it doesn't mean anything when he flirts with me. Because I'd fall for him, if I could—if he weren't in love with someone else, if I weren't Mormon. But he is, and I am. So we dance, and we dive. Every day we dive until it's time to drop him at the airport, where I stay as long as he'll let me in his arms, in the embrace that says it's time to get back to real life.

The LDS church on the island is a sweet yellow chapel a mile or two inland from Georgetown's famous seven-mile beach. The congregation is small, comprised of a few locals, a few expats, and a weekly swell of vacationing families, usually from the United States or Britain. This week, I've gathered with my fellow ward members to watch the April General Conference in Salt Lake City. I've been watching these broadcasts from the tabernacle twice a year, or reading the reprints of them in the church's *Ensign* magazine for as long as I can remember. Conference is when the prophet and his twelve apostles speak directly to their membership worldwide. They give counsel as well as revelation, just as biblical prophets did.

This time, though, I can't make it through the opening hymn, sung by the Salt Lake City singles choir. I'm sitting on the edge of a row of folding chairs, because the chapel has no pews. The room is multipurpose. I'm concentrating on particles of dust in the telescoping ray of light stretched from the projector to the screen. I can't bear to look at the screen itself, the women in pastels, like so many Jordan almonds. The men in suits, wearing equally angelic expressions. Members just like me, ostensibly. Who have vowed to be obedient to God's laws, and to repent of their sins. They've promised to be honest, true, chaste, benevolent, and virtuous; they've promised to be hopeful, and to endure all things, to seek after what is lovely, of good report, or praiseworthy. Only then will God provide a lasting solution to their loneliness and frustration.

I imagine they comfort themselves, like I do, with the game of "wouldn't it be worse." Wouldn't it be worse to have a sick child, ailing parents, or a flesh-eating virus? Wouldn't it be lonelier to be trapped in a dying marriage, scarier to have crippling financial problems or to spend one's retirement fund on failed in vitro treatments? Wouldn't it be worse to live a life absent of faith, absent of purpose, absent of the love of God? I imagine they tell themselves, like I do, that a soul-crushing loneliness is a small price to pay, given the big picture. Everyone suffers. Loneliness is the human condition. And after the tests of our faith, we will triumph.

But today, I can't access even one of these well-practiced platitudes. When the camera focuses on one after another of the choir members' faces, what pounds in my head and through my body like an intermittent blast of white neon is panic, like that Mother's Day Sunday, years ago. It puts its face over mine and sucks the breath from my lungs. Without willing it, without thinking it, I rush for the outside door. Blinded by the burst of sunlight, I keep my head down, feel my way along the exterior wall until I round the corner where there aren't any windows. I hold myself around the waist, straining for air. My shirt snags each time I rock back against the thick, sharp swirls of yellow clay.

I can't go back inside. Can't listen to what I know is coming: a voice so sincere, so full of love it verges on pandering. A close-up of a grandfatherly man insisting I want children, when I don't. Insisting my talents are other than what they really are. Insisting I be placated by the polemic I've heard since I was a girl, burned into my consciousness for the first time in 1988, when the prophet Ezra Taft Benson said, "I would like to express the hope we all have for you, which is so real, that you will be exalted in the highest degree of glory in the celestial kingdom and that you will enter into the new and everlasting covenant of marriage . . . Dear sisters, never lose sight of this sacred goal. Prayerfully prepare for it and live for it."

I don't *want* to live for something I can't control, that might never happen. What good would it do to measure my success or worth by something so arbitrary? And I can't sit through the sentence that always comes next, as if it could be a boon, as if it is not the most soul-crushing aside. Some version of the same emphatic promise: "I assure you that if you have to wait even until the next life to be blessed with a choice companion, God will surely compensate you."

My eyes are turned upward, squeezed shut against the piercing sun. When my breath finally comes it is a ragged series of sobs that take the strength from my knees. When someone comes to find me—a newlywed college student visiting from Utah for the duration of her husband's three-month marketing internship—I'm sitting on a curb in the parking lot. Rocking back and forth, concentrating on the taste of tar wafting up from the hot asphalt. Trying to breathe steadily, to assuage the twisting ache in my chest.

She asks what's wrong, and I shake my head. There's no way this girl can understand how infuriating it is to be told to live for marriage. How condescending to be told that the time before marriage is a time of "preparing" or "creative waiting." To be reminded that nothing I have done is good enough, nor will it be, to grant me access to the highest level of exaltation. To be told that my life has consisted of a series of placeholders.

How can she understand how frustrating it is: on the one hand to *want* marriage—because it's the vehicle to love, sex, and intimacy—and on the other to know that the word "wife" is defined so narrowly in our community that it can't fit me. There is no room for what I feel, what I'm drawn to, what I'm good at. My leaders tell me what my gifts are, and they're wrong. They tell me what my nature is, and they're wrong. They tell me what my purpose is, and I feel nothing.

How could she understand what it feels like to hear the word "companion" over and over again, as if *companionship* is what's missing. A dog is a companion. A friend is a companion. I could buy a dog, and I have friends. Companionship is not the issue. *Eros* is the issue. And were I married, my sexuality would be acknowledged, and valued. It would be holy, fully sanctioned, God-given. But as it stands I must pretend it doesn't exist. I must keep myself apart from it, rise above it. Sexuality is destructive, for a woman like me. How would this girl, at twenty-one, understand what it feels like to be told that after death I'll be given what I don't want now, and be expected to feel encouraged? How can I explain the futility I feel, and the fear? How can I explain the terror taking root in my stomach, hungry for the faith I want to keep believing?

I can't speak, and she doesn't try to make me. She puts her hand on my back, makes slow circles with her palm. Her touch is kind. Like a mother's. Like my mother's would be, if she were here. She would trace patterns on my shoulders with her fingernails, run her fingers through my hair. Every Sunday of my childhood, my mother's was a sweet, absentminded affection; she would scratch my back during sacrament meeting, and I would try on her jewelry, feeling the warmth of her hand in the gold and silver bands. Brandishing her rings, I imagined myself a movie star, a queen, an ambassador, shimmering in diamonds and amethyst.

I smile apologetically at the girl next to me. I dry my tears, and stand up straight, ashamed of my existential angst. There are people with real problems in this life. There is war, and poverty, and genocide. There is economic downfall, hunger, hate crime, and violence. So what if my heart aches. So what if I'm suffocating. I hear our prophet's voice in my head: *I do not minimize your problems, but I do not hesitate to say that there are many others whose problems are more serious than are yours.*

I agree, but I also can't go back inside. Instead I drive until I see a pull-off to the right of the two-lane road, a small patch of beach fringed by mangroves. Thigh-deep in the water, I lift my skirt to my waist, training my breath to match the measured sighs of the waves easing past me. To love God is to keep his command-ments.

I let my skirt drop into the water and press my palms hard into my eyes. I stand still in this manufactured darkness, listening to the small swells break softly against the sand before receding to begin, again, like the questions in my head: Can I stay, if it's like this for-ever? Could I forgive myself, if I turned out to be too weak to endure? Could God forgive me, if I quit, if I fail, if I fall?

When I can fill my lungs fully without shuddering, I turn back toward my car. My skirt clings and flaps wetly against my legs, like a mark of punctuation. *I'm fine.* I remind myself with every measured step through the warm sand, *I'm fine. I'm fine, I'll be fine.*

Chapter 10

Wait on the Lord and he shall strengthen thine heart:
wait, I say, on the Lord.

—PSALMS 27:14

———— ❖ ————

*E*veryone on Grand Cayman, it seems, has traveled to Cuba except me. When I ask people if it's safe, they scoff like I've asked the world's most asinine question. So when Danielle—a hilarious, voluptuous LDS singleton with a 1940s fashion vibe—says she's coming to visit me on the island, I convince her to go to Cuba with me. She'll have her passport on hand already, and on the off chance we become imprisoned, she's the person most likely to make that experience bearable.

Danielle and I met when we attended the same singles ward, years ago; we lost touch when I bought my house in a different town, but reconnected a few years later at a party for LDS singles over twenty-five. I knew I'd love Danielle forever after that night: she burst into a scream when she saw me—Macaulay Culkin–style—and then serenaded me with the chorus of *Reunited* by Peaches and Herb.

When Danielle and I board the plane to Cuba, I'm at the mercy of two of the strongest forces within me—the desire *not* to be incarcerated in a country that has threatened the United States with nuclear war, and the desire to see Havana—once known as "the Paris of the Antilles"—in all the vestiges of its former glory. It's the birthplace of the rhythms I have danced to so often they feel like the music of my home country. It boasts a rich history of culture, corruption, and glamour, and persists despite the near-perpetual threat of destruction via invasion, revolution, and hurricane.

Danielle has brought a guidebook, has studied maps and dog-eared interesting, or instructive pages. All I did was book the trip, so without her I would've missed our first accidental discovery—one of Hemingway's former haunts: El Floridita, La Cuna del Daiquiri. The neon sign burns green and blue into the darkness outside the bar. It's late enough that the chairs are stacked on top of the tables, all the lights are turned off. But through the window, we see it—just as Danielle's guidebook promised. Sitting coolly at the bar is a life-size statue of Ernest Hemingway, cast in bronze. I imagine that dashing bombast, drink in hand, regaling the bartender with tales of fishing, writing, and the second ex–Mrs. Hemingway.

The following night, Danielle announces we're going to the Tropicana, that paradise under the stars: once the largest, most beautiful nightclub in the world, an open-air structure surrounded by towering royal palms. Inspired by the rustle of their fronds in the breeze, I close my eyes just enough to blur my vision. In that romantic haze, it's easy not to see the torn pantyhose, the shabbiness of the showgirls' sequined costumes, not to notice the girls I suspect may be boys. Around us, music blares over the crowd. Hundreds of dancers shimmy and spin in feathered headdresses, onstage and on catwalks among the trees.

Danielle and I fan ourselves in the languid night air. Our round, white-draped table is set up with two complimentary Cokes and two small bottles of rum, which we leave untouched. I sip my Coke and imagine how it must've been in the 1950s, when this place was the pinnacle of celebrity glamour. I imagine Danielle and me, back in time, Marlon Brando sitting at the next table, admiring one or the other, or the both of us. I imagine we've flown in for the night from Miami, on Cubana Airlines' Tropicana Special, and that our plane was packed with starlets and diplomats, musicians, politicians, and gangsters. I picture us dancing in the aisles throughout the short flight, to music played by a pared-down version of Armando Romeu's orchestra. In real life, the cab that brought us here was a shimmering, caramel-colored 1957 Chevy Bel Air, and I infuse that detail into my fantasy, imagining it's the car that picks us up after we've exhausted ourselves with dancing, gambling, and exchanging glances with Holly-wood's tuxedoed leading men. I imagine us wilting blissfully into the backseat as our driver whisks us off to catch the 4:00 AM return to Miami.

The morning after our night at the Tropicana, Danielle and I wake up early and walk to the artist's market on Calle Tacon. I am looking for a souvenir to take home, and am not brave enough to smuggle cigars—as Danielle plans to do, for her boyfriend in New York—in the false bottom of her weekend bag. I wander through the tight rows of paintings, drawings, carvings, and collages, disap-pointed by the impending rain clouds, not wanting to leave before finding the perfect memento. But just as I am about to give up, just before the blast of tropical rain that prompts the artists into a well-choreographed throwing on and tying down of plastic tarps, I find three small collages assembled on rough, asymmetrical squares of homemade paper. The bright, strange images remind me of the mag-ical realism of Gabriel García Marquez. Of the way I feel every time I read *Love in the Time of Cholera*—again and again, to see if it will ever stop breaking my heart.

In my favorite of the collages, an olive-green car drives on a road next to the sea. The roof of the car is loaded with fruit, and the fruit is larger than the car. Watermelon and papaya, mango and banana reach nearly to the second floor of an apartment building where a woman with rollers in her hair looks out the window into nothing. Her eyes have no pupils. They are almond-shaped, and turquoise. In the distance, there is a city of domed, white rooftops. Above them the sky is fuchsia, dense with clouds growing darker and redder the higher they climb. A small boy in a blue house flies a kite in that cumulous ruby sky.

It's otherworldly, the way I feel walking around Havana, unable to escape the feeling of being trapped in several different eras at once. In the three-lane street in front of our hotel, during the height of business hours, we see a man leading a pack mule, a man riding a bicycle, and a man driving a pristine 1937 Model A Ford. As for architecture, I don't know what I expected—but I wouldn't have guessed baroque, or neoclassic. Both are everywhere. Our hotel overlooks the National Capitol Building, which bears an ironic, striking resemblance to the US Capitol.

Danielle and I, exhausted from walking, rest in the Plaza Vieja, where a twelve-piece band plays outside a restaurant that serves the best limeade on God's green earth. We drink glass after glass in the shade next to a stray dog lying next to a stray cat. Peacocks wander freely among the tables in the cobblestone square. And from the balconies of the surrounding apartments—a patchwork of ruined buildings nestled between others beautifully restored—laundry flies from lines, like rows of bright flags. *Books couldn't teach me this*, I think, with the sharp tang of lime on my tongue. No picture, no movie, could show me this place.

At night, we walk along the Malecón, surrounded by couples staring first at each other, and then at the sea. I don't know why I'm surprised to see romance flourishing despite the poverty and dictatorship and diapers full of shit lying open in the streets. But it feels, somehow, like a blessing—a reminder that love can exist anywhere, in spite of any obstacle. And that alone feels like a lesson worth breaking the law to learn.

For our evening meals, Danielle and her guidebook wisely point us to *paladares*: family-owned restaurants, which must limit seating to fewer than twelve, and must be staffed by members of the family. We'd been warned before we came: food in the government-owned restaurants is literally inedible, not to mention expensive. Danielle decides, based on her research, on the paladar *La Cocina de Lilliam* for our last night in Cuba, but the cab ride seems to take forever. I wonder if she is also having visions of windowless rooms, men in dirty uniforms, concrete floors, trays of small, dirty tools. I imagine us held indefinitely, Americans having entered illegally, with no embassy to call, and no way to get more than what money we've brought.

I'm worried also about the ear infection that has bloomed overnight—a fairly common ailment for divers. The pain has worked its way into my jaw, throbbing and hot despite the over-the-counter drops I picked up at a Havana pharmacy. I'm uneasy about not being able to seek treatment from a doctor, though I've been assured that the flight home won't reach an altitude to potentially burst an eardrum. Also on my mind is the ten American dollars I offered a chambermaid in our hotel to stay a few minutes after her shift and press the dress I'm wearing—a bubble-gum pink, Marilyn Monroe–style halter. Ten American dollars will feed that woman's family for a month, according to the guidebook, and I don't quite know how to feel about what a small sacrifice that amount is, for me.

The thirst for American dollars in Cuba is like nothing I've ever seen. As is the poverty. We've been harassed on every corner by people ready and willing to take us sightseeing or to museums, to the boardwalk or Havana's famous ice-cream shop, Coppelia. Do we want to see the bar where the Buena Vista Social Club plays—for a dollar, or two, or three, for milk, for medicine, for formula, please, please?

My concerns are all replaced by curiosity, however, as our cab enters a spacious, rich, and residential neighborhood. The kind of place diplomats would live, and entertain other diplomats, whose wives would daintily sip sherry, and wear silk chiffon. The paladar is in one of these houses: a large Spanish colonial built in 1937. We are welcomed, graciously, into a fragrant backyard garden scattered with water features—a koi pond, even. The food is simple, spicy, delicious: fish with beans and rice. Danielle and I stay for hours, letting ourselves melt into the warm night. We let the mosquitoes take what they will take, mesmerized as we are by the rippling of the fountain beside us, and the man playing guitar by a wrought iron gate.

After dinner and the long cab ride back to Old Havana, we're dropped off in front of the wrong hotel, so Danielle and I walk the few remaining blocks. It's late, and the street is lined with men carrying M-16s, all of whom smile politely and greet us with, *"Buenas noches."* Across the street, a man stumbles from his apartment. He stands directly in the line of traffic, though there is none. He rubs his eyes, as if we might be apparitions—two American women, suntanned, flaxen-haired, wearing dresses from a bygone era. He looks for a second more, then tilts his gaze heavenward, calling, *"Ay, Dios mío!"* just before falling to his knees. He clutches his chest and says it again, *"Dios mío."*

My initial rush of laughter turns quickly to embarrassment—at how privileged I am, with my heels clicking along the sidewalk. With a thick fold of dollar bills in my purse and my biggest problem a plague of *ideas*. What right do I have to unhappiness? When I have health, freedom, and financial stability; opportunity, mobility, health care, and equal rights; clean water, central heat, and higher education. I have never gone hungry. I have never been touched by violence, or even an unkind hand. The sight of something beautiful is not so far from my frame of reference that it could bring me to my knees in a city street.

I see the news of Hurricane Ivan online, sitting in my father's office in my parents' house, just weeks after my return from Grand Cayman. Island fever set in not long after I returned from Cuba: after a year, the island had begun to feel small. I found myself craving better books, better movies, better friends, city culture, and conversations more meaningful than small talk with tourists, and the occasional celebrity.

The slow-moving Category 4 storm hit Grand Cayman head-on, according to the news reports. The 150 mph winds, along with an estimated eight- to ten-foot storm surge, caused billions of dollars of damage on the island, and would have put me out of a job—and possibly a house—had I not already chosen to leave. But the fact that I avoided a hurricane does little to make me feel better about living with my parents, even if it's temporary.

They've agreed to let me stay for free, for a year, while commuting to work—back again at Circa—and saving money to buy my own place, which I appreciate. But my mother jokes that part of my "rent" is accompanying her to every Relief Society function; I think she thinks I'll feel more valued if I'm more involved with the women of her ward. She doesn't understand that the Relief Society—with its focus on strengthening families and homes through faith and service—is designed to perceive a life like mine as less than ideal. A life without a family simply can't be equal or complete. And my mom can't see that the well-meaning, ill-fitting community of LDS women chafes, no matter how kind its members are.

In November, my mom insists I go with her to the Relief Society holiday party. The hostess's house is a well-groomed suburban McMansion, tastefully painted, tastefully landscaped. Inside, every light is on, and through the windows I can see dozens of women decked out in cashmere, sequined scarves, rhinestone earrings, and holiday pins. Their laughter carries through the open windows to the front walk, where I'm carrying a regifted bag of homemade toffee. The wife of one of my dad's business partners delivered it earlier that day— luckily, as neither my mother nor I felt like cooking or baking.

Before we can knock, the door bursts open with a merry "Helloo-ooo," and "You look so pretty!" and hugs from my tenth-grade seminary teacher, my Young Women's advisers, and nearly every other woman in my mother's ward. I'm happy to see them—these women who helped shape my childhood and adolescence. In the kitchen, there's a crowd of ladies bustling around the marble-topped island, where plates of hors d'oeuvres lie waiting to be devoured. While everyone is busy admiring one another's outfits, I see the bishop's wife playfully lift the collar of another woman's blouse. "Patricia!" her friend shrieks through laughter, and slaps her hand away.

"How are you wearing your garments with that neckline?" Patricia asks, and only then did I notice. Her friend's top *is* lower cut than temple garments generally allow. Still—whose business is it? I pour myself a mug of spiced apple cider and move through the throng to the living room. Perched on the arm of the family room sofa, I'm on the periphery of a conversation that vacillates between recipes for yams and the latest Harry Potter book. I don't know anything about either subject, so I listen, and drink my cider. The woman next to me leans over. "How'd you manage to get a tan in November?" she asks.

I look down at my arms, surprised any trace of it is left. "I went diving in Aruba a few weeks ago, for my birthday," I tell her. The dive company I worked for in the Caymans has a branch in Aruba, where my timeshare also has a property: I couldn't pass up the employee discount, and free hotel.

"Ooh, fun!" she says, leaning closer. "Who'd you go with?"

"Myself," I reply.

After three full seconds of silence, she sort of laughs and says, "What a waste."

I look up from my mug sharply. A waste of *what*? Money? I'd earned it. Time? Also mine, and well earned. And I'd had a glorious vacation, including a weeklong PG-13 romance with an incredibly fit, trilingual, Greek Orthodox Aruban dive instructor who didn't drink and respected the fact (or pretended to) that he wasn't getting laid.

I saw Lorenzo the first full day of my vacation, at 8:00 AM on the dock at the marina, where I checked in for my dive. He was shirtless, lean, and muscular, tasked with *lifting* things: getting tanks of air on board and arranging bags of gear. I tried not to notice the musculature of his back. And his chest. And his legs. His dark hair was cut short enough to highlight his round, slightly comical ears. When it was time to board, I heaved over the duffel bag that contains my mask, fins, snorkel, buoyancy control vest, rash guard, board shorts, towel, sunblock, lip balm, dive log, camera, water bottle, wide-toothed comb, and spray-on leave-in conditioner.

He took the bag in one hand, and held out his other to guide me over the gap between the dock and the boat. "Watch your head," he warned, right before I smashed my skull against a metal bar so hard it rang like a bell. Everyone aboard, crew and passengers alike, stopped midsentence, waiting to see if I'd bleed, or fall down.

Lorenzo came to check on me when the boat was anchored at the dive site, all of us squirming into wet suits, balancing against the slight rocking of the boat. "Your head, it's okay?" he asked, smiling. "I would be sad to lose you at seventy-five feet."

"I'm fine," I assured him, handing back the ice pack that had long since turned to warm blue liquid.

"Let me see," he said, scrutinizing the lump above my temple. "I was thinking, maybe you have a disease."

"Excuse me?"

"Something terribly wrong, to make your skin so pale. And make you not see so well." He imitated me crashing into the metal bar, then stumbling blindly, arms out like Frankenstein.

"Nice," I said, over his laughter. "Charming."

"I am even more charming at dinnertime," he assured me, handing over my fins.

That night, he took me dancing, and to a candlelit restaurant that boasts the island's most delicious plantains. Afterward, ignoring all my mother's warnings about strange men, the cover of night, foreign countries, and deserted expanses, we walked holding hands along the edge of the surf outside my hotel, until Lorenzo guided me to a picnic table in front of a darkened cabana. I sat with my feet dangling. He stepped between my legs, and tilted my face toward his. He kissed me slowly, gently until I felt hypnotized by his breath and body, the waves rolling to shore, and the breeze in the palm trees nearby.

I only had to wonder momentarily what he was doing with his hand in the waistband of his pants. I didn't even have time to say, "Is that a gun in your pocket?" before he *pulled out a gun*. He set it down on the table beside me, and leaned in again, as if I wouldn't notice the deadly weapon three inches from my thigh. As if my mouth had not gone dry, a cold surge had not gone running through my body.

"So this is the part where I get raped and killed?" I asked, pulling away. Feeling a rush of disbelief more than fear. "*That's* what's happening?" I said.

"No!" he said, loudly. And then softer. "No. Cariño." He moved a stray hair from my face. "I'm a police officer. The island is small; I carry my gun."

"*No*," I corrected him, as if he were deaf or stupid. "*You* work on a *dive boat*."

"On weekends, I work on the dive boat." He put a hand over my heart. "I thought I told you this. I'm sorry to frighten you."

"So why didn't you just *keep* it where it *was*?"

"I was afraid you'd find it on your own. And then *I* would be frightened." He laughed, running a finger lightly over the bruise on my head. "Darling. You are not so coordinated."

I smiled grudgingly, and he leaned in to kiss me again. To pick up where we left off. I let him. And later, I took him upstairs to my hotel room, gave his hands and mouth permission to wander. Because he did not need anything, he said, except to please me. Because I needed to be reminded, if only for an hour, that I'm a woman, in possession of a woman's body.

Since then I've—again—been waiting to feel the guilt I've been told I should feel, given these sins of the flesh. It's been conspicuously absent. Though I do feel bad about not being able to return the favor, so to speak. I don't like to feel selfish. So that's worrisome, as is my *lack* of guilt: does it mean I'm too sinful, too far removed from the spirit to be able to feel its promptings? Or is it just that those sixty minutes felt like a healing balm, a brief and necessary oasis? That I'm thirty-three years old, and something's simply got to give?

I look back at the woman next to me, unable to respond to "what a waste" as a conversational gambit. I don't blink, either; I sit still, bug-eyed, trying to figure out something polite to say. The church lady, whose name I don't even know, finally says, huffily, "Well. I guess I just don't like myself that much," and turns her attention elsewhere.

I stand up, ostensibly to refresh my mug of spiced cider, and am intercepted by Miranda, a friend of my mother's, who greets me with a hug and "Congratulations!" My mom was just telling her I've had my first poem accepted for publication.

Caught up in Miranda's hug, I'm embarrassed at how emotional I feel. At how much this tiny accomplishment means to me. I laugh and put a hand over my face to hide the blush that's risen to my cheeks. Miranda gives me another momlike sideways squeeze. "I'm so happy for you," she says.

Another woman from the ward walks by just then, someone I don't know well. She hasn't heard the conversation, just sees the blush in my cheeks, my bashful pride. The woman's eyes light up, and I think she's simply saying hello when she reaches for my hand. Until I see the confusion on her face. Until I realize she's looking for an engagement ring—the thing she's sure Miranda and I must be talking about.

"It's not that," I say, quickly pulling my hand back. "I write poems. One of my poems is getting published."

"Oh. Like children's books?" the woman asks.

"No," I say. "Like *sonnets*." Even though the poem about to be published is not a sonnet.

"How nice," she says, with an encouraging smile. "It's good you have something to keep you occupied."

I smile stiffly and turn away from her. Because I'm this far from asking what the fuck she thinks I *do* all day. But even through the surge of anger that's rising, I remind myself of what I know is true: she means well. They all do. These women want me to receive *all* of God's blessings, many of which can be bestowed only after my temple marriage, which should be my first objective. Everything I've done so far (my two graduate degrees, my international travels, my teaching career, my friendships, my creative pursuits), is "preparing." Treading water, keeping time, staying busy until real life begins.

I tell my mother on the short ride home from the party—the *what a waste* story, not the one about the man with the gun. I'm irritated she made me come to this party, that she can't go anywhere by herself. These are *her* friends; this is *her* sisterhood, not mine.

"Oh, phooey," says my mother, looking over from the driver's seat. "You had fun. I saw you smiling. Besides, who cares what Sister Baxter thinks; you don't even know her."

I stare blankly out the window. "I'm saying it's always the same." My breath appears in a cloud against the window, quickly fades to nothing. "I'm saying I'm exhausted."

My mother doesn't respond.

Needing a distraction from these thoughts, this mood, I suggest a movie when we arrive home. My mom doesn't like to watch anything sad, which eliminates most of my favorites. I refuse to watch gratuitous explosions, which eliminates most of hers. My father, in a house with two willful women, generally doesn't get a vote, so the movies we end up watching are different versions of the same story: the heroine, after a series of comic misadventures, inexplicably finds herself in the throes of real danger—just in time for the hero to arrive. The characters and the situations are interchangeable; it might be Joan Wilder and her lonely heart traveling to Cartagena to save her sister from the clutches of Colombian drug lords. We don't need to be afraid when she is kidnapped. The man will save the woman. When Ronny Cammareri, love-struck by his brother's fiancée, shouts into the freezing night air, "We are here to ruin ourselves and to break our hearts, and love the wrong people, and die," we respond with an ache in our hearts. We follow him inside, with our hands outstretched. When Willie Scott, a glamorous Shanghai nightclub singer is locked in a cage and prepared as a human sacrifice, we know. The man will arrive, sweaty and bleeding. When she cries out, helpless and terrified, we do not doubt him.

When the movie's over, I'm alone in the room. My parents have gone downstairs to bed, left me alone with the question, hanging heavy in the room. *What happens in real life?* I press Stop, flip on the overhead light, and stand at the top of the stairs, waiting for my eyes to adjust. The question thumps ahead of me, into the pool of darkness below. *When no one is coming, what then?* When it's my fingers being pried one by one from the edge of a cliff; when the mountain I am climbing turns to shale. Who will be the one to save me?

The stairwell before me is lined with a photographic history of my family, beginning in 1968, with my parents' marriage. I find myself looking there for the answer. Going back to 1973, when my brother and I wore matching OshKosh overalls. To 1974, when a pink gingham dress partially obscured my scabby knees. My brother sits unscathed beside me, wearing red shorts and sneakers. Across from our senior class portraits, he and his bride stand in the sun-drenched gardens of the Oakland temple. In the frame next to them, their daughter is ethereal in a white dress and cloche hat—a miniature Daisy Buchanan. Her brothers—dressed as a fireman and a sprite—follow shortly after. At the foot of the stairs, I linger in front of my slim, green-eyed mother—fifteen years younger than I am now, and about to be married. Next to her, my young father is a premonition of me. His mouth is mine—full, almost smiling. His eyes are mine, though brown.

The light from his office is a dim glow at the end of the hallway, and I follow it until I'm standing in front of the built-in shelves above his computer. I don't know what I'm looking for until I see the un-marked, faded black spine. My father's Bible. He uses a different one now. This is the gift he received at his baptism, and used throughout my childhood. I lift it from its place among the relics, run a hand lightly over the cover. This is the book that carried my father from a house haunted by alcohol, and—as a nineteen-year-old missionary—through deep, white drifts of Wyoming snow. Through his sister's first suicide attempt, and his own coming-of-age during the harrow-ing early years of his and my mother's marriage. A given, considering what damage each of my parents brought to that union.

I sit in my father's chair, and in the quiet, half-lit room, coax the zipper carefully, beginning at the top of the spine. The worn black leather opens with a sigh, and I bow my head to breathe in the scent of my childhood. Caught between the tissue-thin pages is the mem-ory of my father's sleeve against my cheek, the weight of his watch spinning on my eight-year-old wrist during sacrament meeting. I can summon the smell of vinyl and gasoline inside the Volkswagen Beetle he drove, can feel myself rushing through the garage, upstairs to change my clothes in time to watch *The Hardy Boys*. I planned to grow up and marry Joe, so no one could ever ask me to change my name.

Holding his Bible, I can feel my father's hand between my shoul-ders in a white-tiled font the Saturday after my eighth birthday. We are dressed entirely in white. The water chest high and cold: the heater was broken that day. I remember holding on to his forearm, tattooed with a gray-blue dot of ancient pencil lead. I remember the rush of water around my ears as I went under, baptized in the name of the Father and the Son, and the Holy Ghost. I remember the warmth of my father's hands on my head, later, as he confirmed me a member of the church. And knowing that after that day, I would be responsible, always, to choose the right.

Glued into the spine is a black satin ribbon, a bookmark placed in Matthew, near verses so familiar I can almost recite them by heart. I can almost see the packed sand of the dusty road, hear the crowd pushing, asking, needing, like the man begging for his daughter to be raised from the dead: "And Jesus arose, and followed him, and so did his disciples."

I picture the press of bodies, bereaved and desperate for a miracle. On the outskirts, the woman brave enough to take what she couldn't ask for. To answer the question for herself, when he couldn't hear her voice among the clamoring. She "came behind him, and touched the hem of his garment: For she said within herself . . . I shall be whole."

Jesus turned. And when he saw her, he said, "Daughter."

I was afraid he would be angry, every time I read the story, as a girl. I waited for a voice like thunder, a punishing hand raised to the heavens. But what he said was *daughter*. The echo of the word runs through me, and prompts me to steal, despite the commandment against it. I take my father's Bible back to my room, praying this pilfered inheritance will heal me. Holding the book to my chest, I become like them: asking, needing, bereaved, and begging. *Give me faith enough to fix what feels fractured. Make me whole again.*

Chapter 11

Let me go to the window,
Watch there the day-shapes of dusk
And wait and know the coming
Of a little love.

—CARL SANDBURG, "AT A WINDOW"

———— ◆ ————

S ex isn't everything," my mother says lightly, from the kitchen of my new condo. She means to be encouraging. But I stiffen reflexively against her words, as if to defend myself. I've heard it too many times from too many people—that sentence, so reductive it's offensive.

How easy it is for my mother, who married at twenty, to dismiss what she's never lived without. I can't help but feel like she's being purposefully dense, simply refusing to consider anything beyond the surface. My first impulse is a fierce rush of frustration—the urge to roll my eyes, shout a blistering, condescending "no shit" in the direction of the kitchen, where she's unpacking boxes. *Obviously,* the problem is not just the absence of sex. Obviously, there are more complex issues at the heart of my unplanned celibacy.

But when I turn to meet my mother's eyes, I work hard to keep my voice from veering into sarcasm. "Do you think I'd be a virgin at thirty-three, Mom, if I thought sex was everything?"

As if on cue, the CD we've been listening to reaches the last notes of the final track. The silence in the room highlights the trepidation we both feel. "I know you're struggling," my mother says, resting her hands on the counter. An impotent kind of energy is humming around her. She wants to help me, I know. She's trying. For the first time, she's asking.

Seconds pass before I trust my voice not to waver, before the burn in my throat subsides. "I don't know how to fix it." Ashamed by even that admission, I hold in the heaviest secret, the sentence that frightens me at night. Outside, a container ship slowly barrels through the shipping lanes. The north end of Vashon Island is nearly obscured behind its towering mass of orange crates, its hull plowing a wake toward the breakwater below. "I don't know how much longer I can live like this," I say finally, half-hoping my mother won't hear.

The Mormon Church is a system of absolutes. There is only one right way to live. One complete truth. Either I believe the doctrine of my church was revealed by God to a living prophet, or I don't. And if I believe, I must live the way I've been commanded. I must endure to the end. If I am floundering, drowning, or desolate, my faith should be the solution.

I can feel my mother's fear from across the room, the exaggerated stillness of her body. How can I tell her that over the past two years I have *willed* myself into depression? The relief of numbness, that saving grace. How can I say I am glad to feel myself withering? That I can almost stop needing what I can't have, if I don't allow myself to feel anything.

If I say no, sex isn't everything—those mechanics, that act—but it affects everything, she will say, "Be faithful." If I say sex casts a monstrous shadow over my life: the visceral wanting of it, the religious sanctions against it, the looming threat of disfellowship or excommunication, and the damaging ways I've devised to resist it, she will tell me to follow the prophet's counsel, and his apostles'. If I say

sex keeps me from getting near enough to a man to fall in love, because nonmembers are the ones who want me and I can no longer
trust myself around them. If I say I'm unmarriageable in the Mormon
community. If I say the crisis of celibacy is a crisis of isolation, that I
am wrong in both places, judged by both sides, she will say wait for
my spiritual reward. "Look to the afterlife," as if this life means
nothing.

There will be no way to respond that isn't sacrilege. No prophet or
apostle has lived a celibate life is what I'd like to tell her. No one
who's ever told me celibacy is a viable option has ever been celibate.
They don't even use the word. They say "abstinent," which implies
there will be an end. They don't consider what my life will be like, if
I never marry. Which is likely, given who I am, and the ways I'm different. People stand at the pulpit, or they come to my house, and tell
me not to need what every human needs. Afterward, they go home
and undress. They lie down next to the person they love most, or
once did. When they reach across the bed, someone is there.

The ship outside my window has traveled all the way from China.
I imagine it's full of laptops, T-shirts, lipstick, or toys; I imagine a
crate full of telephones or headphones—some advanced technology
that could help my mother hear me. Make her understand. One of
the apostles recently warned against withdrawing from others. "Such
retreat," he said, "may ultimately lead to the darkening influence of
the adversary, which leads to despondency, loneliness, frustration."
He's got it backward, I remember thinking. Withdrawal is a *survival
tactic.* Because if I can't get numb enough, if I can't withdraw far
enough from my body and the need to feel human, I will end up
clinging to a stranger on a deserted beach, again. I will find myself
tangled in the arms of another somebody, anybody, on my entryway
floor. It will be some weary, medicinal surrender that destroys everything. One moment of weakness is all it would take to make myself a
hypocrite, or a failure.

I open my mouth to explain, or try to. But there is nothing I can say. I listen, instead, to the steady, rhythmic crash of waves against the seawall. And I listen to my mother's voice, which sounds as if it's coming from far away. "Everyone has trials, honey. You just love God. You keep the commandments, and you say your prayers." She turns back to the dishwater, as if that is all that needs to be said.

I sink into a chair, knowing I shouldn't have tried. Knowing she'll never understand how insulting it is to have my problems waved away with asinine suggestions: Get a pet, people say. Get a hobby. As if *knitting* could fix this. She won't believe me if I tell her how often, at church, I'm reminded as a single woman not to feel worthless. "Why *would I?*" I am tempted to shout. Or if I told her about my bishop, who just after I moved to my new ward asked me to teach a class of five-year-olds. "Fine," I said, and tried to say more, but he stopped me short. Held my gaze. "It will be *good for you* to be around the children," he said, pointedly. As if I am suffering from some deficiency, need a weekly dose of toddler therapy.

"Think about your patriarchal blessing," my mother suggests, still trying to be helpful. She's not worried. She's waiting for the man who will provide the children she saw in the dream she had nearly twenty years ago. She is waiting for her vision to become my reality.

"What if your dream was just a dream, Mom?" I start unpacking a box of crystal water goblets. "Because the *math* doesn't work. Say some man fell out of the sky right now. By the time I fell in love, got engaged, got married, got pregnant, gave birth, I'd be thirty-six at the soonest, and who knows if I could even have four children. Never mind I can't imagine wanting one."

My mother opens her mouth and I cut her off before she can say it. "*Don't* tell me I'll change my mind!" I shout. "I know who I am. I know what I feel. No one would ever roll their eyes at a woman who's dying for a child, and say, 'Don't be silly; you'll change your mind.'" I stand up to face her fully. "Don't *dismiss* me!"

She sighs. I am trying to calm down, trying to remind myself it won't do any good to shout. She won't hear me, no matter how loud I get. She can't hear me. "I never wanted kids, either," she offers. "Until I had you two. When we were engaged, your father said he wanted five kids. *Five.* I told him if that were true, he'd better hurry up and marry someone else."

"Mom!" I want to smash every one of my goblets against the glass top of my table. I want to take a sledgehammer to the table, watch it explode into a million glittering shards. "You were *nineteen!*"

"I was twenty by then," she corrects. "And believe me, I kissed my share of frogs."

My phone ringing is the excuse I need to go outside to the balcony, despite the chill, the puddles of rain on the tile beneath my bare feet. It's James, calling to tell me he's decided to join me for my upcoming dive trip in Belize. When does the tour company need his deposit?

Belize, I think, and let the tension drain from my body. I face into the cold wind coming off the Sound, look to the expanse of saltwater stretched out in front of me. A ferryboat is inching toward the dock nearby, sounding its low, mournful horn. Beyond the ferry, the snow-capped peaks of the Olympic Mountains rise in the distance—and in the opposite direction, the Cascades.

I fell in love with this place the minute I saw the view from the steep, tree-lined drive. James, who moonlights as a Realtor, is the one who showed it to me. From the passenger window of his car I spotted Puget Sound glittering blue in the late afternoon sun—hints of it, peeking through the trees. We parked ten feet from the breakwater dividing us from Puget Sound, and I stepped into this scene knowing I needed to live inside it.

"Unless it's infested with vermin," I announced, "I'm buying it." But I was already thinking, *That's what exterminators are for.* Once inside, I rushed straight to the balcony to watch the sun morph into a red ball of fire before sinking into the horizon. "Make an offer," I told James, choosing, again, to see a sign where I wanted one.

"Maybe you should look around first?" suggested James, but the rest was unimportant. I slept on the floor, on an inflatable mattress, lived out of trash bags, and showered at friends' houses during the four months of remodeling required to transform my condo from a stained and sagging rental into something glamorous, chandeliered, vintage-inspired. My mom didn't understand why I didn't want to stay at her house for a few more months—but I couldn't bear to not wake up to this view every day, to the briny smell of the sea wafting in from outside.

My feet are freezing by the time I hang up with James, my anger dissipated. I don't know if it was his voice or the thought of Belize that calmed me down. But I need to apologize to my mom, who is only doing what she knows to do: mother me; protect me. Even now, if I sleep over at her house, she sneaks in after I've fallen asleep and puts an extra blanket over me—the yellow wool one, with the cream-colored stripes. She knows how easily I get cold. And she's worried about me. She's hoping that what I'm going through is a phase. Something I'll grow out of or work through. She's counting on the right bishop, the right husband, the right scripture: someone, something to help me see things differently.

I wonder, though, if she understands the fundamental differences between us. For her, the motivation for marriage was love, yes—but also it was escape, safety, freedom. My mother, in direct response to her volatile, violent upbringing, can't think of anything better than being safely ensconced at home. Few things are more precious to her than a night light, a deadbolt featuring ANSI Grade 1 protection, and a year's supply of food storage in the garage. Not to mention a husband to walk the dog after dark and bring home a dependable salary including medical, dental, and vision. There is nothing more rewarding, for her, than to have created the loving, traditional, functional family neither she nor my father had.

But none of those things are factors for me, besides love. What I need—access to my sexuality, a less prescriptive definition of womanhood, a wider view of the world, time and solitude to write, respect for my current life and creative pursuits—may never have entered her consciousness. I wonder sometimes, as well, if she's able to understand desire the way I feel it. If, given the abuse she suffered, she gets the extent to which sex *does* matter. *Is* an integral part of life, relationships, and identity. My mother talks about her body in the third person: if you ask her how she's doing, she'll say, "The knees are a mess," or "The back is killing me," or "The gall bladder has to come out." I snapped at her one time, told her it's irritating, the way she refers to her body. She didn't know what I was talking about. She was surprised at first—and then not surprised at all, by her unconscious choice of words. "I've been trying to escape my body my whole life," she said.

I immediately felt ashamed. Suddenly it seemed obvious: she survived her abuse by dissociating. She needed the disconnection I find myself railing against. If she could exist separately from her body, then the crimes against it would exist separately from her. I have to consider this too, when she says sex isn't everything.

"What are you doing later?" I ask her, by way of apology. "There's a chaise lounge I want you to look at. We can go to dinner after. It'll be fun." I grab a towel and dry the dishes she's washed. I put them where I think they should go, knowing full well she'll wait until I've put them all away to tell me how they *should* be arranged, and make me redo the whole thing.

It's the day before my thirty-fourth birthday when James and I arrive at Captain Morgan's Retreat, a short water taxi ride from San Pedro, Belize. Our concierge welcomes us with congratulations: we have chosen the most luxurious resort on Ambergris Caye, she says. Are we familiar with the TV show *Temptation Island,* she wonders, handing us each a complimentary glass of rum punch. I hand mine to James, who drains both his glass and mine. She continues, saying the television show was filmed at this very resort.

My *life* is a temptation island, is what I'm thinking.

I didn't *intend* to end up alone with James when I began planning this trip six months ago. I sent out an e-mail to twenty-five friends inviting them to San Pedro; how could I have known the only one who would respond with more than an "I wish" was James? And now I'm walking behind him and the white-shirted porter leading us, travel weary, plane rumpled, down a brick path shaded by giant palms. I savor every breath of the Caribbean air as I walk. I close my eyes. Imagine it filling out the empty spaces inside me.

This trip is about the necessity of being underwater, though I will accept James as a welcome benefit. I needed, when I began planning, something decidedly wonderful in my immediate future, something to drown out the sound of wheels spinning beneath me, to soothe the dry ache inside, so persistent it feels like my familiar.

When the porter stops walking, we're at a villa on the top left corner of a fourplex featuring brightly painted walls and a verandah overlooking the sea. There's a bedroom for me, and a sofa bed for James. There's no question, this time, of who will sleep where. Though there is still an undercurrent of flirtation between us: a look he gives me, sometimes, that says he would if he could. I know already that I will listen through the wall before I fall asleep. Let the sleep-rhythm rise and fall of his body be a lullaby for mine. I will linger over the smell of his shaving cream in the steam of the bathroom after his shower, over the sight of his towel hanging to dry on the bar beside mine, and the casual way he changes his shirt in my presence. I'll have that much of his body, at least, available to me. These will be crumbs enough to live on.

James and I drop our bags, tip the porter, and head straight to the

dive center. We've each logged hundreds of dives—including the fifteen or so we've done together. Much of what is strange and beautiful
underwater, we've both seen at least once: sea turtles, moray eels, spotted eels, Christmas worms and parrotfish, tarpon, barracuda, octopus,
spiny lobster, lionfish, angelfish, stingrays, eagle rays, giant schools of
silversides. Jellyfish, nudibranches, groupers half as big as ourselves.
Brain coral, fan coral, fire coral, black coral, tube coral, and a hundred other wonders of the sea. James, who also dives in cold water,
has seen even more than I have, has captured much of it on video.
But every diver looks forward to the next rare or exotic sighting: a
manatee, a cuttlefish, a manta ray.

So it shouldn't be a surprise that James, standing in front of the
poolside dive center, is holding a brochure for the shark dive. Or that,
after perusing the brochure, he starts asking *questions* about the shark
dive. "It's pretty simple," says the dive master. "We chum the water.
The sharks smell blood and come up for lunch."

I want to know how he can be sure they won't want to eat a tall
blond lady for lunch. Rather than get into it, he hands me a FAQ
card in regard to Caribbean reef sharks. According to the laminated
page, they're one of the most abundant large sharks in the area.
They're between six and nine feet long, and weigh around a hundred
fifty pounds. Generally, they're unaggressive toward divers, since
we're neither food nor threat. Therefore, the sharks often approach
quite closely during dives, terrific for photography and videography.
Nevertheless, divers should keep their hands close to their bodies or
tucked under their arms, since competing sharks could mistake
hands for pieces of bait. I hand the card to James when I'm finished
reading, hoping he'll find the endeavor unnecessary. And also hoping
he'll suggest we go.

I've seen a few small white-tipped and black-tipped reef sharks,
no more than three or four feet long. I've seen plenty of nurse sharks,
dopey- and sleepy-seeming, cartoonish in shape and expression. But

no big, toothy, scary sharks. I did see a large, murky shadow once, far below me on a dive off Cayman Brac, but I looked away quickly, pretending it didn't exist.

The Libra in me comes out at times like this: on one hand, I wonder if it's wise to take part in an activity that teaches sharks to associate humans with food; on the other I am afflicted desperately, incurably with FOMO—the fear of missing out. And the Great Blue Hole, the site of the shark dive, is one of the most astounding dive sites on earth, according to the literature at the dive center. It's in the center of Lighthouse Reef—a limestone sinkhole nearly a quarter of a mile in diameter, nearly perfectly round. It's over four hundred feet deep, close to five hundred by certain accounts. It looks, from above, like a "giant pupil in a sea of turquoise." The walls are sheer, flat rock, until about a hundred feet down, where spectacular, prehistoric stalactite formations begin. The Great Blue Hole is one of three stops on an all-day trip to the Hol Chan Marine Reserve. The boat leaves at 6:00 AM on Mondays, with a check-in at 5:30.

I look at James, and I look at the guy behind the counter, who are both looking at me. I sigh heavily and reach back into my pocket for my credit card. The shark dive is $350, in addition to the $1,000 I've planned to spend for a ten-dive package. But when will I get this chance again? And why say no when there is no reason to say it?

The night before the shark dive I sleep fitfully, like it's the night before Christmas. Except there is dread laced through my excitement. Because coming down the chimney is *sharks*. I wake before my 5:00 AM alarm so anxious I feel irritated by the sight of James, calmly drinking coffee in a rattan chair. As if this is just another day at the office.

During the four-hour boat ride to the marine reserve, full-on fear burrows into my abdomen. There's only one thought in my head. I'm repeating it like a mantra, so it will be instinctual when the time comes to use it. *Keep breathing.* Divers die when they panic; it's dangerous to hold your breath. Full lungs are like balloons. They make you buoyant, send you shooting to the surface without the benefit of a safety stop—three to five minutes spent hovering at a depth of fifteen feet, required to balance the nitrogen in your blood. I'd much prefer not to use the international dive insurance I've recently purchased. I would prefer not to be airlifted to a facility boasting a recompression chamber for hyperbaric oxygen therapy, nor to require the expertise of a surgical staff trained to amputate shark-bitten limbs.

I try to distract myself by counting: in the middle of the deck are fifteen duffel bags full of gear. Behind the benches lining both port and starboard sides are thirty full tanks of air; each of us will need two today. I tap James on the shoulder, lean close so he can hear me over the boat's roaring engine. I hold my hair away from my face, in opposition to the wind.

"You have to stay right next to me," I shout. "When the sharks come. You might even need to hold my hand. I don't think I'll freak out. But just in case."

"You'll be fine," James says casually, offering me a water bottle.

"I mean, I get it. You can't save me if a shark wants to eat me. I'm just saying stay close."

"I hear you."

"I mean *really* close. Like annoyingly close."

"Got it," he says, with a slightly sarcastic pat on the shoulder. I stop talking, though I'm still not convinced he understands that I am *serious*.

Upon our arrival at the Great Blue Hole, the dive master gives us his usual safety speech and outlines the dive profile on a dry erase board. We'll go straight down to max depth for five minutes, then slowly ascend to forty feet, where we'll wait for the sharks—if they decide to show up. If not, we come straight to the boat after our safety stops—he recommends a full five minutes—and we'll go on to the next dive site. Part of me is hoping the sharks won't show; the other part is thinking I just dropped $350. I *better* see some freaking sharks.

"Pool's open," the dive master says, clicking the cap back on his marker—the international sign for us to spit into our masks, fasten our fins, and tighten our vests. One at a time, we stand awkwardly, balancing against the weight on our backs; we shuffle, flat-footed, to the back of the boat and take giant strides into the sea, hands flat against our faces, holding our regulators and masks in place.

James and I descend within sight of each other. He stays close. I'm grateful, though still not particularly at ease. Our dive starts near the limit of safe diving—beneath which nitrogen narcosis can set in—and since there is no ocean floor to tell us when we've reached our depth, we keep a close eye on our dive computers. Also within sight is one of the limestone walls of the Great Blue Hole. The transformation is spectacular when we reach 120 feet. Monstrous-looking, craggy stone fingers reach into the blue void—like something from a postapocalyptic sci-fi film. I think of these formations as they once were—aboveground, shooting into, or dripping from the sky.

I hear our guide tapping something metal against his tank: time to ascend. We float slowly up to a ledge at forty feet. Some divers stand on the ledge, but I've been too conditioned never to touch anything underwater. James and I hover, slightly apart from the group, but connected by our shared anticipation. I steel myself against the fear I don't yet feel, but predict: the involuntary clench and release of muscle, a sense of loosening within my body, thick lava of dread emanating from the tight knot low in my stomach.

There is a deckhand on the boat above us. One stays behind, whose task it is to dump buckets of chum into the sea. To summon the sharks. Give us what we paid for. I picture him brown and bare-chested, balanced on the undulating bow. Backlit in the blinding sun, like an eclipse, a shadow casting bait in the form of blood.

It's not long before we see the results of his efforts. The sharks come when they're called. Fin following scent, they slice up from black water to blue. They appear at first like a mirage, a vision so unreal I blink hard against it, willing it to focus. In seconds the sharks are in sharp contrast, almost impossible to comprehend. I'm overwhelmed by the size of them, the shape and number of them, their dorsal fins cutting through the sea. Maybe there are seven, maybe twenty; I can't tell. They are circling, snacking, their blunt heads so large they seem magnified. I'm enthralled by their slick musculature, the matte-looking gray of their skin. They are electric in their energy, gruesome in their teeth, but the pull of their dead-looking eyes is hypnotic.

I can feel the tunneling of my vision, the dilation of my eyes in response to the elegant strokes of their tails. James and the other divers evaporate from my consciousness. I forget about not breathing, about being eaten alive. I drift toward the sharks, without thinking. I feel drawn, somehow—unaware of danger, though I am fully aware of the violence implied in their mouths, the deadly potential of a sudden sideways grip and thrash. Still, I drift, though the swirl of sharks is thinning, disappearing so quickly I'm afraid it will feel like we never saw them at all. I am reluctant to ascend, and do so only after the last shadow has faded into the deep.

The dive master had to hold me by a fin, James tells me once we're back in the boat. He can't believe I didn't notice, teases me about being a spazzy tourist diver. Why was I swimming toward them? I couldn't feel anything but the sharks, I tell him. On the long boat ride home, I'm grateful for the noise of the boat's engine: that excuse not to talk. Because I'm still trying to process the contradictions in my head. How is it I can feel peaceful, glorified, connected in the literal presence of sharks? That next to them, I can forget to be afraid? And sitting still in the house of God, I feel myself drowning. I'll be singing a hymn or bowing my head for a prayer and there it is: the absence of air, the collapse of lungs rushing me into a hallway, into a parking lot, gasping, fighting the feeling of a hand holding me under. Desperate for something solid to push up against—anything to stay the frantic, ineffectual churn of my feet.

And James—offering me fresh water, a slice of orange to cut the salt in my mouth—how can I feel so drawn to him, when he is everything wrong for me: work-obsessed, atheist, unavailable. With him, of all people, I feel appreciated. Challenged, and seen. Admired for my mind, my choices, my humor, and my body. He pushes me to write more, and better. To read more, and better. To think more, and better. He has never implied I should be anything other than a better version of who I am now, that I am incomplete, or a failed version of any ideal. Unable to reconcile these contradictions, I lose myself in the deafening roar of the engine, the sun warming me deep down, and James's expression of sheer wonder, playing and replaying the video of our dive.

Chapter 12

He hath destroyed me on every side, and I am gone: and mine hope hath he removed like a tree.

—JOB 19:10

———— •— ————

Last Sunday, the bishop's wife—who's also the Primary music leader—cornered me behind the piano where we were stacking chairs at the end of our meetings. "Isn't it such a joy to serve in the Primary?" she said, sighing beatifically. "Thank goodness you have these children in your life." She reached to pat my arm, and gazed at me earnestly. "It must be so *difficult* for you, not to have your own."

I stepped back and said, "No. It's not difficult." To her horror, I continued. "I've never wanted kids. Thank goodness for that. Think how I'd feel, Mormon and single at thirty-four, with no prospects and a tick, tick, ticking biological clock."

The bishop's wife has eight children. She married her high school sweetheart, was engaged by seventeen, so it's no wonder she looked at me like I'd flipped her the bird. Or that she delivered her response in the same tone she uses with the three-year-olds: "If you were truly living the Gospel," she said, "God would bless you with a desire for children."

If I were *truly* living the Gospel.

I must not be worthy. If I'm different, I must be wrong, or doing something wrong. Everything at church seems to eventually trickle down to that conclusion. But it was that conversation—that particular sentence—that finally cut the cord connecting me to the brothers and sisters of my ward. I'm simply too tired to listen to it anymore, too aware of how little good it does to argue.

And the thing is, elsewhere, I am valued. Elsewhere, my community—my found family—is real, and loving. I'll cleave instead, to my chosen tribe. To Danielle, and my two writers' groups, my Bennington classmates, and the Circa girls, who have become family as much as my family is: Willow—a preacher's daughter, and a songwriter—who understands my spirit, and my poems. Melissa and Corina, my confidantes, and comic relief. John and Alphonsine, Circa's husband-and-wife chef team, who live just down the road and fondly refer to me as Aunt Jackie—Roseanne's single sister, who stops in all the time for snacks and gossip. And Gretchen, so protective of my innocence she once practically flew across her kitchen—horizontal and in slow-motion, screaming a desperate "Nooooooooo"—to swat a pot cookie out of my hand before I accidentally ingested my first-ever illicit substance. "I'd never forgive myself," she said, breathless, "if you ended up stoned on my watch!"

These are the surrogate husbands and the sisters of my heart. They're Republican, Democrat, pro-life, pro-choice, gay, straight, married, single, divorced, remarried, rebounding, recovering. Mormon, atheist, Buddhist, agnostic, pantheist, and Catholic. This community—my true relief society—is the antidote, the healing balm, the life ring keeping me afloat.

Diving, too, continues to buoy me. The day after I arrived home from Belize I wrote FIJI over a long string of squares on my calendar twelve months ahead. Those four letters, written in capitals, circled in red, inching closer every month, feel like the next reach in a row of monkey bars. Something solid to grab with one hand, before I let go of what's gripped in the other.

I sigh myself to sleep most nights with visions of islands more beautiful, and farther away, than any I've seen. Halfway around the world, in fact. *If I can just make it to Fiji* is the current that carries my prayers. Driving away from the bishop's wife last week, I imagined Fiji, and felt my anger dissipate like fog in sunlight. During slow lunchtime shifts, I daydream into the pages of my *Fodor's* guidebook, savoring the syllables of "archipelago," "Melanesia," "Vanua Levu."

In the months leading up to Fiji, I'll keep doing what I'm supposed to do: go to church, teach the five-year-olds, have Sunday dinner with my parents, avoid dating, avoid dancing, avoid every other conduit to what I can't allow myself to feel. I'll wait tables, meet with my writers' group on Monday nights, and share the poems that have begun, despite my best intentions, to circle around my fears. They're beginning to tell the terrifying truth—as much as I am able to acknowledge. They are attempting the impossible—a revision of what's been carved in stone.

I've written a poem about the parable of the ten virgins in the book of Matthew: the wise five who came prepared with oil enough to wait through the night for the bridegroom, not knowing what time he'd arrive. And the foolish five, who did not have enough—who were sent away to get more or do without. In my poem, one of the wise virgins shares her kerosene. She howls revolution until all ten lamps burn halfway full.

In another poem, this same virgin goes to the party for the prodigal son, just back from a spree of riotous living. She toasts to the brother who stayed behind and did what he was told. She glances toward the prodigal:

Sure, I'm glad you're back, but how hard is it to come home, when the money's gone? I'll raise a glass to your brother instead, to knowing what it's like, playing every rule; waiting—days tasting

shades of vanilla—for the promised Christmas bonus. Always
good always home, instead of upstairs with whoever's asking,
fence-sitting on a fall somewhere in the gray between always good,
always home the words say themselves in the same night prayer for
who knows how long, how many years, just in case he's still listen-
ing: Dear God, please. Please.

Beneath these poems, and my predictable patterns of behavior,
beneath every one of my prayers I feel a sense of contradiction. The
urge to open my hands battling the need to keep my fingers pressed
tight—to contain what's turning to sand so fine it will blow away if I
let it. These opposing forces are what lead me toward my first outright
rebellion: an afternoon outing to see *Brokeback Mountain,* now playing in select cities. I know many, if not most, members of my faith
consider the film a symbol of our society's eroding values, a rational-
ization of the perversion of homosexuality. Regardless, I need to see
it. Though I don't understand why, until after.

Less than half an hour in to the movie, I'm as close to the fetal
position as I can get: I've got my feet on the seat in front of me, my
knees in my chest, and my hands in my sleeves. I'm curled into myself in the darkened theater, fully engrossed in the story, though not
expecting to relate to it: what could I have in common with two gay
cowboys in 1963?

The first shock comes during the sex scene. It feels frightening,
such aggressive physicality. I look away, not knowing how to process
such a fierce, sudden penetration. Given my inexperience, it seems
disconnected from pleasure. But what devastates me is not the sex, not
the homosexuality, but the unexpected depth of my empathy. For a
full hour, I am unable to take my hands away from my mouth, unable
to predict when sobs will rise, unbidden, from my chest. I muffle
them, afraid they'd be audible, afraid someone will touch me and
break the spell.

When Heath Ledger as Ennis Del Mar falls to his knees on the frozen ground, weak with grief and yearning, my chest feels like it is cracking open. When he collapses into the sleeve of his shearling coat, my stomach tightens so fast I lose my breath. When his mouth is a gruesome twist, I cover the ugly, sideways openness of mine. His unrelenting anguish is a dare, urging my heart to break. Because I know what it is to be fundamentally bound to an ill-fitting life. And to have no choice but to be what makes me other. I know what it is to be told that if I pray hard enough, if I *try* hard enough, God will fix what's wrong with me.

After the movie, we are all puffed and weary—Melissa, her girlfriend Jessie, and I. We're emotionally spent, trudging toward the car like zombies. I'm grateful for whatever thoughts have each of them preoccupied, because all I can think about is a beautifully framed gift my mother gave me for Christmas years ago—a copy of *The Family: A Proclamation to the World*, which all LDS people are encouraged to display in their homes. In my first townhouse, I hung it where I knew I'd never see it—in the powder room next to the washing machine. In my current home, it has stayed, still in its beautiful frame, facedown under a pile of blankets in my closet. It's taken until now for me to acknowledge why.

A large percentage of the people I love most in the world are gay or bisexual, and that document is what church members and leaders use as evidence to support the stance that gay people—who are sinful, threatening, deviant, or misguided—should be denied marriage. Should be punished by God if they engage in homosexual behavior. The party line is that such views are *pro-family*, not antigay. But I believe in equal rights, and I've never bought that rhetoric. I've also wondered where the line is: would it be a sin for a gay person to date members of the same sex? To hold hands, or kiss, or even hope that someday they'll be loved? That feels like the worst part: denying people hope. I don't know where I'd be if I couldn't tell myself that any day now, five minutes, or an hour from now, everything could change.

Which isn't to say I've been brave enough to speak out against any doctrine of my church for fear that I might be wrong. I might be deserving of censure, judgment, or punishment. I've been taught that if the prophet speaks the words, they must be God's words. My solution has been to remain supportive of my friends, and keep that proclamation in the closet.

We drive in silence for a mile or so, until Jessie swerves quickly to the curb, with a maniacal cackle. Babeland, that bright yellow storefront on East Pike, is directly across the street. As in, *toys* in Babeland. As in sex toys. "We're going in. *You're* going in," Melissa commands gleefully, turning to point a stern finger at me. "I can't wait to see this."

Once inside, I have an entirely new understanding of what it means to be a stranger in a strange land. This is what it means to be unashamed of sexuality, I think, perusing a flyer advertising weekly classes on bondage techniques, fellatio, and stripping for lovers. Wandering through the store, I am literally flabbergasted. There are such things as prosthetic *flaccid* penises? That people just walk around with, when they feel the need for a bulge? I hold one up, and point it at Melissa. "I don't get it," I say.

She answers matter-of-factly. "It's for women going through gender reassignment." She shifts into the voice and mannerisms of the boys of her Philadelphia youth. "You know. So they can feel all masculine and shit."

I am overwhelmed by how much there is *to do* with the anus, and I zoom past those displays as well as the wall of leather bondage gear. I am dying to get on the phone with Danielle, who is possibly the only person in the world who can understand the series of explosions erupting in my brain.

I call her the minute I get home.

"Dahling!" she says.

I announce without preamble, as if it's all one word, "OMG I just went to Babeland!"

She bursts into laughter. "What was it like?" she asks. "I want details."

"It was well lit and nicely laid out, with colorful, tiered table displays and information cards next to every product. There was much attention paid to merchandising. It was staffed by the loveliest androgynous pixie, who provided all kinds of interesting facts."

"Such as," she says, drawing out the vowels.

"Did you know Babeland opened in 1993 in response to the lack of women-friendly sex shops in Seattle?"

"No I did not."

"Did you know they're part of the First Thursday art walk with boudoir photography shows?"

"We have to go!" she shouts.

"I know. Also, there is an entire wall devoted to condoms. I had no idea there were so many kinds of condoms. They're neatly labeled, multicolored, in clear, reach-in containers. Like you'd see at a candy shop. And there's a whole bookshelf full of resource materials; there are books on every topic you could think of. There's really no excuse for anyone to be having bad sex in this town. And every customer in there was all suburban and straight, looking for ways to "spice things up." It was a lot like shopping at Target, except for all the vibrators. Though I might have felt differently if someone were next to me shopping for strap-ons."

"Yikes," says Danielle.

"Yeah, that was a lot. They just seemed so . . . *large*. And weirdly shaped. And who knew so many people were into nipple clamps? But that stuff was all in the back, and you could easily avoid it. Most everything was just regular stuff for regular people, doing, you know, regular stuff."

"Did you buy something?" Danielle demands.

"No!" I shout, laughing. "Melissa made me go. I was just *browsing*."

I hang up and reach for my laptop to check my e-mail. I'm not expecting a message from James, and the sight of his name on the screen makes me blush—as if he's somehow been conjured by all this talk of vibratory toys. Or as if he knows my secret: I haven't invited anyone but him to Fiji. His e-mail confirms his plans to join me for the entire two weeks, and my short note back—about dates and flights and expenses—is propelled, as always, by the impossible wish that James could be the someone who changes everything.

Before we even arrive on the island of Viti Levu, however, that fantasy crashes hard against reality. When we check in for our departing flight at Sea-Tac, James stands at a separate kiosk, though our tickets are booked together. Same at customs, upon our arrival at Nadi International Airport. My brain registers it right away: he is shifting me, from the nebulous middle space we've inhabited for years squarely into the friend zone. I've been waiting for this. Expecting it: the point at which a platonic flirtation loses its appeal.

When the customs official asks who I'm traveling with, I point to James, in line at a different booth. He asks why we aren't together, and I can't think of a simple reason, a sentence to explain it. "I'm not his wife," is what I come up with.

During our first days on the island, in the hotel and on the dive boat, James continues to set boundaries. If I ask what time it is, or ask him to wake me when his alarm goes off, he says wear a watch. Buy an alarm. He is treating me like he would a guy friend. He lets the crew be the ones to carry my bag, to offer a hand to guide me on or off the boat. When on one of our first dives, I ask him to fix the Velcro tab that's tangled in my hair at the back of my neck, he claps me on the back, hard, after he's finished. As if to say, "*Readyyy,* break!"

I try to get the hint. I don't ask to borrow sunscreen or toothpaste when I realize I've forgotten mine. I buy more, for twice the normal price, in the hotel gift shop. But despite my best efforts, I feel wounded. Rejected and lonely. So when a woman on the dive boat very obviously wants to get to know James better—a woman who is not as pretty, not as smart, not as young, not as funny, not as anything as I am (including Mormon, virginal, fragile, unavailable), I say bitchy things about her bandanna do-rag: "What, is this a Snoop Dogg video, circa 1992?" And her conspicuous posing on the bow of the boat—the taking down of straps, the arching of her back. "Wait, who invited Rebecca Romijn?"

Instead of laughing at my adolescent barbs, James flirts back. If I sit too close to him, he inches away. If I brush by him in the narrow aisles of the dive boat, he shifts to avoid my touch. I know he can't breathe, and what I do is lean in closer. I am desperate for the attention he usually gives me—a small, vital element of these two tropical weeks per year when I need to pretend my life is different from what it is. I can't back off, though I know I should. Because James is standing closest to my need to matter most, to someone.

After our dive, back at the hotel, he hooks his camera to our television and invites this woman—the back-arching poser—to watch the video of this morning's dive. Something he has never, in three years, done. James is not a joiner. Nor a sharer—*I've* never even seen video of our dives. But here he is, sitting beside this woman on the couch. And on the TV screen, she and her white bandanna glide into the frame. Immediately I see why she's been invited: James has filmed her emerging from a tunnel in the reef, amazed to find a sea turtle swimming beside her, matching her pace. Of course she wants a copy of the video. Of course she and James exchange contact information. It turns out they live within driving distance from each other, back home.

Of course they do.

I ask myself what I'm doing, sitting miserably in a room with them, and why. I head to the pool, lecturing myself during the elevator ride to the ground floor. I know it's not fair to expect James to treat me like a girlfriend in all ways but the physical. I know it's unreasonable, and that if he were to give me what I'm acting like I want, if he were even to try, I would push him away. There's no way for him to win.

And yet I do. Expect him to. I want him to want me, though I can't give him anything in return. Which is why, the next morning, I snarkily bring up the subject of The Video. Though as soon as I've done it, I wish I hadn't. I wish I could be graceful about accepting the inevitable shift in our relationship. Especially when James looks at me pointedly, shrugs, and says, walking out of the room, "It ought to at least get me a blow job."

But it's not until we're packing to move from our hotel to a 104-foot sailing yacht for a seven-day live-aboard dive trip—beginning in Natewa Bay, to Kioa and Rabi Islands, and finally the Ringgold Atolls—that I pull the thread that starts everything to unraveling. James is finishing the two remaining beers in the fridge, meticulously packing the suitcase he's set open on the Murphy bed. I'm shuttling back and forth from bedroom to bathroom to living room, gathering the things I've strewn everywhere: sunglasses on one table, wallet on another, water bottle here, travel documents there. I make a move to throw the black jersey dress I wear every day into the machine with James's laundry. He moves to stop me, and I complain, "It's such a waste. Why would I do a whole load just for this one dress?"

"Church and state," he says, pointing to me, and then himself.

"I'm going to check e-mail," I say, feeling petulant and rejected. I grab the room key and make for the door.

In the week we've been here, I haven't contacted anyone back home. No news is good news, I tell people. If I were dead, someone would call. Still, I know my family would appreciate knowing I've made it here alive. My mother can't help but devise hypothetical scenarios of abduction, terrorist bombing, or pirate attack, and in the case of any or all of the above—since I am unmarried and childless—my house would go to the state of Washington rather than my family, unless I specify otherwise. She insisted I make out a *will* before this trip; if she couldn't protect me, she at least could safeguard my property.

Without thinking—or because I'm hurt, and acting flip—I say, "Ardith will appreciate knowing you haven't raped and killed me."

"Excuse me?" says James. His face is a warning I don't take.

"It's nothing personal. She thinks every man's a rapist." And almost before the words have flown from my mouth, I see James's eyes go flat and hard. I'm mortified when I realize what I've said, when I realize I've forgotten, for a moment, what he does for a living. That he has had experience with rapists, and victims of rapes. For James, my offhand comment is worse than inappropriate: it's an insult and a betrayal. Not having his back, not being loyal—these are deal breakers for him.

I feel nauseous with regret, and apologize before he can say a word, or I try to. But he cuts off every one of my attempts. "*I am not a rapist*," he repeats, his voice rising louder each time, his jaw clenched tightly, his eyes boring into mine. He won't let me talk, and eventually I stop trying. I don't know how to unsay what's been said.

What is already bad between us becomes worse on a morning dive trip from our live-aboard yacht, called the *Tui Tai*. A small launch takes us twenty minutes or so from the boat to a reef featuring stunningly bright purple coral. Eight of us, not including Ravi, our dive guide, descend to about sixty feet without incident. Then at seventy we're caught in a powerful, fast-moving current. Before I fully realize what's happening, one couple in matching blue-and-black wet suits disappears. Still holding hands, they're pulled suddenly sideways and deep, as if taken by some invisible force, or sucked from the open door of a crashing plane.

They had been swimming farther from the coral head than James and I, where the current was unobstructed. When it becomes clear we can't swim against it, James and I do as Ravi does —something we've been taught never to do. We cling to the reef. I know I am killing the coral, and still I grip hard with one hand. With the other, I press my mask against my face to keep it from being torn free. I wear my mask loose as a rule, counting on water pressure to keep it in place, and now the current is pulling the seal away from my face. Seawater is rushing through from the side, and I'm terrified—afraid I'll panic if I lose my mask, if I'm forced to open my eyes, or worse, swim blind. My hand is crushing my nose beneath the thin layer of silicone rubber. I close my eyes and repeat like a mantra, *Breathe in. Breathe out. Don't panic. Breathe in. Breathe out. You're fine.*

When I am calm enough to open my eyes, when I realize my mask stays on just fine if I face *against* the current, I look to find James. He is also clinging to the reef, but twenty feet higher than I. He must have been climbing upward, trying to get free of the current. He is watching my breath—the fearful rush of bubbles flying from my regulator. I'm trying not to hyperventilate, but does that mean I should breathe faster or slower? Deeper or shallower? James makes eye contact with me. He points at me, gives me the OK sign. Am I okay?

Yes, but I can't return the OK sign—can't let go of my mask, or the reef. I give him a slow, exaggerated nod, and he gives me a thumbs-up before letting go—the sign that he is going to the surface. I should follow. That's the rule when separated from one's buddy. Ravi has done the same, has let himself be swept off out of view, but I can't let go. What if the current drags me down too far, too fast, causing nitrogen narcosis or my eardrums to burst? What if it shoots me to the surface and I get the bends? What if I bash into a reef, what if?

I watch James. In seconds he is gone, and I am even more terrified now that I'm alone. I can't move and I don't want to stay. I'm scared I'll stay frozen here until I run out of air. I'm scared no one will look for me, or notice that I'm gone—like those backyard games of hide-and-seek at my cousins' house I never wanted to play. Summertime, we'd hide in the waning light among broken-down storage sheds and cobweb corners, each game an experiment in how much stillness we could stand. Winning meant dissolving into the plane of a wall, becoming indistinguishable from the hiding place.

A few times my cousins and my brother left me hiding. They forgot me, or it was meant to be a joke, their going off to another game, or home to slake their thirst. I learned then about the joy to be found in losing. In simply standing up, walking back to the willow tree that served as home base. I'd part the parachute of green-leaved branches and lean my back against its trunk as if to receive the salicylic acid Egyptians discovered could heal both pain and fever. *Dear God don't let me be good at hiding* was my prayer then, and I've felt it Sundays, too, sitting alone in a pew: the terror of hiding for no one to find.

Here it is again, the same question in my white-knuckled hand clutching the reef: stay or go? Hold out for a rescue that might not come, or force myself to trust the current? Trust myself to release what keeps my hand clenched tight.

Finally I exhale, close my eyes, and give in to the letting go. The air from my lungs leaves an ephemeral trail behind me, and seconds later I am spat out into calm water cut with long, diagonal rays of light. Above me, the surface is shimmering bright. Twenty feet deep, according to my dive computer. I resist the urge to kick to the surface, and stay—for the sake of safety—counting the longest three minutes of my life. Before it's over, Ravi is beside me, an angel in a bright-blue wetsuit.

He offers his hand to me, and I take his fingers loosely in mine. A swell of gratitude floods my body. I know I am safe, but still, I'm thankful for this gesture. He gives me the thumbs-up. Time to ascend. The boat is waiting. James is waiting, as are the other seven divers, who all managed to get there before me.

The boat is quiet while I struggle out of my gear. I'm shaky with adrenaline, can't focus on anything, can't find my towel among the maze of bags and gear. It is Ravi who drapes it around my shoulders. Another gesture so small, so perfect, it brings tears to my eyes. I sit down, trying to keep my legs from shaking. Most of the divers are couples, and all I want is what they have: a hand on the small of my back, a chest to lean against, a steady heart rhythm to soothe my racing pulse. I want James to comfort me—and maybe he's trying, when he imitates the rush of air from my lungs underwater, the hand covering my face.

When he asks if I was *scay-ewed*, he most likely means to lighten the mood. Maybe he is used to being in danger, or braver than I. Maybe I wasn't actually *in* any real danger. And on another day, his impression might have been funny. I might have said an emphatic "hell *yes* I was scared," and laughed, relieved by surviving, amused by his spot-on imitation of me. But today, his question feels cutting. I turn away to hide the tears I feel rising. Tears are the last thing James wants to deal with.

I close my eyes and will my sadness to recede. I remind myself of where I am, what majesty surrounds me. I take comfort in the view, like nothing I could have imagined. Colors I could not have imagined. Lush, verdant islands in the distance. The sea, in patterns of aquamarine, turquoise, and indigo. The three wooden masts of the *Tui Tai*, like spires piercing the azure sky.

It is lunchtime when we get back to the yacht, and I eat in the shade resting against a giant orange bolster near the bow. James has gone back to the cabin to deal with his camera equipment. One of the other men points out, with his mouth full of ham and hard bread, that James isn't much of a dive buddy. Says he doesn't stay close enough, doesn't take care of me. I immediately feel defensive. I get that this guy is trying to make me feel better; he may have heard James's remark, or seen my reaction. But what he's saying isn't true. I don't want someone in my space, tugging at me, blocking my view. James always knows where I am, is never too far to swim over and share his regulator, if a situation turned dire. This morning, he did what we were both supposed to do. He just was calmer, acted before I could summon the courage to do the same.

I tell James this story after lunch, in our cabin where I've gone to rinse the salt from my hair and skin and change into dry clothes. I'm thinking we'll laugh about this guy, who doesn't know anything about anything. This will be the opening I need. I'll assure James that I trust him. I'll say I'm worried that I've ruined things between us. But before I get to the punch line, James flashes into anger. I'm accusing him, again, he thinks. Criticizing, again. Proving, once again, that I don't have his back.

"Why do you *say* shit like this to me?" he demands, before stalking out of our shared cabin. I don't see him for the rest of the day. He's elsewhere on the boat, avoiding me. I go to bed around ten, but lie awake, waiting. When he doesn't come back by midnight, or one, or two, I go down to the galley, pretending to want a cup of tea. James is there, alone; I'm relieved on one level, but all I want is for things not to be falling apart, spiraling outward from this fragile, needy version of myself, this girl who keeps pushing and pushing, making things worse.

I start to say something, and he shakes his head once, to silence me. "You don't *learn* quickly, do you?" he says cruelly. It's a sentence that strikes me dumb, sends me out of the galley, back up to the stairs, into our cabin, where his bed will remain empty for the rest of the night. James sleeps on the deck of the boat, rather than return to our room. He catches a cold, and is unable to dive for the final days of the trip.

We're booked on the same flight home, but there's one seat left on an earlier connection, and he takes it. I say good-bye to him at his gate, and we don't hug. I'm fairly certain this is the last I'll see of James. He is finished with me, and this pointless dance we've been doing for years. All I can think is how could he not be weary of the adore me, confide in me, touch me, but stop. Come closer, but stop. Love me, but stop.

Three days after my return from Fiji, I still can't get out of bed. I've not been eating, not been bathing, have spent the jet-lagged blur of days and nights in a cycle of sleeping, weeping, and staring blankly at the thing in front of me, invisible, but real, illuminated by the chandelier-cast rainbows that glint on the ceiling, floor, and walls of my room.

I'm dizzy every time I stand up, and so ashamed of my reflection—greasy, puffy-eyed, listless—that I can't bear to look at myself. I haven't told anyone I'm home. I haven't returned the phone calls of my friends, or my parents, who have left messages threatening to call the police. *Just tell us you're okay,* my dad writes, resorting to a text. But I'm not okay. When I can no longer avoid going to work, I drive without my seat belt on. I run yellow lights.

After five days, my shame urges me out of my stupor. I'm not this person. I can't be this person. I force myself into the shower and scrub my skin nearly raw. I increase the heat, by increments, until the water verges on scalding. And after I'm clean, I sit down in the tub, holding my knees tight to my chest. *This suffocating can't be right,* is all I can think. *This absence from myself, this floundering, the years of disconnection and despair: none of it can be bringing me closer to the spirit of God.* I sit under the steaming flow of water until it begins to run cool.

My naked body is a blur in the fog of the mirror. When I'm finally ready to meet my eyes, I wipe my hand across it. *You are the one who takes care of you,* I tell myself. *Who will, if you don't?* I say it again like a promise, into the blue-rimmed gray of my irises. *You are the one who takes care of you.* The words inspire a tectonic shift, a click like the spring of a lock, exposing what's been lying in front of me for days, unassuming, and cataclysmic: I am finished with my church.

Still watching my eyes in the mirror, I see them soften, reflecting a swell of gratitude, surrender, relief as every what if, every fear and doubt go blessedly silent. Finally, I've decided. I won't continue in a belief system that gives me nothing, any longer, that feels like light. That force-feeds my identity and surrounds me with a mob that professes its love, every time—*we love you*—just before the trampling.

Once I've acknowledged my decision, a series of smaller revelations rushes forth—truths I've been afraid to speak, until now: I no longer believe that there is no such thing as lasting happiness outside the LDS church. I no longer believe it'll be worse if I leave, or that there is only one right way to live. There cannot be only one way to be loved by God. If he made me who I am, there must be a way for me to flourish in this life as well as the next. Even as I allow them, I know these thoughts are a mutiny. They are a revolution I am imagining already. I flip off the bathroom light, thinking that if I can allow myself to believe differently, I might survive intact.

Sunday, I go to church to tell the Primary president she'll need to find someone else to teach the five-year-olds from now on. She's a freelance illustrator with an irreverent sense of humor. Not long ago, she mentioned desperately wanting to extricate herself from a group of Mormon women who gather weekly over mocktails and *The Bachelor*. "*The* Bachelor?" she said, rolling her eyes. "They should just call it *Everything Bad About Being a Girl*."

"I'm not coming back," I tell Valerie. There's no need to mince words. This isn't a cry for help and she's got company coming for dinner in an hour. The two of us are sitting on miniature folding chairs. Church is over, and the Primary children have all been shuttled off to their parents, who are busy shuttling them to the parking lot. Valerie's three-year-old daughter, done with sitting still, is racing in circles, holding her red corduroy dress above her head.

There's a long, heavy silence before Valerie says, "I understand. Believe me I do. I just don't think leaving can be the right thing." She reveals the story of her father, who left the church and left her mother, then remarried and redivorced. He lost his family, and his friends, and his business—each epic collapse propelled by the one before.

"I just need you to cover my class." I say it kindly, but I shut her down. Valerie nods, stands up, and gives me a hug that feels real.

"I've been where you are," she admits. "Please call. If you need anything. Whether or not you change your mind."

Released from her hug, I'm speedwalking down the near-empty hall to get through the foyer, through the double doors and onto the pavement before she has time to tell someone who might follow me, corner me, try to convince me not to make the most terrible mistake of my life.

When I push through the outside door into a burst of noontime sun I feel a magnificent wash of relief, an expanding within, as if my lungs have doubled in size. I jog to my car, amazed at the lightness I feel, the near giddiness of my head and clamorous heart. I'll be free to write or not, marry or not, breed or not, squander or not my inheritance. I'll have a life absent of *categories*—single adults and young single adults, members and nonmembers and less-active members, and part-member families. I'll be surrounded by people who inspire me, who value my choices. People for whom my childlessness, my marital status, or an odd number—three or five at the dinner table—is utterly inconsequential. I will be free to engage without defense or sabotage in the company of a man I love. Let me be *cherished*, for fuck's sake. I am worthy of that, I think, watching the steeple shrink in my rearview mirror.

In the weeks since my break from the church, I've felt a surge toward action—an impulse to address everything in my life that's gained the wrong type of momentum. First, I write a letter to James. I don't expect a response, but I tell him anyway: I've been in love with you. I fold the letter inside a book of stories, *The Things They Carried* by Tim O'Brien—because we talked about it, before things fell apart. And because some gesture feels necessary: a peace offering, a parting gift, a balloon let go in a sunny sky.

I don't expect to be forgiven for my bad behavior, though I've already forgiven his. I don't tell him I've left my religious practice, either—lest he think that decision was somehow strategic: a move intended to make him move. Ironically, the day after I mail it, everything bound up in the letter—its longing, its declaration—dissipates. I don't need James to read it, I realize. I only needed to release it.

Next on the agenda is my Visa bill. I imagine cracking under Suze Orman's interrogation previously recorded from her studio set at CNBC. *Yes,* I went to Fiji when I couldn't afford it. *Yes,* even before that I'd racked up charges related to my move and remodel, and *no,* I did not pay them off before traveling halfway around the world. That high-interest debt is a lump in my stomach that churns when I think about it.

I have Suze to thank, really. She's the one who leads me to the online ad which leads me to the tutoring company which leads me to Ben. He answers the phone when I call to say I'm eager to help high school students nights and weekends with their math, reading, writing, and grammar. I conveniently forget to mention my own abysmal math performance in high school. Nor do I offer up the fact that I haven't *done* math beyond simple arithmetic in nearly twenty years. I was right in thinking I'd never need most of the math I choked down like medicine.

There's a group interview in four hours, Ben says, if I can make it. I'm to give a five-minute teaching demonstration in front of twenty other applicants. Several of us will be hired. Choose any topic, he says. Just show your personality, your teaching style.

My lesson is on how to be everyone's favorite waitress, which includes but is not limited to:

Carrying Four Plates at Once: two in the hand, one on the forearm, one in the other hand, with a step-by-step demonstration.

Making Bad Waitress Jokes: when there is nothing but a piece of parsley on the plate, say, "Would you like me to wrap that for you?" When the old man orders another beer, say, "Okay—you wait here."

Wearing Silly T-shirts: TALK NERDY TO ME, or I LOVE YOU, BUT I'M NOT IN LOVE WITH YOU, or I'M JUST HERE FOR THE FREE DRINKS, which is especially funny if you're Mormon.

"Weak sauce," says Ben, who is swiveling in his chair with his hands clasped behind his head. It's hard to take his critique seriously. He's wearing flip-flops and a Rolling Stones T-shirt with holes in the armpits. I shrug. And despite my subpar teaching demonstration, I am hired. Even more shocking is that despite the ratty T-shirt and harsh critique, I've already developed a mad crush on Ben.

We spend hours together in the next few weeks, in coffee shops and on the phone. He needs to be sure I understand the math I'll be required to teach. When he is the student, he plays dumb, asks ridiculous questions, makes me explain and re-explain the problems. I can't do it without laughing, because whenever I talk he hums the chorus of Van Halen's "Hot for Teacher."

"Stop it," I say. "I'm trying to learn this." But what I mean is *I am in love with the way you never make fun of how bad I am at parabolas.*

I'm alone at home on a Tuesday morning when a box arrives from UPS. My heart stops when I see the return address: my first book of poems. Fifty copies of the slim, perfect-bound chapbook (a volume shorter than the forty-eight-page minimum for a "full-length" book) that didn't win the first book contest I entered, but nevertheless was chosen for publication. I hold the box and spin in circles, not knowing what to do. I want to open it, but I want someone to be here when I open it, to witness this first tangible success, which will bring no tangible income. Still, it's evidence that I wasn't crazy to downgrade my career, to continue writing despite the drawer full of rejection letters beside my bed.

I call all my close-by friends who work nights and should be home, but all I get is voice mail—except for Melissa, who says she's vacuuming. I force myself not to ask how long vacuuming could possibly *take*, and say it doesn't matter if she's in her pajamas and hasn't showered. She helped with the cover design. She took my author photo. She should *come over*. How about tomorrow, she says, or bring one in to work tonight.

I push my disappointment aside, telling myself this is a personal accomplishment. Few people understand what a big deal this is: the years of work it takes to make a book that hardly anyone will read. I did this for myself, so maybe it's right that I should celebrate alone, sitting on the floor beside a tall stack of copies. I push it over, just to watch them spread out in a glossy black fan.

Danielle calls when she gets home from work, and proposes brunch the following Sunday at Café Campagne, in Pike Place market. It's French, and fancy—the perfect place, she says, for a poet to celebrate.

"Dahling!" she shouts, when I walk into the restaurant. She stands up to hug me and jump up and down, and demands her copy immediately. She sets it upright against the window, so we can admire the cover throughout our meal. So she can gesture to it every time a server, or host, or busser approaches our table. "My friend wrote this book!" she keeps announcing, and though no one cares, they are charmed by her and tell me congratulations, which is all I want to hear.

"What should we get?" Danielle says.

"Ooh, croque madame," I say into the menu.

"Sick. Runny eggs," she replies.

"I'm getting it." And because I'm feeling giddy, and empowered, and like I am a grown woman who should be allowed to celebrate in whatever way she pleases, I order a glass of champagne. "I'm doing it!" I announce, as if challenging Danielle to try and stop me. She doesn't. Rather, she proposes a toast, to poetry, and friendship, and all things sparkly and fabulous.

I am *impaired* after my one glass of champagne—my first taste of alcohol ever—so we walk around Pike Place Market eating mini-doughnuts and trying on ridiculous hats. We put coins in the machine that tells your fortune. We watch the men throw fish at Pike Place Fish Co., and take silly pictures in the photo booth at the magic shop. I feel joyful, and proud of my poems, and not at all like I deserve to be punished by the hand of God.

Though I'll admit there was one moment, after the busser took my empty glass. Our elegant, effeminate waiter asked if I'd like another. It's a big day, he pointed out, but my family history, and my father's voice, flashed in my mind: "No one plans to become an addict. Who wants to take the chance, find out the hard way?"

The night before I'm to teach my first tutoring session, Ben comes in to Circa to have a beer and go over my math. He thinks I've invited him here so my friends can check him out, give me the thumbs-up; an obvious current has been running beneath our study sessions, a flirtation he's implied he'll act upon as soon as I can teach trigonometry well enough not to need him in a professional capacity. But the truth is my friends are suspicious. They want to know why Ben won't tell me his age or his birthday, why he doesn't want me to text, though calling is okay. Why he won't come to my house, or invite me to his place, though we've been seeing each other a couple times a week outside of work. There are perfectly logical explanations, I assure them. Except for the birthday thing, which Ben brushed off with an allusion to an absent, possibly abusive father.

Ben moved to Seattle on short notice to take care of his mother, who's recovering from a stroke and needs live-in help she can't afford. He can't leave her overnight, or for too many consecutive hours. He took a pay cut so he could at least have a job when he got here. Money's tight, so texting isn't in the phone plan. The Circa girls suspect "mother" is code for "wife" and think Ben is a big fat liar.

I find him sweet and generous—a man who loves his mother. And I'm looking forward to the time, a week or two from now, when I'll be finished with my training, and he'll be allowed to become my boyfriend. I haven't dated anyone since I came back from Grand Cayman three years ago, with the exception of a three-week interlude with a guy who lived three hours away—a friend of a friend I saw five or six times before the virginity issue decided things between us. So I'm allowing myself the luxury of seeing what might happen between Ben and me. Now that anything can happen.

When Ben arrives, we commandeer one of the big booths, spread out our books, and share a burger, getting the business out of the way quickly, so we can use the rest of our time for flirting. At least that's what I had planned. But Ben is getting serious. "Have you talked to your parents yet?" he asks. He and I have had a lot of long phone conversations over the past few weeks. He knows my whole story, including the part where it's been two months since I left the church and I still haven't told my family. When I shake my head no, Ben says what everyone says. "You'll feel better afterward."

I shrug and look away, feeling emotional. Wondering if my brother will try to keep me away from his kids when he finds out. Wondering if my parents will ostracize me, quit speaking to me, shame or accuse me. Thinking of my friend, whose family didn't allow her to sing at her sister's funeral, because she left the church. Ben reaches for my hand. "It'll be worse the longer you wait," he says, and I know he's right. I don't want to lie to my family. I have no interest in keeping up a complicated charade, and already, they're under the impression that when I show up for dinner on Sundays, I've just come from church.

"I'm afraid they'll be ashamed of me," I admit, and Ben moves to my side of the booth, puts his arm around me.

"That'll never happen," Ben says, pulling me closer. "Sunday," he says. "I'll be home all night. Call me after."

I know he's right, but still, driving to my parents' house, my head is full of the things I'm not sure I should say. How much do they need to know? Should I mention that even though I know so many people who have found joy in the Mormon faith, have been healed by it, literally saved—my parents included—I am uncomfortable with the church's missionary program? That the more I see of the world, I feel its beauty is more marked because of its differences. That when I see missionaries abroad, I sometimes feel the itchy underside of words like "assimilation."

Should I tell my mother, whose presence as a stay-at-home mom was invaluable to me, that I rail against the church's inability to separate the words "woman," "wife," and "mother"? Let women choose those things, if they want to. But don't say there isn't equal value, or God-given purpose elsewhere. There are women who have changed the world—who *are* changing the world. Don't tell me that the impulses that drove them, even if they eclipsed the drive to procreate, were misplaced or inspired by the adversary.

I'm wary of the LDS church's go-to response if its members disagree with doctrine: our mortal brains can't comprehend the entirety of God's plan. If the polygamous model of the afterlife feels fundamentally wrong, don't worry. One day—like all points of doctrine that don't make sense now—it will be made clear to us why a man can be sealed to more than one woman, but not vice versa.

How do I say I don't believe sex is important enough to take on such an epic role in LDS people's lives? That this one element of our humanity shouldn't be so magnified that it becomes destructive for those of us whose lives don't fall into the prescriptive model. How do I bring up the disproportionate numbers of gay LDS youth who kill themselves? Or the fact that Utah leads the nation in online pornography subscriptions and prescription antidepressants? My parents don't want to hear these things. Their lives have been shored up by their membership in the Mormon Church. They live LDS lives because they've had spiritual confirmations of its truth. I don't want them to feel I'm trying to place doubt where there is none, trying to rob anyone of what beauty and benefit faith can provide. I don't want to debate, either. I just want them to know about me. What went wrong, for me.

At my parents' house, I put off initiating the conversation, wondering if this will be the last Sunday I'll be invited to dinner. I can't imagine that happening, but I know others whose families have shut them out completely after an admission like mine. So it's not until after I've helped my mother make dinner and helped my father do the dishes that I ask them to come into the family room. My mother sits on one of the two couches with her back to the window. My father is in a wingback chair next to the fireplace. I sit on the couch between them, take a deep breath, and say I'm taking a break from church. I can't say the whole truth, even though I should be clearer about not intending to return.

And in the silence that follows, I pretend not to know what they have just heard: that they will lose me in the hereafter. Everything they've spent their lives building is about to crumble because I am too weak to endure.

When she finally speaks my mother's voice is full of panic. "But we're all supposed to be *together*." My father, my brother, and I—the small circle she has created—are her family. My brother has a wife, has children; they will be there, too, in the celestial kingdom. But I am her child. She needs me with her. She has earned that privilege, she's done everything right.

"I can't do it," I say, shaking my head. I cover my mouth with my hand, unable to stay the tide of emotion that carries the words, that cramps my diaphragm and steals my breath. It doesn't matter that I'm grown. My parents have always been proud of me, and my next sentence could change that, forever. "I would have left years ago . . ." my voice trails off. *If I'd been able to bear the thought of disappointing you* is what I don't say.

"We love you," says my father. "But this is a mistake." He shakes his head, then asks, "How's your testimony?" My father is asking: Do I believe Joseph Smith was a prophet of God? Do I believe that an angel appeared to him, and revealed the fullness of the Gospel of Jesus Christ?

I tell the truth: I believe in God. I don't know how to live without that as the guiding principle of my life. But I don't know about the rest. The Mormon church brought me joy. It made my life feel purposeful, and centered, and right—until it didn't. Until I felt myself suffocating.

"I'm dying inside," I say quietly. "Haven't you seen it?" My voice cracks when I ask the question that hits him like a fist. "Didn't you *see me,* Dad?"

"The Gospel is perfect," he finally says. "People are flawed. You have to ignore them. You have to be strong. Everyone has trials. Everyone."

"But the *doctrine* excludes me, Dad. I know you don't think it does. But it says I can't be fully exalted the way I am. I'm not complete, unless I get married. Imagine hearing that, every week, and not being able to change it. The doctrine tells me what womanhood is, in a way that excludes me. The doctrine tells me that everything I do is 'preparing' for something I don't want. The people I love most, the life I want—none of it counts. And I can't listen to it anymore, can't be told who I am and what I want, when those things *aren't true.*"

"I want to fix it," my dad says, with his head in his hands. "It hurts me, that I can't fix it. It feels wrong. That you should be so unhappy. It's not right, that *you*—"

"But there *is* no fix. There's no way to change it: I can stay and be miserable, or leave and be damned. I've stayed for years because I've been afraid. Afraid to leave, afraid to be punished, afraid to feel lost, afraid you'll love me less."

They both rush in with *no, no, no, no* they will never love me less.

"You're my *baby*," my mother says with a sob, and in the exposed, awful silence that follows, all I hear is the echo of my father's helplessness, my mother's tears.

When she can speak, Mother says, "Your life might be easier now, if you leave. But think about the eternities!" She's so frightened she sounds angry. She's trying not to think that by choosing to abandon our faith, I'm choosing to abandon her.

"If you truly believe I'm the kind of person who deserves eternal punishment, then, respectfully, that will have to be your problem, Mom. I don't believe it. I just don't."

She covers her face with both hands.

"This is not what I planned," I tell her, though she still can't look at me. "It's not what I *wanted*. I've done everything. I've changed everything. I changed cities. I changed countries, careers, friends, boyfriends, hobbies. But after everything I've done to make my life feel right, the one consistent is I feel like shit when I go to church."

There is a long pause while that blasphemy hangs in the air. "I don't want to ruin our family—to be the one who failed, and ruined everything. I don't want to fail you." I take a deep, steadying breath and force myself to say what's both awful and true. "But I am doing this. Love me and keep me. Or don't, and we'll grow apart. It's your decision. You choose." I mean it, and they know I mean it. Though the words feel like they are ripping something loose, inside me.

I am lying curled in my bed, exhausted, when Ben calls late that night. I know he's been waiting to hear from me, but I've been too upset to talk. Hurting my family feels like the worst thing I've ever done. I'm terrified that I have just sunk a wedge between us. That they'll have to pretend to love me as much as they used to. And I still have to talk to my brother. It's not fair to leave that to my parents. But I haven't been close to him—haven't had a conversation beyond news and

small talk since he married ten years ago and moved to California—
since our lives began veering in opposite directions. I don't know how
to say I've left without it coming off like some big pronouncement, or
awkward admission.

I answer Ben's call after I have practiced breathing steadily for the
length of several rings. After I've convinced myself there are no more
tears left in the world. But the second I hear his voice, they rise again,
hot and salty, trapping my voice behind the tightness in my throat.

"Tell me," Ben says. "Tell me anything." His words enter my ear,
and seep into my bloodstream. They course through every cell in my
body, easing the tension from my shoulders and stomach and legs. I
stretch out and lie flat on the bed, staring into the patterns on my ceiling. There could *be* someone. The possibility takes root, perhaps for
the first time. There could be someone to help me through this. Help
me take care of me. Make sure I arrive safely home.

"I'm right here," Ben says, "I'm not leaving." The words inspire a
loosening in my chest. A fissure opening just wide enough to let in a
blinding ray of hope.

Chapter 13

The question, O me! so sad, recurring—What good amid these,
O me, O life?

Answer:
That you are here—that life exists and identity,
That the powerful play goes on, and you may contribute a
verse.

—WALT WHITMAN, "SONG OF MYSELF"

———— ◆ ————

My mother calls, Saturday afternoon. "I'll pick you up at eleven for church," she says, with a frenetic, affected cheer.

I sigh heavily into the phone. "Come over if you want to, Mom. I won't be here. I have brunch plans."

"Next week then," she trills into the phone. She sounds manic. I can tell she's forcing back tears. This is the kind of behavior I was dreading; she doesn't see that what she's doing is for *her,* not me. She doesn't see that it's disrespectful. Dismissive. Condescending. As if my reasons aren't real. As if the problem is only that I don't have someone to sit with.

I call my dad a few days later—to ask him to ask her not to do it again. I don't want to dread her calls for the rest of my life. He tells me she means well. "Cut her some slack," he says, and I hear an ache in his voice. I'm putting him in the middle, I shouldn't, I know. "This is scary for her."

"I know she means well," I say, pacing. "But that's not really the point, Dad."

To make him understand, I tell him about the e-mail I received, after returning from Fiji. When I felt everything falling apart, when I had to force myself to get out of bed, when my heartache was painted in dark circles beneath my eyes and my whole body felt tender as gums that bleed under the slightest pressure, my former bishop wrote to me.

He could not help but notice my absence from church, he said. And couldn't help but correlate that absence with my recent vacation. He knows I traveled alone with a man. And while he is not *accusing* me, I should know that if I had committed a serious sexual sin— which seems likely, given my absence and the vacation and the man—I should keep in mind: the shame I must feel, the feelings of abasement that accompany such sins should not get the best of me. I *should* feel ashamed, he assured me. And guilty. Guilt is simply the spirit of the Lord speaking to my conscience, encouraging me to repent.

Anyone, no matter how heinously they have sinned, he wrote, can pray. Anyone can come to church. "Do not let the adversary convince you that you are unworthy to call upon your Heavenly Father. You must not put off the day of your repentance."

The letter went on for two pages. Single spaced. It ended with that hackneyed story of a man in a stormy sea who asks God for help. A boat comes by, and the man waves off the boat. "God will save me," he says. A helicopter comes by, and a life ring is lowered down. The man waves off the helicopter. "God will save me," he says again. The helicopter leaves, and the man dies. In heaven, the man is chastised by God, who *sent* the boat and the helicopter.

"Do not reject my effort to help you!" wrote the former bishop. "Do not be ungrateful to God, who works through the efforts of his disciples. *I am your friend*," said the former bishop, who is not my friend. "I love you," the letter said, in closing.

There is a long silence on the other end of the phone. I have to ask my dad if he's still there.

"I'm so angry I can't see straight." His voice is tight and fierce. "That guy's lucky I don't know where he lives. What is *wrong* with people? How is that Christian? How is that fellowship?"

"I know, Dad."

"And this guy, he just seems creepy. Do you think he's *interested* in you?"

"I think he's a socially awkward, sanctimonious asshole, who thinks he's doing the Lord's work."

"I'm calling your bishop. What's the number? What's the name of your ward?"

"It won't make a difference, Dad. And the *last* thing I want is this guy on my doorstep apologizing. I don't want you to do anything, Dad. I'm just saying this is what it's like. This is how church is, for me."

"He's so far over the line he can't even see the line."

"Yeah, Dad. But he means well, right?"

I feel him bristling, on the other end of the line. Wondering if I'm lumping my mother in with this man. "I'm just saying everyone means well." I sit down on my couch, exhausted. "Just let me be, Dad." My voice is wavering. I am on the verge of begging. "That's all I want. Please, just let me be."

"Be allergic to the soul scrapers," says the poem by Ann Darr. The line runs through my head after I hang up the phone. After my dad tells me he loves me, and that he hopes I'll change my mind, come back to the church. Cling to what matters, he says. Ignore the rest.

Be allergic. I print a copy of the e-mail, and then block the bishop's address from my account. I don't know why I've kept his message so long in my inbox, emanating its plague of energy. I open the drawer next to my stove and take out a box of blue Diamond matches. I hold the letter by a corner, and watch the long narrow flame eat through his accusations, watch the curling black edges creep over each repugnant syllable. I hold on until the heat forces me to drop the remains, still flaming, into the deep white square of my kitchen sink. I focus on the fire, how it stretches black at its tips, turns to smoke that thins as it rises.

I think of those biblical cities, those destroyed and cleansed by fire. And Lot's wife, who turned to face the flames, despite the command to look away. She was the sinful one, they say, who loved what was evil in Sodom and Gomorrah. But what if she simply turned to bear witness? What if she needed to see her city—and all that was beloved within it—engulfed in the grip and roar of flames? Needed to see her life reduced to skeletons and cinders, in order to believe it. I imagine her standing just outside the city walls, illuminated in a terrible orange light. I drop the burning letter from my hand, listening, through the hiss and crackle of fire, for the killing rush of salt. Its slow push through her veins, bulldozing every path to her heart.

The following week, Ben brings Shelby, his chocolate Lab, when he comes by for trigonometry practice. On the rocky beach outside my house, he and I hold hands and wear thick sweaters against the wind. Shelby chases tennis balls, and later, naps on the rug in front of the fire, while Ben and I practice maths; he says it like the British do. Eventually, I throw my books on the floor and we make out on the couch until he says, "Shit, look at the time. Gotta run."

Of course I am thinking about having sex with Ben. But I'm nervous. Like that scene in *The American President*, when Michael Douglas—the president—is about to be seduced by Annette Bening. "My nervousness," he says, "exists on several levels." Ben knows I'm a virgin, knows why I'm a virgin, and says it's no big deal. He also knows there's a lot of stuff leading up to sex that I've never done and would like to try. And yet, he hasn't made any moves. I feel strange initiating, given my lack of skills. So I've been waiting for him to suggest something. Remove some item of clothing—mine, or his. Only he doesn't. He hasn't, in four months. He hasn't slept over, or stayed late, not once.

"What's his problem," Melissa asks, at the end of our Friday night shift. "Are you sure he's not gay?"

Corina and Melissa and I are in one of the large booths, doing rollups, like we've done together every Thursday and Friday night for the past three years: First, lay the napkin on the table, turned so the square is like a diamond. Pull the bottom corner up to meet the top and smooth the bottom seam. At the long base of this triangle, lay the knife down and a fork on top of it. Fold the right corner into the middle, and then the left. Roll it up *tight*. "Like a doobie," the owner of the restaurant said, the first time he showed me—a metaphor he couldn't have known was entirely wasted on me. Repeat, until all three bins are heaping full.

Melissa—foulmouthed and angelically beautiful—is desired by every man and woman in the free world. No one else exists when Melissa is around. It would be easy to hate her, except it's impossible not to love her.

"You think everyone's gay because you're gay," I joke, handing over half a bottle of wine that's been open for two days, too old to sell for nine dollars a glass. I take a sip, trying to train my palate, while Melissa and Corina share the rest.

"No, I think he's gay because he doesn't want to *do it* with you."

"Seriously," says Corina. She has a smile like a movie star and is obsessed with bizarre estate-sale jewelry: a locket with teeth in it, a walrus pin with fur and tusks. She'll run a credit card through your cleavage while you're asking whether she sold the last special, or pinch the loose skin of your elbow while you're trying to talk.

"What's up with that?" continues Corina. "Every guy has a virgin fantasy. It's like he's hit the mother lode."

I point a finished roll-up at the two of them. "I'll bet you one million dollars Ben, if he has a virgin fantasy, has not cast a thirty-five-year-old as its central character. Maybe he doesn't want to mess with the fantasy virgin. She's a powerful archetype."

"Fucking fantasy virgin," says Melissa. "All fragile, and waify. Natalie Portman, in *Beautiful Girls*."

"Brooke Shields, in *The Blue Lagoon*," says Corina.

"Marcia Brady," says Melissa.

"Ariel," Corina shoots back.

"Ariel the *mermaid*?" I ask, doubtful.

"Yeah. Gavin's obsessed with her."

"Your fiancé's obsessed with a mermaid," says Melissa. "She doesn't even have a *vagina*."

"On *land*, she has a vagina."

"Excuse me?" I say.

"Oh, yeah!" Melissa shouts, slapping her palm on the table. "The evil octopus queen gave her *legs* in exchange for her voice."

"So she gets a vagina but loses the ability to speak?" I ask.

"It's the ultimate fantasy," says Corina, drily. "Good one, Disney."

"That's some fucked up shit," says Melissa.

"With someone like Ariel, Ben can be the crusader: the first to plant his flag in fertile ground. Her only pleasure is to learn to please him," I say. "With me, while he might *initially* be intrigued—"

"Maybe he could sense it," says Corina. "Like how deer and birds sense earthquakes. Ca-*caw!*" She jumps up, inexplicably doing a series of karate kicks, accompanied by bird calls. "Ca-*caw!*"

Melissa laughs with a mouthful of wine, has to struggle to keep from spitting it on me. "I'm just saying with the fantasy virgin, there's no problem with the irony: that the thing he most wants is the thing he most wants to annihilate."

"With his penis," says Melissa.

"Right. He's free to fetishize. To also become a caricature: math teacher by day, wolf by night. Big and bad—"

"Wearing grandmother's bonnet," interjects Corina.

"He can imagine that the only reason *she's* still a virgin is that she has not yet met *his* penis, superior to all other penises, named something like The Mighty Thor."

"That, and the missing vagina," says Corina.

"And then there's *my* virginity, the actual reasons for it. He's probably imagining I've got large, scary issues."

"Nah," says Melissa. "He's just hoping it's a big charade. He's picturing himself all sweaty and ripped, giving it to you up against the wall, like Patrick Swayze in *Road House*. Yeah, boyeeee."

"He's probably scared he *will be* that good," says Corina. "That he'll rock your world so hard you'll go crazy, show up in his kitchen one day, ready to boil some bunnies."

"He grew up Catholic," I say. "Maybe de-virginizing a virgin is just too much."

"He's picturing you crying hysterically afterward," says Melissa. "And then, every argument you'll ever have: 'I gave you my *virginity*, you bastard. And you can't even replace the fucking *toilet paper*?!' "

The conversation devolves into a series of hypothetical fake arguments, each beginning with "I gave you my virginity, you bastard." But despite all this conjecture, I have no idea what's going on in Ben's head. He's not talking, and I'm afraid to bring it up. Afraid one or more of the above theories will turn out to be true, and will be far less hilarious when real.

Besides, I have worries of my own. Namely, his past. I don't feel intimidated or jealous that he's been with a number of women. I expect that he's been with a number of women, and while I do not want to *know* the number, that knowledge brings me a certain amount of relief. I want him to be in charge. Teach me. Make sure it's good. But then again, he's *been with a number of women*. Who knows who *they've* been with. So even though we're not sleeping together, and have made no immediate plans to do so, I've demanded he get the full battery of tests. Because what if things get carried away, one night? What if there is some unforeseen condom-breaking drama, or he has something condoms don't protect against? Imagine if the first time I had sex, I ended up with genital herpes?

I've already made an appointment to deal with the issue of birth control, which Ben doesn't want to attend. He doesn't want to sit in the waiting room, even. Doesn't want to give me a ride, have a cup of coffee, pick me up in an hour. "It's too much," he says, but I'm going, regardless. It would be nice to have the moral support, but the appointment is for me. For *my* peace of mind.

There's no way I could deal, right now—or possibly ever—with the kinds of choices pregnancy would require. I remember a weekend trip I took with Leila to Santa Cruz, where she had a date with a guy from LDSSingles.com. They'd been carrying on a virtual romance for months, but it was all over when he revealed that he and a former girlfriend—unmarried, uninterested in a long-term relationship, and opposed to abortion—had given up a baby for adoption. "They're adults!" Leila insisted. "They should be *responsible*." Meaning they should keep a baby they didn't want; stay in a failed relationship; lie in their bed. She railed about his immaturity, his selfishness. About what kind of people would do such a thing.

I would do what they did. I would do it in a minute. I suspect I might do worse.

My mother, at age thirty-two, had a fibroid tumor in her uterus the size of a cantaloupe. There is a picture of it in our family photo album, which she refuses to remove. Sometimes I *envy* her hysterectomy. What a relief, to never have to worry about becoming pregnant. To never have to defend the decision not to have a child. To never be accused of lying, being selfish, messed up, or broken when you say not all women want babies.

The paperwork in the waiting room says 90 percent of what Planned Parenthood does is primary, preventive care. If only I'd known that seven years ago. I stopped getting my annual exam after I left my teaching job, lost my insurance, and joined the ranks of those who can no longer afford primary, preventive care. I never considered Planned Parenthood—for the same reason many religious people don't: I dismissed it outright, because women can get abortions and teens can get birth control there. I assumed, when I was actively Mormon, it was a place I shouldn't go. But now I have access to an affordable annual exam, and breast cancer screening. Not to mention the birth control I assume I'll one day need. Now I can go anywhere I like, without fear of judgment or reprisal.

The intake form in my lap takes thirty seconds to complete. It is an epic failure in the game of "have you ever": Have you ever had unprotected sex, a partner with urethritis. Do you smoke, have a history of drug use, a current or past partner who's an IV drug user, a new sexual partner in the last two months? Ever had gonorrhea, herpes, syphilis, an abnormal pap, migraines, pelvic infections, German measles, anemia, diabetes, varicose veins, stroke, digestive problems, anorexia, bulimia, thyroid problems? It is a test I stop reading halfway through, a Scantron form bubbled in a string of *B*s. No. No. No. Nonono. No Nonononono.

In the exam room, I steel myself for a repeat of indignities past: the nurse who accused me of lying about my virginity, who rolled her eyes, and sighed derisively. Another who snapped at me, said she didn't have time to play games. This time, I tell myself, I won't snap back. I won't say you'd think she'd be more *patient* and *professional* with someone who's making a decision that is pretty *freaking difficult* to manage, not to mention *really good* for her reproductive health. I won't point out how I am actually *saving* her time what with my lack of pregnancy tests, STDs, cervical cancer, abortions, morning-after pills, hormone injections, and/or birth control pills. This time, I will not let my eyes well up in frustration, humiliation, or rage.

The physician's assistant enters, carrying my paperwork. She talks in a soft voice. "It's important for the clinician to have accurate information," she says.

"It's accurate," I say. I smile, despite the breeze in the back of my gown. Despite how absurd it is to be wearing nothing under it but a pair of striped, knee-high socks. To be trying to make *her* feel more comfortable.

She blinks, starts sentences, keeps stopping. Finally, she says, "But you said no to everything."

"Story of my life," I joke, and she looks confused. "I'm a virgin," I say, shrugging.

She steps closer. "You're safe here. Everything is confidential." Her eyes tell me not to be afraid.

"It's not that," I say quickly. "I promise." She seems so worried I want to reassure her, so I say the next sentence slowly. Deliberately. "I'm *religious*."

She smiles like a light turning on, and leaves the room again. The clinician who enters next is about my age. Petite, pretty, in a no-makeup, Pacific Northwest kind of way. She doesn't know I have heard the murmuring outside the door.

"So," is what she says, sitting down. She crosses her legs, and sets her clipboard on her lap.

"I know, right?" I laugh, because the situation suddenly seems ridiculous. "I'm guessing you don't see a lot of thirty-five-year-old virgins around here?"

She smiles in a way that says we could be friends on the outside. That says now she may have *actually* seen it all. "Do you have any questions?"

"I have comments," I say. "I am not a person who can be trusted to count, keep track of, or bring anything. I don't have routines. I can't do things at the same time of day, every day. Or even every week. I forget to brush my teeth some days. So there goes the pill, the sponge, spermicide, the diaphragm, the cervical cap, and the ring.

"Ninety-nine percent effective is not effective enough," I say. "When I say I don't want babies, I am not one of the people who's just *saying* that. Who could be convinced, once she's pregnant, if the father is happy about it. I'm not afraid of being a bad mother, haven't suffered some trauma I don't want to deal with. I just don't want children. So I *cannot* get pregnant." I hope she understands what I'm implying.

The clinician has stopped trying to take notes.

"I don't want a bunch of hormones coursing through my body, don't want to go insane with mood swings, and breakouts, and weight gain, none of which I currently suffer from. So I'm not interested in the patch or Implanon. And condoms, are you joking? I can name twenty people off the top of my head who have had babies while using condoms. And the pull-out method? The rhythm method? Ha. Good one."

"Okay," she says. She is waiting for me to continue.

"So what do you think about an IUD? I read the statistics are equal to having my tubes tied. Those are odds I can live with. Short of having my tubes tied. Short of you giving me a list of single men in the greater Seattle area who have had vasectomies."

She explains the differences between the two kinds of IUDs, the benefits and risks associated with each. She apologizes that I'll have to undergo (and pay for) STI screening, which is mandatory, to ensure *her* safety. I appreciate the protocol, so that's no problem I say.

During my exam, she explains every move before she makes it, asks permission to touch me during the most routine procedures: when she tightens the blood pressure cuff, when she puts a stethoscope to my lungs. I am mystified by the level of attention paid to my body—as if it is fragile, or sacred. As if to repair what might elsewhere have been damaged.

Only then does it occur to me how many terrified and abused women she must see every day. And I am suddenly sorrowful for the ways in which we all suffer, in whatever ways we do, grateful for the safety of my upbringing; for a father who has taught me the standard by which all men should treat me; for being treated with care and kindness in a place I'd been warned vehemently against. I'm unprepared for her hand on my back to feel so opposite of those condescending, encouraging pats I received at church.

More than anything, what I didn't anticipate was for this day to feel seminal: but here it is, a feeling of settling, and release. The end of every futile attempt to keep my body separate from my spirit. I feel peaceful, and hopeful, in claiming my sexuality. Acknowledging it as an integral, elemental part of the whole. I have the bizarre, inappropriate urge to send a thank-you note.

A week later, I open my mailbox to find a wedding invitation from my friend Kim, from Bennington. She and another of our classmates, Eric, are getting married in a month in San Francisco. I'm invited—along with a plus one—so I call Ben right away to invite him. We'll be out of town together, for the first time. Spending a night together, for the first time. *Two* nights, in fact. In a hotel. I'm prepared, physically, since my appointment at Planned Parenthood, so all that's left is to buy new underwear and a fabulous dress, and wait for what feels inevitable.

Friday nights, Melissa and Corina continue to offer advice about My First Time, which they, too, are convinced will happen in four, three, two, one weeks from now. "Expect it to be horrible," Melissa says, breezily. "It's horrible for everyone the first time. Seriously. Horrible."

I can't tell if she's joking. "Really?" I ask Corina, when Melissa gets up to put away a bin of roll-ups.

"No," Corina says. "You're not a kid—you're not going to get pressured into it, you're not going to do it with some creeper who only cares about himself. It'll be great," she says. And then grins widely. "Or it'll be horrible, and we can laugh about it."

"Oooh. I got it!" Melissa says, sliding back into our booth. "What if you pretend you're just pretending. So it'll be like a hot role-playing game."

"You should hire an escort," Corina says. "Just get it over with, so you can be normal with someone you like."

"Do it!" shouts Melissa. "It could be all Richard Gere in *American Gigolo*." She takes a long sip of her beer. "Or," she suggests, "you could just get really, really drunk."

"Super helpful," I say drily, as they clink their glasses across the table. "Great advice."

I decide the best thing to do is go back to Babeland. Buy something, just to be sure everything works. Avoid the pain I've been told to predict. Danielle has volunteered to go with me. Two minutes after we walk in, she holds up a purple, glittery vibrator. "You remember this," she says. "It inspired an entire episode of *Sex and the City*. Charlotte stayed in her room for so long her friends had to stage an *intervention*."

"Holy crap," I say, looking at the price tag.

She hands me the information card: "While the lavender shaft twirls for G-spot stimulation, the rabbit ears flutter along the clitoris and the 'pearls' stimulate the sensitive opening of the vagina. Separate variable speed controls power each of the two components."

"Whoa," I say, cringing. "That seems like a lot."

"I know, right?"

Just then, the androgynous pixie I met before walks over. She asks if she can help, if we have questions. Danielle immediately clams up, and I let loose. "Yes!" I say, relieved. "I have so many. Like, what's the difference between the curved ones and the straight ones, because if curved were ideal, wouldn't real penises be in the shape of a letter C? I mean that seems crazy, right? And how important is it to be waterproof? And do I want hard plastic or something more . . . bendy?"

"Oh geez," says Danielle, busting into laughter, and walking to the shelf of books by the entrance of the store.

I point to a display by the window. "Are those made of *glass*? Do you use them, or just display them? I'm just imagining . . . that," I say, because I cannot say the word "dildo," "sitting on the coffee table, when your mom comes over for lunch. Or worse, your dad." I'm off again before she can respond. "How do couples' vibrators work, and do you need *so many* settings in regards to pressure and speed?" I point to something gigantic, industrial-looking. I can't help but cringe. "And—tell the truth—do I want the part that goes inside to vibrate? Because wouldn't that just make you feel like you have to go number two?"

Danielle groans in horror from across the room.

"And the G spot—does it really exist? If so, does it need this much *attention*?"

The pixie smiles and guides me to a display nearby. "Let's start at the beginning," she says.

When Ben calls later, I tell him all about my field trip, including a play-by-play of Danielle's profound mortification. "So what did you get?" he asks. "And have you tried it?"

"I got the one made famous by *Sex and the City*. Because they should know, right?" It's still in its package. "I just don't see how it can work. Geometrically speaking." I look at it dubiously. "I'm sort of intimidated. And is it even *necessary*? Can it really have powers beyond those of a bathtub faucet?"

"Dear God, some days I wish I were a woman," says Ben. He asks for measurements, for comparisons to this or that household item. He assures me, as did the pixie at the store, that it is well within the range of normal. That it will totally work. "Call me in half an hour," Ben says. He is waiting for a full report.

It's comforting to hear Ben joking around, asking to be involved in this part of my life, ridiculous as it may be. Because not long after my visit to Planned Parenthood, he freaked out a little. Went on a weeklong road trip by himself, saying he needed time to think about our relationship. When I didn't hear from him for eight days I figured I had my answer, but on the ninth he arrived on my doorstep unannounced. Said halfway up the California coast he realized I'm the person he wants to tell everything to. I'm the person he wants to be with, every day. I realized I love you, he said. And what girl doesn't want to hear that?

A week after my trip to Babeland, I've still not given Ben the report he requested. We're on a plane to San Francisco, and he's joking about getting me drunk so I'll tell all my secrets. I'm game I say, laughing. Mostly because I've never had a drink on an airplane, and it seems somehow glamorous—a throwback to times when flight attendants were called air hostesses and wore uniforms created by designers like Armani, Pierre Cardin, and Balenciaga. I ask Ben if he'll drink whatever I order if it turns out I hate it—which has been the case with most everything I've tried. Despite my best efforts, I haven't yet found my signature drink. Generally, I let bartenders make what they think I'll like best, knowing they'll just make what they like. Both ways, it's fun. Especially with Ben as my partner in crime. And my driver. Because after three sips of a cocktail, my motor skills are in serious jeopardy. After an *entire* cocktail I will for sure try to sit in someone's lap.

My friends have all laid bets on sugary, girly cocktails: blueberry lemon drops, cosmos, mai tais, and green apple martinis, all of which I found revolting. I'm hoping I land on something sophisticated—a drink a woman would order, as opposed to a girl. Though I'm prepared for the worst: to be the one who can't lay off the exotic berry mini-mart wine coolers. Mostly, though, I'm hoping to figure it out fast. Drinking is *expensive.* Given all the things I've tried and hated, I could just as easily have lit a hundred dollar bill on fire and thrown it into the toilet.

When the flight attendant comes by, Ben orders me a vodka 7Up, and for himself, Jack Daniel's on the rocks. "What do you think?" Ben asks, after I take my first sip.

"Gross." I slide my plastic cup across the tray table. I snuggle into

him, and sigh. I have a date to a friend's wedding. It's a first, since
Murphy.

"Try mine," says Ben, indicating his tiny bottle of Jack Daniel's
and cup of ice. And there in the dreaded E seat, on a Boeing 737
somewhere between Mount Adams and Mount St. Helens, cruising
at thirty thousand feet, I find everything I've been looking for. Two
sips of Ben's smoky, sweet, Tennessee whiskey become three. Three
sips become four, and five, and six.

"Easy, Tiger," says Ben.

"This is the one I like," I announce, when there is nothing but ice
swirling in my plastic cup.

"You just went from zero to straight whiskey."

"Aaaaah, yeah," I say, closing my eyes. I am in love. In sweet,
sweet love with the lingering burn in my throat.

"I'm dating a sixty-year-old man," says Ben.

"I'm immune to whiskey," I say, a few minutes later, swaying in
my chair in the manner of Stevie Wonder. "Look," I say, pointing at
Ben, then me, then Ben. "See? *Immune.*"

"Right," says Ben, turning my finger away from his face.

"I feel as though you are placating me. Ben. *Benjamin.*"

"It's hard to take you seriously when your eyes are only half
open."

"Whiskey's *awesome.*" I say. It is crucial that he understand this
most salient point. "You know, Ben? Do you *know*? Ben. Ben." I am
poking his arm. "Ben. Ben. Ben."

"Oh, boy," says Ben. "You just stay on your side of the armrest,
Fancy Pants."

I lean back in my seat, enjoying the warm fuzzy feeling inside.
Though underneath it hums a slight worry—whether it's good to enjoy a drink so much. To want another, so soon after the first, even if I
have no intention of ordering another. But I've not started drinking
to medicate, or because I feel lonely, anxious, unworthy, or unloved.

I am enjoying one of life's small pleasures, in moderation: learning about wine pairings at Circa, dabbling now and again in the silly fun times provided by a low-level buzz.

Having sorted that out, I move my empty cup over to Ben's tray, and lock mine in the upright position. I scoot low into my seat and position myself under Ben's arm to nap the rest of the way to San Francisco. It's not long before he extricates himself. "Give me some room," he says, grumpily.

"Sorry," I say. "I didn't mean to be annoying." I take my *Vanity Fair* out of my bag, and open to the last page first, like I always do. "Guess what Ron Howard considers the most overrated virtue," I ask, and Ben shoots me a look that says he *said* give him some room.

We arrive at our hotel late and hungry, which doesn't help Ben's mood. There's no place nearby to eat, except a pricey steakhouse, which sends us back to the hotel for vending machine snacks. When Ben flips the TV on to SportsCenter, I decide the next night will be a better night for sexy shenanigans, and fall immediately to sleep.

The next day is the wedding day, which starts with brunch. Ben and I, Sariah and her boyfriend, as well as six other friends from graduate school meet at a restaurant nearby, and chat nonstop about writing, and old times at Bennington. Sariah and I only realize on the drive home that our boyfriends had nothing to say to each other, and were left out of almost the entire conversation. We both apologize, and when we get back to the hotel, I ask if Ben wants to take a walk or something. He says he's fine and flips the TV on to SportsCenter, again, while I take a shower. The wedding's in a few hours, and I might as well start getting ready. Maybe we can get a drink with the others, beforehand.

There are only two towels in the bathroom, and I use them both: one for my hair, the other for the rest. I realize the problem just when Ben's about to get in. "Sorry," I say. "I didn't notice. Let me find the housekeeping cart; I'll get you a fresh towel—*two*, if you like." I smile, picturing him Carmen Miranda–style, one towel on his head, and another like a sarong.

"You're just like my mother," he says, suddenly irritated. "You don't think about me."

My head is spinning. Because *what?* I'm just like his *mother?*

"I've lived alone for fifteen years. I use two towels," I say, totally confused. I can't figure out why he's upset. "It's just a habit. I'm not trying to be a jerk. And there are so many towels." I point outside. "On the cart." I am dressed by now. "I'll be right back," I say, and walk toward the door.

"Stop trying to fix it!" He raises his voice. "This isn't about *towels*."

Only I have no idea what it *is* about, and he won't say. He ends up using the less wet of the two towels I already used, insisting I shouldn't get a fresh one, yet angry about having to use the damp one. Or angry about my general thoughtlessness. I'm sifting through everything that's happened since yesterday morning, trying to figure out what I could have said or done, to inspire this reaction.

We've never had an argument before—though it's true he went virtually silent last week. I assumed he was just busy at work, but now it feels like there must be more going on, like the more of my friends he meets and the closer we get to the wedding, the more he wants to turn around and go home. We should talk about it, but I still have to do my hair and makeup and then Sariah comes in to have me help her with *her* hair, the back of which isn't working right, and then it's time to leave. When I tell Ben we've got to go— Sariah and Charlie are waiting in the lobby—he is visibly irritated at having to turn off SportsCenter, though the clip of Tiger Woods making an impossible-looking putt is one they already played, an hour ago.

At the wedding, everything seems to work itself out. We drink some wine, and chat with our tablemates. Ben is charming and funny, and visibly grateful I haven't asked him to dance. After the reception, my feet are tired and my dress feels tight, and I am glad to be back in our honeydew-colored room with the tacky bedspread, desperate to slough my shoes and strapless bra.

Ben looks handsome in the dim light of the bedside lamp. I loosen his tie, unbutton the top two buttons of his shirt. I rest my face against his chest. He takes me by the biceps, straightens his arms, so I'm standing three feet away from him. He says nothing, but squeezes hard before letting go. I balance all night on the edge of the bed, replaying every conversation, trying to figure out what I did, what I said, what he did, what he said—something to explain what's going on.

Last week, Ben called to say we'd spend the whole day together Saturday. He'd drop by my house at ten, he said. Maybe we could take a long walk or go to a museum or have brunch at that new place up the street; we could wander around downtown, check out that pie shop I read about. But when Saturday came, there was a NASCAR race he needed to watch. I spent two hours on the sofa next to him, watching cars drive in a circle. When he fell asleep, I went to my bedroom to read. "Gotta get back," he said when he woke up, and headed for the door.

When I first invited him to the wedding, he mentioned wanting to introduce me to his nephew, who lives two hours from where we are now. When I told Ben about the string of wedding-related events to see if we could fit in a day trip or dinner with his nephew, he never made plans. It's getting too complicated, he said. We'll meet up with him another time. I assumed he meant it when he said it was fine.

A few weeks ago, when we were stopped at a traffic light, I alluded to our overnight stay and what could happen in the still of the night. He sighed heavily and said it feels strange to him. Backward, somehow, that he fell in love first. I wondered then if I should be worried, if it were more than just a joke the way he always refers to sex with me as "the dirty, dirty sex." Does *he* have some unarticulated notion of sin, or of ruining me?

And then there's his scandalous, intriguing habit of touching me in public. When I'm standing in the hallway in the office where we work, where no one knows we're dating; when I'm asking where should we meet for dinner; or at the store, I'll get the wine and you get the bread; or in the parking lot, see you tomorrow, when I walk past him, he keeps his hand low, brushes his fingers lightly between my legs. There is never anyone else around, never anyone looking, but the erotic pulse is a shock, an unexpected thrill. It happens at Target, Home Depot, Marshalls. Lying on the edge of the bed, listening to Ben breathe, it registers clearly for the first time: he has never touched me there when we're alone at my place, when the door is locked, and I have invited him. When I've whispered, "Yes, please, I want you to."

Not long after the wedding, I suggest a weekend getaway. A do-over. A room without a TV and with towels stacked to the heavens. There is a hot tub on the porch of the cabin that overlooks Puget Sound, where Ben and I are naked together for the first time in water steaming through the evening air. It's a surprise to see eczema on his calves. How is it I have never seen his calves? It's been months now. We have been together for months. I think about all the things that we haven't done, and maybe should have, before this. Why has there still never been a late night together at my place, or his, do you like this and what if I touch you here?

The sun is about to set. Seagulls take flight above the marina. Sailboats rock gently in their slips in the harbor, and I am in love with the cool, briny smell of seaweed. Ben pulls me toward him, through the steaming water. He puts his hands on my shoulders, presses down. It seems like he wants my face below the surface. But I've never given a blow job before, and I'm nervous about it in general. I can't fathom doing it underwater, both blind and unable to breathe.

My body goes rigid, and my mouth stays closed. Ben looks away, releases my shoulders. "Water's too hot," he says, and climbs out, dripping. He reaches for his jeans. I don't know whether or not I should follow.

Eventually, I decide on a compromise. Inside, in the shower, I rinse off the smell of chlorine, hoping Ben will join me in the movie-star bathroom. That he will notice the door purposely left ajar. I imagine he'll enter quietly, and flip on the heat lamp above me. I picture the light cutting through the steam and the glass walls of the shower. And him, leaning against the marble countertop, watching. I tip my head back. I arch my back and lift my arms to rinse my hair. I imagine he unbuckles his belt then, and opens the door. He blocks the spray with his body, and traces every curve of mine with the wet bar of soap. He does it slowly, paying close attention. Soon, his mouth is on my shoulder, then the hollow of my neck, making the hair stand up on my arms. His hand is on my thigh, moving slowly upward. I press my body against the length of his. He is ready, waiting for me.

But when my shower is finished, Ben is still in the other room, reading a book in bed. I drop my towel and climb under the white down comforter. When he asks absently how was my shower, I put a hand beneath the covers. What happens next—the touching, the climbing, and kissing—I am somehow removed from it. His hand seems always in the wrong spot, too cold, slightly uncomfortable. I scoot toward his waist, thinking I could do what he wanted before. I ask how he likes it. "Tell me what you want," I say. He doesn't answer, and I wonder, *Is it me? Am I the reason his body is not responding?*

I think of something James said once: "You're in trouble, sweetheart. No man wants to be your teacher." I look up, confused, when Ben shifts to roll me away from him. "Maybe later," he says. His voice is tense—irritated, or angry.

"I'm just happy to be alone with you," I say. I've waited this long, what's another day, a week, a month? I get up to dry my hair, again not understanding why he's so upset.

We miss our 7:00 AM ferry the next morning, by one car. We're first in a line of cars parked bumper-to-bumper waiting for the next boat, which won't arrive for two hours. The itch, the pain of the silence is like a rash between us—he hasn't said ten words since last night, and I'm afraid anything I say will make things worse. So I get out of the car, sit on an ancient, sun-dried log on the rocky beach. I don't go back for my book, or my sweater, though I wish I had them both. I wish I could be sleeping against Ben's shoulder, that I knew what to say to diffuse his baffling anger.

On the other side of the Sound, finally off the ferry, beyond the small streets crowded with stoplights, the air is warm on the long stretch of I-5 between us and our separate houses, separate beds. I close my eyes against the speedometer—the needle's steady climb. Ben's gripping the wheel hard, with both hands. I could almost laugh. If he presses the gas pedal hard enough, he can get farther away from me. It almost makes perfect sense. I feign sleep, uneasy about asking him to pull over, even though the convertible top is down, even though I feel a brutal sunburn blooming across my chest.

Later, at home, looking at my body in the mirror before the cool bath I hope will be a balm, I study the diagonal slash of white where the strap of the seat belt laid against skin now painfully red, blistered on the ridge of my collarbone. I look at myself directly, so I can't pretend I don't already know what a mistake it was to believe Ben could swoop in and be the solution. So I can't pretend not to know he said it weeks ago, for the last time: I love you.

Whatever this was between Ben and me has already begun its slow slide off the rails. It won't be long before the phone call, or the cup of coffee, or the short visit on his way home from work that makes our breakup official.

Needing a distraction from these thoughts and the pain of my sunburn, I stop in to Circa for moral support. I help with roll-ups, drink a half glass of wine. Of course, my co-workers begin to speculate, trying to figure out what the hell happened to my romantic weekend.

"Your 'first' is a big deal," Melissa says. "Maybe he doesn't want to have to feel like the world's biggest asshole if he breaks up with you someday."

Corina pipes in. "He probably freaked himself out, thinking you've spent every night of your life watching the Brad Pitt scene in *Thelma & Louise*. You've been waiting, like, *twenty years* for sex. That's a dangerous thought, for a man." She holds up a sad, drooping finger.

"I guess I never considered he could be nervous," I say. And as soon as I say it, I flash back to him in the hotel room, nearly shouting, "You don't think about me."

"I mean, everyone's always saying a man always wants it, doesn't matter who, when, where, why. I guess it didn't occur to me that I could be *turned down*." I sigh, resting my head on my arms. "It's just hard not to feel like a freak. Like I'm just not sexy, or I waited too long, and now it's just too weird, too complicated. What if no one ever wants me?" I say. Not wanting to cry, I walk to the bar to rinse and stack my glass.

Willow, who's breaking down the bar, takes me aside. She knows the whole story; the whole Circa staff has been tuning in for every weekly installment. "I hope you don't mind, but I asked Kevin what he thinks." Kevin is Willow's husband, and my friend. He's known for saying it like it is, for better or worse. "He says you'll meet a man, and it won't be an issue."

"But—"

"Nope!" she cuts me off, perfectly imitating Kevin's inflection. "You'll meet a *man*," she repeats. "It won't be an issue."

"Thanks, Kevin," I say, hugging Willow. I move to let go, but she holds me tighter. I'm embarrassed of the grateful tears I feel rising. At what a difference it makes to know at least one man in the world thinks I'm attractive and normal enough. Even if he is someone else's husband. If I already know one, maybe another man exists who won't think I'm broken, crazy, or simply too much trouble.

Chapter 14

He brought me to the banqueting house, and his banner over me was love.

—SONG OF SOLOMON 2:4

———— ✦ ————

Tonight I've put my hair in a 1950s high ponytail. I'm wearing red lipstick, the best disguise for the exhaustion I feel after having been in the weeds for three hours straight during my lunch shift. I had an hour and a half to put my feet up and stare blankly into space before changing my shoes and starting again at dinner. Like every Friday night, it's busy, loud, and fun. We see the most regulars on Fridays, and everyone's in a good mood: they've just gotten paid, the weekend has begun, and the specials tonight include cornmeal-crusted, pan-fried oysters and an eight-ounce filet mignon with red wine gorgonzola butter. "Save room for chocolate cake," I'm telling everyone in my section. "It came out of the oven two hours ago."

When someone has the audacity to ask how good can it be—it's just *cake*—Melissa leans over from across the aisle. "The cake is no joke," she says, emphatically. "Crazy Cake Guy called from *Europe* last week to be sure we'd have it the minute he arrived from the airport."

"It's true," I say, pointing to a table near the door. "See that woman over there? When I asked, 'How's the cake tonight,' she closed her eyes, and said, 'This cake? Is my. New. Boyfriend.'"

Melissa keeps going, can't help herself. "This one guy, who's been on the Atkins diet for something like three years—who eats nothing but bacon and mayonnaise—makes us describe it to him. '*Slowly*,' he says. 'Use more *adjectives*.'"

Unable to resist such an assault, my table orders the cake, but on my way to ring it in, I stop by table 31 to say hello and recite the specials. Before I can say anything, one of the two guys at the table sits up straight and says, "You're the girl."

"I'm a girl, yes. Good eye." I smile, thinking he'd be handsome if it weren't for the bad haircut. The white socks and Dansko clogs peeking out from under the table. Still—he's got that square chin I like. Cute smile, nice forearms.

"No," he laughs. "*You're the girl.* The poetry girl." There are copies of my chapbook at the bar for regulars to read while they wait for tables. "I always look for you," he says. "We met once before. I was reading your poems out loud? At the bar? At lunchtime?"

"You're *that* guy," I say, finally putting two and two together. I'd avoided him the entire time he was here, doing that. His date was in hell listening to him, and so was I. "So how's the girlfriend?" I ask.

"Not so much my girlfriend anymore. *Nicole*," he says, and I can't figure out how he knows my name. Until I realize I'm wearing the apron my mom made, with my name embroidered on it. She made one for all twelve of the Circa girls last Christmas. Excited by the features of her new sewing machine, she went through a stage where she monogrammed everything in sight. Meaning she assigned my dad to figure out how to program the machine, and had *him* monogram everything in sight. It was a sweet gesture, followed closely by the phone call she made to tell me she'd had a spiritual impression over breakfast. I'll come back to the church one day, she's sure of it. In the meantime, it won't do any good to push me. She should just relax and accept this stage of my life, and did I want to meet for lunch the following week?

"I'm Scott. Thatcher," says the guy at table 31.

Another bell goes off in my head. "You're on my mailing list. Family@Thatcher.com."

"Yeah," he says. "Except I lost the 'family' in the divorce."

"Yikes," I say. "Not your best year."

"Want to see a magic trick?" he says. There's a deck of cards on the table beside his beer.

"Later," I say, glancing around my section. "I've got six other tables, and I need to make a loop. So," I look at him closely, squint like a B-movie fortune-teller. "Two steak salads? Medium?"

"Nice," the friend says.

"Not my first time," I say, and step across the aisle to ring their orders in. The next time I circle around my section I stop to see the trick. It's called the Ambitious Card. I write my name on a card with a Sharpie, and no matter where he puts it in the deck, it jumps to the top. Even when I slide it into the middle, Scott makes a swirling motion across the top, snaps his fingers, and my card appears above the others.

"Good trick," I tell him, impressed in spite of myself. "What else you got?"

"It's horrible," he says, feigning shyness. "It's juvenile. Embarrassing really," and then he goes into a routine where two separate rubber bands seem to be joined, then disappear up his nose.

Corina smacks me on the ass when she walks by, not so subtly telling me to get back in the game. But soon I'm looping back around to see the trick with two red sponge balls the size and shape of a clown's nose. They appear and disappear from his hands, and finally end up in mine. I scream when I see them leap from my hand.

"What the hell's going on over here," says Melissa, not one to be left out of the fun.

"Watch this trick," I say, as Scott starts again. I rush back out to check on all of her tables as well as my own. But soon, I'm standing in front of 31 again, listening to the sad story about the girlfriend who left, who he dated right after the divorce. He thought she would stay forever, fix everything. I mention my breakup with Ben six months ago, which was harder to move past than it should've been—for the same reasons. We compare theories about the human impulse to fictionalize, in relationships: to assign people qualities we want them to have. And after the breakup, we grieve for those things, not wanting to admit they may never have existed.

He says we should get together sometime and talk for real, so I take my business card from a stack next to the computer and set it on the edge of his table. He doesn't notice. He's talking nonstop about a documentary he can't wait to watch—it's in production now—about Philippe Petit, who walked a wire strung between the Twin Towers of the World Trade Center in 1974. He met Philippe Petit at a club for magicians in New York a few years ago, and *yes*, he's a pathological egomaniac but—"

"Here's my card," I say. Scott looks at me blankly for a minute, until I slide it toward him. Deliberately. "Because you said we should get together. To talk. O-ver cof-fee." I'm speaking to him as if he's 147 years old.

"*Ohhhh*," he says, finally getting it.

"Yes," I say, nodding.

"Pardon my friend," his friend says, shaking his head. "He's so smart he's dumb."

Since leaving the church, I have not embarked on the wild romp of experimentation that's been feared by my family and few remaining LDS friends; the same romp that's been encouraged by others, who feel a sowing of oats is in order. I feel like one's late thirties isn't the time to start shooting black tar heroin, binge drinking, or having orgiastic sexcapades with randoms from Craigslist. The point never was rebellion; I never craved excess. I don't see the point in delving into the kinds of self-destructive behaviors that will send me straight to anything Anonymous.

I haven't dated since Ben, except for a thirty-day spree on Match .com, where I went on nearly thirty first dates. I found it depressing. Felt like I was going on a series of interviews, a few of which turned creepy. A simple question—"so what'd you do all day?"—could elicit the dead-serious response: "I did a lot of coke and surfed electrostim porn sites." But what I learned from that experience is what I love most about my non-LDS life. It's a dream, not having to care about dating. Not having to care about marriage. Not having anyone in my life who'd think to judge my worth by whether I have, or don't have, a relationship.

I don't mind being single, it turns out: what I minded was having singlehood be my defining characteristic. Emancipation from that idea is the equivalent of nirvana. How glorious, to not feel rushed, forced, or directed. So I'm having fun, for the first time in years, in the company of men. Flirting with everyone I meet, not wasting five consecutive seconds wondering if I should or shouldn't, what it might lead to, at what point I should detach.

But Scott, I like. Scott, I want to go out with. I'm not surprised when I don't get a call from him over the weekend. But then Monday goes by. And Tuesday. Right when I'm about to write him off, he calls.

"You've been playing it very cool," I say, answering even though I'm driving seventy miles per hour down I-5.

He laughs. "I'm not the least bit cool. I swear. I've been out of town, and didn't have your number." He tells me he's a pilot, that he flies Saturday through Monday mornings. Sometimes Friday nights. "What are you doing now?" he asks, and despite the fact that it's 9:00 PM and he's a virtual stranger, I agree to stop by for a glass of wine.

His place is on the way to mine. I'm sure to let him know, however, that I'll be calling Melissa to leave his address and phone number, just in case I turn up dead or missing.

After a glass of wine Scott and I lie down fully clothed on his bed, telling each other our stories. He fakes a backache to orchestrate this move, which is more hilarious than threatening. And I do love a good story. His is of a fairly recent, very ugly divorce. His career in the air force. His childhood, as one of three adopted kids. His parents were kind and they loved him, but they clearly preferred their biological son—the miracle—who came last. At the dinner table, when Scott said pass the butter, they passed the margarine. When Craig said pass the butter, they passed the butter. So Scott always wondered about his worth, his place in the world, and what he deserved. Those doubts followed him into adulthood—probably informed his choice of marriage partners. So there's that to learn from, he says.

I tell him about my religious upbringing, my summer in Chicago, my absconding to the Caymans. I tell him about my recent break from the Mormon Church, the issues that precipitated it.

Scott reveals that as a kid, he was sent to live for a summer with relatives who were devoutly religious. He read his Bible daily, and tried to believe. He wanted to, he says. "It would be nice to have that, I think. Helpful. Hopeful. I wish I was someone who could have faith."

"I wish I *were*," I correct, with a pang. Wouldn't James be proud.

"I have trouble with tenses," Scott says, and I immediately feel like a jerk—who corrects someone's grammar on a date?

"The subjunctive is tricky," I concede. "It's not a tense; it's a mood."

And then he kisses me. Eagerly, boyishly. Evidently, I am not the only one for whom grammar is an aphrodisiac.

"Go on," he says, after the kiss. I tell him more, and I'm surprised at his reaction: an atheist who is not dismissive of faith, who wants to understand what I loved about my religious life, what I risked, and what was lost in the leaving. He takes in the fact of my virginity without judgment, without a condescending eye roll, or the ravenous, slavering expression that admission sometimes inspires. There is not one moment when I feel like a sideshow freak, or when I am put on the defensive.

Scott doesn't ask me to justify my belief. Doesn't challenge this or that aspect of LDS history or doctrine. It doesn't occur to him to use words like *brainwash*, *cult*, or the offensive, condescending *magic*. *Magic book, magic glasses, magic underwear*. He doesn't imply that to believe in the spiritual or miraculous makes a person imbecilic. He is admiring of my commitment—the sacrifice required to live a religious life. He tries to empathize with what I've done to my family: how I've knocked them off balance, threatened their sense of security.

I tell him I can feel my mother's trepidation every time she and I talk, can sense a fearful wavering in her voice and body. It's like I've shoved her onto a tightrope, where she can't catch her balance, doesn't know how to get back to solid ground. My father chooses his words carefully now. His sentences are mincing. We are tentative with each other, for the first time ever. As if the smallest interaction could cut or leave bruises. My brother, already distant, has withdrawn even further.

I stay late at Scott's house, but drive the five remaining miles to my house when the effects of our nightcap have evaporated from my bloodstream. The following week he takes me to a Thai restaurant in our neighborhood where he tells a funny story about his parents, who insist on pronouncing it "thigh food." We order cocktails at the dogged, eager insistence of our waiter, who's talked me into a cosmopolitan. It's atomic pink with a lime green umbrella, a paper-thin sheen of ice floating on the surface. Scott's is a Manhattan. He takes a sip and nearly chokes. "Pah!" he gasps, and says in the croaking voice of an eighty-year old, "Smooth."

I take a sip from my martini glass, and my face is a twist of sugar-coated misery. Scott and I look at each other, and in an unspoken pact, each pick up the drink the other ordered.

"Heaven," I sigh into the dark, seductive pool of Maker's Mark.

"Mmmmm," he says into the umbrella still perched in his drink. "I hate whiskey. I was trying to be manly."

"I have zero things in common with Carrie Bradshaw."

He looks at me blankly.

"So this is your daughter?" I ask, pointing to the screen of his phone. His wallpaper is a photo of a little girl wearing his pilot's hat.

"My youngest. She's five. Her sister is eight."

"Do you want more kids?" I ask, and a choir of angels erupts in my head when he tells me he had a vasectomy four years ago. He could not have become more appealing in the space of two seconds had he told me he was the crown prince of an obscure, obscenely wealthy European country. I've often wondered, even with the IUD I've not yet put to use, if I'll be able to put my fear of unwanted pregnancy out of my head. The vasectomy makes Scott a strong contender, as does the next revelation.

Scott's first time was a big deal, he says. He was nineteen, and in love. He wants me to have that, too, regardless of whom I choose. He's worried I'll feel cheated if my first time isn't like a scene out of *The Notebook*. Scott is very concerned about things not measuring up to scenes from *The Notebook*, which his ex-wife watched fourteen times shortly after it came out. *Fourteen times.* Afterward, she developed a habit of berating Scott in regard to the long, distinguished list of ways he fell short of the fictional Noah Calhoun.

"I'm a thirty-six-year-old virgin," I say, over a bowl of Panang curry. "I don't need Ryan Gosling in the pouring rain. If anyone's got connections with George Clooney, maybe we can talk. But what it comes down to is I'm a grown woman, and I'm ready."

In the next weeks, Scott and I fall effortlessly into a relationship. There's an endless stream of jokes about him becoming my Svengali.

"Teach me this," I say. "What about this?" I ask and make him lie naked while I look, and touch, and ask questions more indicative of a science project than a den of sexual deviance. He finds it endearing. He enjoys being helpful, and it turns out James was wrong: there *are* men who want to be my teacher. "Man, that guy was stupid," says Scott, laughing, as I unbuckle his belt one afternoon for the second time in three hours.

There is much I want to know about his body, about men, in general—the myths and truths I have read in *Cosmo* while getting my nails done—because who can actually *subscribe* to *Cosmo*? I get a lot of pedicures, do a lot of reading, and subsequently, a lot of experimentation. I am intent on developing skills, catching up quickly. And I'm grateful for my utter lack of self-consciousness in Scott's presence, and his, in mine. I'm grateful, too, that Ben resisted what I was trying to force with him. I see now how uncomplicated things can be, given the right chemistry, the right partner.

But even Scott is holding out when it comes to *sex* sex. "I don't want to take anything from you," he says. "I can wait."

What he doesn't know is that I've already decided. I made up my mind one Saturday morning late into the first month we'd been dating. I'd slept over, and we rolled out of bed late, both starving. I put on one of his sweatshirts, and we walked holding hands, up the street to Circa for eggs and toast, a mimosa for me, just coffee for Scott who had to fly later. We sipped like we were drinking ambrosia of the gods, like we were hypnotized by the blue of each others' eyes.

For the first time ever, I was one of those people I've waited on at brunch every weekend for the past five years—whom I've envied, with their bed head and musky morning glow. Neither Scott nor I could remember falling asleep the night before. We woke up still dressed, sharing the same pillow.

I turned quickly when I felt a hand grazing my bare shoulder, beyond the strap of my tank top—thinking someone was playing that game: touching my right shoulder, hiding to my left. I felt myself blush, realizing it was Scott. My boyfriend. Whose elbow was resting on the back of my chair, whose fingers were drawing light patterns on my skin. I felt tears spring to my eyes, and turned away from him, embarrassed. *How long will it take*, I wondered. How long for my body to become unsurprised, to feel entitled to the act of being touched?

I leaned into Scott, who continued to trace invisible designs on my shoulder, and I knew he'd be kind in every way he knows how, and honest. He'd be generous, and careful. We ate in silence, utterly content, and I let my mind wander to a sandbar on Grand Cayman: a shallow out-of-the-way place where for fifty years, fishermen would come to clean their catch. Hundreds of stingrays became conditioned to feed there, having learned the patterns of the boats, and the men who drove them. The tour companies named the shallow place Stingray City, and tourists followed in droves, paying top dollar to stand chest-deep in the sea, intrigued and frightened by the eerie softness of a stingray's wings.

By nature, stingrays are playful. They'll brush against your body, bank across the plane of your back, spin quickly around and between your calves. The barb on their tails is defensive, nothing to worry about unless you behave as a predator would. This is what our dive master told the group of us preparing to dive at a slightly deeper spot near the sandbar. It was one of my first scuba dives; I'd completed my certification just the week before.

Underwater, we knelt in the sand, fifteen feet below the sparkling surface. We gathered in a circle, held our palms flat under thin pieces of raw squid: deliberate in our attempt to summon stingrays, whose eyes are on top of their heart-shaped bodies, whose mouths are slits in the white planes underneath. They are guided by scent, rather than sight. I held a pungent scrap with my hand outstretched, waiting. For a strange, pale body to flutter and glide against me, for a chance at that thrilling, frightening caress.

I did as I was instructed: held still, kept my palm flat. Still, fooled by the scent of squid in the water, a stingray's mouth latched on to my arm, thinking it was food. The vacuum of its mouth formed a seal on the muscle of my tricep, gripped nearly from elbow to shoulder, before pulling with force enough to rip a conch from its shell. Release came a few terrible seconds later. Only after the blood rose, after the bruise formed, dark and brutal. For months it remained—at first a purple so deep it was nearly black, then a faded yellow-green shadow. A jaundiced watermark, painful to the touch.

I leaned farther into Scott, wondering about the metaphor. If the same kind of bravery—the same waiting, with baited hands—is required, when we avail ourselves to love. When we dive in, knowing we may be injured regardless, or because of, its rare, mystifying beauty.

I've been shopping for weeks, in secret, to find the perfect little black dress. There's a date on my calendar chosen, but left blank so as not to jinx it: a Monday night in mid-June, when neither Scott nor I have work the day of or after, and his kids are at their mother's. I'm looking for a dress that's comfortable, that won't wrinkle, that plunges but doesn't cling, that doesn't require hideous, nude-colored, squeezy underthings. I find one that comes astonishingly close to meeting every requirement, and take it straight to my tailor. I ask her to make the V-neck significantly lower. She raises her eyebrows after she pins it. "Like this?" she asks, and I say, "*Lower.*"

"Very expensive," she announces sternly, and I wonder if I'm imagining her glance toward the picture of Jesus she has tacked to the wall. "Twenty dollars."

I hand over a crisp stack of fives.

Years ago, I bought a pair of cherry-red, patent leather peep-toe shoes with four-inch stiletto heels, and put them away for this occasion. That's as close as I ever came to assembling a hope chest. I've pinned my hair up, which Scott thinks is sexy, though it feels a little schoolmarmy to me. When my doorbell rings promptly at 7:00, I open the door to see him looking nervous and awkward in a navy sport coat, with his hair still wet from the shower. He's given himself a superclose shave, because he won't believe me when I tell him I prefer a day's shadow, its roughness against my skin, that obvious sign of masculinity.

His ex hated the feel of whiskers; she also hated it when he came anywhere near her without showering—another thing I wish he could get past. I prefer him to smell like a man, rather than a bar of lavender-scented soap. I prefer him not to leap up when things are just getting going, in order to lather and scrub. But he is adorable tonight, regardless of the soap, and the shave: he's an overgrown prom date, holding a dozen red roses, that sweet cliché. He hands me a slim box of salted caramels, and a bottle of Veuve Clicquot.

"Hubba hubba," he says in response to my outfit. We both burst into laughter, an overblown, nervous response. I grab his hand and pull him inside. In the kitchen he's jumpy, making me feel jumpy. I put the flowers in water, the champagne in the fridge.

"Ready?" he asks, and I nod, holding my breath. I've been researching for weeks: sexy hotels offering the "Art of Romance": an overnight package including a couples massage, truffles and champagne, and one pair of pajamas to share; I looked online for sexy lingerie, sexy food, sexy wine, sexy music, sexy sheets, sexy kill myself twice with the pressure to be sexy.

Overwhelmed and slightly grossed out, it finally occurred to me that neither of us has a thousand dollars to spend on The Big Night, so I finally broke down and cleaned the house. My condo is as romantic as any hotel when the lights are dimmed, given the fireplace, maple floors, white rugs, crystal chandeliers, sleigh bed, and, the pièce de résistance, a leopard-print chaise lounge.

First on our agenda is a drink at Chez Shea, voted one of Seattle's most romantic restaurants. But it's 7:30 PM in June. Sunset won't come until at least 9:30, and inside, the room is too bright, the corners too square, the linens too stark. The tension is killing us both.

"Want to see a magic trick?" asks Scott.

"Yes, please."

Scott is a surprisingly good sleight-of-hand magician. He perfects his passes and palming techniques in-flight—productively using the would-be wasted hours he spends strapped in a chair, locked in a cockpit, in planes required by the FAA to be on autopilot while at cruise altitude. Scott always needs something to *do*. He can't think of anything nearer to torture than sitting for hours with a book at the beach. He fidgets. Doesn't sleep well, doesn't sleep in. Says he feels guilty relaxing, which is my best talent.

"So, Nicole," he says, leaning toward me, using a mock-serious voice. "May I call you Nicole?"

"You may."

"I'd like you to meet my friend Bob. He's ticklish." He indicates a stick figure drawn with a Sharpie in the right-hand corner of one of the four cards in his hand. "Why don't you give Bob a little tickle?" He moves the card with the drawn-on stick figure closer to me.

"This patter is horrifying," I say. "Did you just say give *Bob* a little *tickle?*"

"I did say that. Bob's ticklish. Go on, tickle him."

I scratch my fingernail on the top of the card, presumably so I can see that the ink doesn't come off.

"Man," Scott says, wide-eyed. "With all that tickling, the problem now is we don't just have *one* Bob, we have *two*." Suddenly, two of the cards in his hand have a Bob on them, and then three, and finally, all four. Scott brandishes the cards, each with their stick figure Bob in the corner. He says, "And that's not even the most amazing thing. The most *amazing* thing is what these Bobs will do for you."

"What will they do?" I ask, taking a gulp of my wine. The Bob trick is killing me.

"*Acrobatics*," Scott says. "So go ahead and choose one of the Bobs, whichever one you like best. Hold it tight, by the top corner. These Bobs," he says, shaking his head. "They get so excited about doing their big act." Scott pulls the remaining three cards away from the one I'm holding, and my card has all four Bobs on it, one in each corner. The three cards in Scott's hand are all blank.

"And that's the trick," he says, which is what he says at the end of every trick. "What do you think?"

Before I can say anything, I'm distracted by a movement out of the corner of my eye. I look over to see a real-life Bob, one of my Circa regulars, waving at me from a table fifteen feet away. Bob and his wife are lovely. I can't wait to get away from them. I need some freaking *privacy*—on this, of all nights.

"Let's get out of here," I say to Scott, smiling toward Bob's table. Scott drains his wine in three seconds flat and lays thirty dollars on the table. He takes my hand and we make a run for Il Bistro, just across the cobblestone walk, below the main level of Pike Place Market.

The restaurant is mostly underground, and plays Argentine tango music; late at night there are dancers, sometimes—couples moving languidly across the floor in perfect frame. Men with their shoulders back, their heads at haughty angles. Women wearing slinky dresses, their faces buried in their partners' necks or shoulders.

The walls of Il Bistro are a creamy white; the furniture is dark and heavy. It's lit by little more than the glow of candles. The vibe is dark and sensual—*Casablanca*, without all the angst and political intrigue. Scott and I give each other the eye, over carpaccio and vintage cocktails.

"Why are you so far away?" I say, running a finger along the back of his hand.

"I'm saving up for later," he says, archly.

In the car, on the way back to my place, Scott gives me a present. Beautifully, meticulously wrapped, is the spectacularly craptastic *Cosmo Kama Sutra*: an excruciating, genius piece of trash featuring "77 Mind-Blowing Sex Positions" titled along the lines of "G-Spot

Jiggy" and "Wanton Wheelbarrow." Each one comes complete with "Erotic Instructions" and an explanation of "Why You'll Love It."

We stop for takeout at the restaurant where we had our first real date, then back to my place to pop the champagne. I kick off my shoes in the entryway, and Scott lays his jacket across the arm of the couch. He untucks his shirt, rolls up his sleeves in preparation for our carpet picnic. There are chocolates, and music. There is firelight, which inspires Scott to read aloud from *The Cosmo Kama Sutra*.

"*The Sexy Scissor*," he says in a deep, affected radio voice. "No other love lock will offer you such a body rockin' range of sensations—"

"Sick." I cover my mouth, laughing. "I can't believe you just said 'body-rockin' range of sensations.'"

"Oh, I said it. 'One second your limbs are in an erotic X and you're supertight for a snug fit—'"

"Please stop. Please, please, please." I put my hands over my ears, weak from laughing. He does not stop, but shifts to an intense whisper voice.

"'Then suddenly you're wide open and able to take him in deliciously deep. We guarantee these thigh-melting maneuvers will lead to mucho bliss.'"

"Ew," I groan. "*Mucho bliss.* I'm imagining someone writing that copy."

"That's not exactly what I'm imagining," says Scott.

I put down my glass, which Scott immediately refills. I take the book from him, and clear my throat. "The Rock 'n' Roll," I say. Quietly, but in my valley girl voice, emphasizing every fourth or fifth word: "'This man on top position makes you feel deliciously *open* and *vulnerable* while his incredibly deep thrusting drives you to *superor*-gasmic heights. This is also a good position for *extrasensual* couples who enjoy a little lip action when they're knocking boots.'" After the phrase "knocking boots" it takes a while to compose myself. "'Since you're face-to-face, it's easy for him to give in to his *primal urges* and lick, suck, or nibble on your mouth while you're *rocking* each other's *worlds.'* " The comedic horror show of this book is the perfect read aloud: intriguing, yet embarrassing—a ridiculous, hilarious turn-on.

"Take off your dress," Scott says, holding aloft the bottle of Veuve Clicquot. "I'm going to pour this all over you." I think he's kidding, until he does it. Until his mouth and tongue follow, tracing the shallow, sparkling streams of champagne on my skin, wherever gravity takes them.

When he decides it's time, Scott leads me into the bedroom. I burst into laughter, turn around, and lead him *out* of the bedroom. We lie back down in front of the fire. "Say when you're ready," he says, and we kiss ourselves breathless. Eventually, I stand up, and hold my hand out to him. He follows, stopping for a second in the kitchen. Before I realize what's happening, he is sprinkling rose petals on the bed. He stands back to look at his handiwork, at the romance he's created, which I'm tempted to tease him about.

But before I can say anything, he dives face-first onto the bed, with his arms outstretched. He gathers up the bedding and runs for the balcony.

"What are you *doing*?" I put on my robe and chase him through the living room. Outside, he is madly shaking rose petals onto the rhododendrons below.

"I freaked out," he says, apologetically. "What if they stain your bedding?"

"Then you can do my laundry."

"Oh I'll do your laundry," he says, dropping the comforter on the chaise lounge.

"Are you trying to make 'I'll do your laundry' into a sexy come-on?" I ask.

He pauses, thoughtfully. "Well. Not if it isn't *working*."

Back in the bedroom, Scott stands looking at me until I take a step toward him. He reaches for the tie keeping my robe closed. We are on the bed then, and his body against mine is warm in contrast to the cooler air of the room. I'm glad there aren't any covers to dull the opposing sensations. And when the moment comes, as it has in the nights leading up to this—when both of us are ready, when it feels imminent and welcome—when one of us usually stops and shouts, "Danger!" neither of us does. It is a simple thing, this coupling. It is effortless, and yet it takes my breath. The pleasure of Scott's body literally takes my breath.

With him inside me, I feel myself opening in every way there is to be vulnerable to another. Let him break my heart, if he will. Let this be a mistake, if it turns out to be. But enough of living on the brittle surface, enough of keeping myself numb, alone, and half-dead from fear. I wrap myself around Scott and feel a sublime letting go of barriers within. Like great slabs of concrete pulling loose and crashing down, the release of every fear and doubt, every hammered-in threat or admonition.

We find our rhythm among prisms cast from the chandelier, and there is none of the pain I've been told to expect, none of the awkwardness, or discomfort. No guilt, no self-consciousness about my inexperience, no loss of self-respect. What I feel instead is something akin to grace. A homecoming.

"Don't freak out," I whisper, feeling tears streaming down my face. "It's good," I say pulling him closer.

"No shit it's good," he says, and then we're both laughing. He wipes the tears from my eyes, makes a joke about "mucho bliss." Another about picturing the Circa girls standing behind him, cheering him on. But it's not funny for long. It is sweet and languorous, building in intensity. His mouth is a caress across my cheekbone, behind my ear. "Don't stop," I say. That plea, that prayer. "Please."

I'm first to fall asleep, lulled into dreams by a hazy afterglow, champagne, and the warmth of Scott's body curled around me. Even before he retrieves the covers from the other room, I've drifted peacefully into a new state of spirit and mind—where not much, and yet everything, is changed.

Chapter 15

*Be strong, and of a good courage; be not afraid, neither be
thou dismayed: for the Lord thy God is with thee withersoever
thou goest.*

—JOSHUA 1:9

———◆———

"Do you feel different?" Scott asks, the morning after. We're sharing an old-fashioned donut at the bakery down the street from my house. Drinking coffee. Smiling dreamily at each other.

"Sort of," I say. "A little like after you get glasses, when you figure out there are leaves."

"Are you sad?"

"No." I'm surprised by the question, that he'd still think that. "I feel weirdly complete." I take a sip of my coffee. "Not in a creepy 'you complete me' way. There's just been so much, for so long, to carry around. So much to feel or not feel, say or not say, think or not think. I just feel thankful to have made the choice of who, and where, and when. A lot of women don't get that."

"Happy to help," Scott says, and I lean over to kiss him.

"Good job, by the way. A-plus, really." I glance at his phone on the table. "So are your friends waiting to hear?"

He laughs, a little guiltily. "Only Greg."

"It's okay," I say. "It's a weird situation—of course you'd talk to him about it. Besides, it'll be all over Circa soon enough."

"The weirdest thing is how *not* weird it was," Scott says, taking a bite of his donut. There is a long silence, in which I assume we're both reminiscing. "Back to your place?" he suggests, and I nod, dumping my coffee on the way out the door.

Weeks later, I wake to find a gigantic dead rat outside my door. I walk right over it on my way to work, shivering with disgust. I am not about to touch it: that's what homeowner's dues and maintenance crews are for. I come home to find someone has kicked the rat *onto* my doormat. Frozen in rigor mortis, it landed upright, so it looks like it's trying to climb inside. I step over it again, holding my breath and call Scott to ask him to make it go away.

"Really?" he asks, dubiously. "But it's already dead."

"Yeah," I say. "But what's the point of having a boyfriend if I still have to touch dead animals?" Not knowing quite how to argue with that logic, he drives the seven minutes to my house and puts on my hot pink rubber kitchen gloves, arranges two compost bags one inside the other, and sets out to vanquish the already dead. Afterward, washing his hands in the kitchen sink, he says, "I actually feel really manly right now." He's walking like a cartoon superhero, with his chest puffed out. "I've just accessed some primal, protective instinct. I'm so caveman."

"Awesome," I say. "Would you like to celebrate your manliness with a delicious glass of Cab Franc?"

"Yes, please. And afterward, perhaps a soothing blow job?"

I'm telling the rat story to Travis, a Circa regular, who I've known for six years now—although I stop at the "I'm so caveman" line. Travis, sitting at the bar, offers me one of his fries, which I take though I'm supposed to have quit cold turkey.

"I saw you two driving last weekend," he says. "Along Alki Beach. You had the top down on your car, and you were wearing a green scarf. I'll never forget it. Like a scene from a movie, both of you laughing as you sped by. You looked so in love."

"I don't know if I'd say love, yet," I tell Travis. "It's only been four months."

I get that love can happen in four months. In four days, or four hours, if you believe those kinds of stories. What I'm really saying is I don't know if I'm *ready* for love, crazy as that seems. I love that Scott's gone three or four days a week. I like doing my own thing in between, and I like missing him. I love reading what I want, watching what I want, saying and thinking whatever I want. Hearing only my own voice in my head, my own conscience in regard to what is enlightening, what is right and good in the world. My life feels thoughtful, still. Deliberate. And blissfully free of orthodoxy.

What I am in love with is having a boyfriend. Our late nights by the fire and our long, thrillingly nerdy conversations. I love having someone to help with wiper blades and my tricky pilot light, having Scott's shoulder when I'm blue and a rescue when I've run out of gas, again. I love having a leg to rest my foot against while I'm falling asleep—a man in my shower, a man in my arms, and in my bed.

What a dream, not to have to manage the future. And what a surprise to find myself wondering, *If I don't want kids, do I need marriage?* That question alone has set my head to spinning. I have a lot to figure out, still.

Scott sometimes says he wishes he could give me more, could *be* more for me. He uses a pained tone that sounds a lot, to me, like whining.

"I don't want you to be more," I say. "I love not having to worry, my head spinning around those exhausting questions: *Will we get married? Are you the one?* I'll be happy the rest of my life if I never again hear the phrase 'the one.' For the first time, I'm not in a rush."

"Women say that," Scott says, in response.

Last weekend, when Travis saw us driving on Alki, we were on our way out of town. Scott had a rare few days without work or kids. Which is not to say he wasn't preoccupied with thoughts of both during the four-hour trip to Orcas Island. He is by nature a worrier, and I've learned not to fight it. I let myself drift off into my own world, imagined myself in a vintage Alfa Romeo zooming along the Amalfi Coast rather than the winding two-lane drive from the ferry dock to the twenty-four-hundred-foot summit of Mount Constitution.

Scott wanted to do some hiking, and I said sure, whatever. I was on a romantic getaway with a man I was sleeping with: a first, unless you count the bungled attempt last year with Ben, which I don't. I was happy to do whatever Scott felt like doing, especially because he was generous enough not to mind that I brought him to the same resort where Ben and I stayed. It would be weird, except I can use my timeshare points there, and Scott jumped at the chance for a free two-day holiday.

At the top of Mount Constitution, Scott chose a hike that works in reverse. It starts at a steep decline from the summit, loops down, and ends at the beginning: next to a medieval-looking observation tower, which marks the highest point in the San Juans. That day it was clear enough to see Canada. The hiking trail, lined with towering evergreens, was scattered with roots and rocks. Birds chirped. Squirrels scampered. Purple flowers bloomed beneath moss-covered logs. The sun shone dusty rays through limbs of trees, illuminated boulders so majestic they seemed unreal—as if made of papier-mâché, a set for some show like *Land of the Lost*.

Scott practiced a sleight of hand move while we walked, a diagonal palm shift pass that will require weeks of dedicated practice to perform without flashing the palmed card. After a mile or so, we stopped at a grassy clearing near the edge of a ravine. I heard a creek below, and looked for it through a tumble of fallen trees. "I used to come to this island as a kid," I told Scott. "Five or six summers in a row, my family stayed in a woodsy resort called Beach Haven. We'd rent paddleboats at the state park, and my brother and I searched for small, pointed rocks, convinced they were arrowheads."

I sat down in a patch of sun, and set myself to the task of staring at the clouds. Scott found a spot in the shade of a towering cedar. "Before that I went to Camp Orkila, which isn't far from here. My parents made me canvass our neighborhood selling butter-toffee peanuts to subsidize the cost of a one-week stay. I dragged cases of them around in a borrowed wagon. My genius sales tactic was a two-dollar loan from my dad so I could open a can and give away free samples. After my first sale, I'd pay him back. One time, this big, bearded guy was tiling his entryway when I knocked on the front door. He asked me to drop a peanut into his mouth because his hands were dirty. I remember thinking how weird it was to touch the inside of a man's mouth, accidentally. Sort of gross, yet intriguing."

"Yeah," Scott said. "I became very aware of breasts around that age."

"At camp I made lanyards in every shape and size, as if people couldn't *live* without lanyards. I swam for hours every day. And at night, around the campfire, I only sang the most dramatic songs. Like 'The Rose.'"

Scott begins singing, comically overwrought. There is a pause before he says, "Ouch. That song hits a nerve."

Allusions like these, I have learned to speed right by. Otherwise I'll be trapped in a forty-minute conversation about his dysfunctional, postdivorce rebound drama with *Pam*. I suspect Scott is still in love with Pam, who by all accounts—including his own—treated him like shit. He talks incessantly about infatuation. His theories about it, the books he's read about it, the ways it controls and ruins people. How he needs to feel that again—though it's the source of every stupid decision he's ever made.

I try not to respect Scott less because of his continuing obsession with an abusive woman he dated for a grand total of six weeks. I keep thinking it'll wear off; he'll get over it. I thought if I asked nicely, he'd stop talking about Pam all the time. Except he didn't. I listened patiently for a couple months: what we have is healthier and better in every way, he kept repeating. So why did he still yearn for what he had with Pam? He wants it, even if it is dysfunctional. He misses that heightened emotional state.

"Never again," I declared one night on the phone. He was on a layover in Chicago, calling me from his hotel, depressed because something reminded him of Pam. I cut him off midsentence. "I'm done. Pam is what *fight club* is for." "Fight club" is the term he and his friends use—for chess club, yoga, radio-controlled planes, or deep relationship talks. It's code for whatever isn't tough enough to talk about in public.

Since I've banned Scott from speaking her name in my presence, he just makes these dramatic allusions, which I refuse to acknowledge. My trick is to pretend like he's not talking. Otherwise, I might punch him in the neck.

"My parents never let me stay longer than a week at camp," I continued, to the clouds as much as to Scott. "Though I begged. I didn't understand the kids who were homesick, crying about missing their moms. What's to miss? Our moms would be there when we got back. At camp, you never had to vacuum and dust. You never had to do dishes or pull weeds. I never brushed my teeth and always peed in the pool."

"Not surprising," said Scott, smiling, though his focus remained on the cards in his hand. I was content to lie back and reminisce, eventually landing on the time a friend and I took one of the rowboats out; they were heavy metal boats with wooden oars. I knew how to row, but the water was choppy, and the boat was bigger than the one I was used to. I was only nine or ten, and couldn't keep us close to shore. I watched the beach shrinking as we drifted too far to swim back; we'd been given lectures on hypothermia, the year-round temperatures in Puget Sound. I remember feeling frightened by the dark water. It seemed menacing, like some creature might be lurking beneath the surface. I half expected a hand to shoot out and grab me by the neck. The lifeguard kept blowing her air horn; we were about to drift beyond a rocky point jutting into the sea. Once past it, no one would be able to see us.

Eventually, two boys rowed out to get us. They were older, thirteen or fourteen. I wanted to cry I was so relieved, but I was too embarrassed to say anything, especially thank you. I threw the bowline over, and they towed us in. They called me names the whole time. Made sure I saw how disgusted they were, by my stupidity. My shoddy rowing skills. I remember thinking how humiliating it was to be saved. To need saving.

But that night one of the boy counselors came into our cabin after lights out. He and my counselor—Joanne of the flowing blond hair—must've had something going. He played his guitar and sang to us as we fell asleep. I remember fighting to stay awake, not wanting to miss even a minute of it. Imagining what it would be like, to have a boy like that be in love with me.

"So let me show you this pass," Scott said, and I turned toward him, dropping the long blades of grass I'd been tying into knots. "Can you see anything?" he asked, shifting the cards in his palm.

It's my job to say *Flash!* when I can see any trace of the palmed card. I enjoy it, usually. I have a special, very nasal voice reserved for the word. But instead of paying attention to the cards, I ran a hand up Scott's thigh, traced the outline of his muscle, well-defined from running and yoga. I looked him straight in the eye.

"No way," he said, half laughing, looking behind him.

"There's no one around for miles."

"I hear voices."

"*Bird* voices."

He sighed, as if he were very tired. "Someone always ends up with twigs in their pants."

"Maybe I want twigs in my pants. Come on. I want to know what it's like, outside."

"Stop!" he said, irritated. He brushed my hand away.

"Wow, you're not kidding." I sat up, surprised. My feelings were hurt. Who cares if *you've* already done it, I wanted to shout. The list of things I would like to do and still haven't would roll out like a medieval scroll. Would hit the floor and keep going, going out the door, across the street, out of town, into a pasture of cows.

When I tell this story to Melissa, who's also stopped at the end of the bar to snack on Travis's fries, she suspects there's more to the story. "What else aren't you telling?"

I follow her back to the wait station. "He doesn't really *kiss* me," I say. "Mornings, he bounds out of bed to make coffee, and breakfast. He brings it to me like a gift. It's sweet. He's being sweet, with the coffee, and the breakfast. But I just wish he'd open his eyes and reach for me."

Just when I'm starting to wonder if our relationship has run its course in these few months, Scott says he wants to join me for my birthday dive trip: his first-ever real vacation, and our first chance to dive together. I originally reserved two weeks in Turks and Caicos, and planned to go by myself. But a series of hurricanes forced me, with only two weeks' notice, to change that plan.

I was at Scott's house, researching "best Caribbean diving" when the island of Saba came up. I showed him the photos of the tiny island, part of the Dutch Antilles, and a boutique hotel with cute rooms and competitive rates. I decided to rebook there, why not, even though I'd never heard of Saba, or met anyone who's been there. Scott said it looked amazing, and he'd meet me for the second week, when his kids were with his ex.

If I'd bothered to check the news or the Weather Channel before departing, I'd have known Hurricane Omar was brewing. I might not be so surprised to find my plane grounded in St. Maarten, leaving me stranded in the airport with no hotel reservations, no food, no idea where I'll be safe, and the task of figuring it all out in minutes, because cabdrivers are disappearing quickly, heading home to board their windows. The airport staff can't help: they've all clocked out, intent on saving themselves.

I fortuitously meet a lovely Frenchwoman, Caroline, also traveling alone, and we find a driver who knows of an unpopular hotel: ugly, run-down, and inland. "Perfect!" I say. Who wants to be beachfront, with nothing but glass and bamboo between you and a hurricane? The cabdriver is kind enough to stop at a half-pillaged mini-mart before dropping us at our hotel, which is everything he promised.

Caroline and I check in, each carrying our luggage and a bag of food not requiring refrigeration: apples, granola bars, peanut butter, water, crackers, wine, and Oreos to live on for who knows how long—during which time we'll be charged the hurricane rate for our room, which is 25 percent *more* than the regularly advertised price. We pony up, agreeing that safety has its price. The two of us sit on the floor of our shared living room eating peanut butter crackers until I drag myself to bed, exhausted from wine and my long day of travel.

I wake to sunny skies. "Weird, the hurricane never came?" I ask, and Caroline's face tells me she'd murder me, if she were the type. I slept right through it. Was no help at all while she laid awake, terrified by the furious, howling wind and walls of pelting rain.

"Sorry," I say, embarrassed. "I sleep when I'm stressed out." I decide it's best not to mention I was no help to my aisle-mates on the airplane either, as the turbulence increased to a level that inspired screaming, vocal prayer, and signs of the cross. I put my earplugs in, shut my eyes, and decided to believe what Scott once told me: that a plane's wings can bend so much they nearly touch before they'll break off. I consoled myself by reasoning that if every plane went down in bad weather, half the earth's population would be dead already.

Last night, there was a shabby-looking golf course next to our hotel. Now it's covered by a series of shallow sand dunes, blown in from the beach overnight. They're glittering in the morning sun, and since there's nothing else to do, Caroline and I set out for a walk. There's been no major damage to the island and no lives lost, the golf course maintenance crew tells us. The airport will open tomorrow they say, and they're right. The next morning I say good-bye to my lovely French roommate, wish her safe travels, and board my flight to Saba.

It's only when I get there, check in, and check my e-mail in the hotel's business center that it registers: Scott's not coming. There's nothing from him. No message about missing me, or about when and where he'll join me. His plans were always loose, since he'd be flying standby and his arrival would depend on empty seats on other airlines. I'm disappointed, but I don't mention it. Why bother? I planned to come alone in the first place. Instead, I send a short, funny note about surviving the hurricane, just in case he saw the coverage on TV (but if he had, wouldn't he have written?). His response to that e-mail comes two days later than I feel like it should, and I know what it means, his pulling away. I spend much of my vacation trying not to picture our breakup encroaching like the images of Omar via satellite—a computerized swirl of orange, red, and yellow surging inevitably toward land.

Scott comes over the night after I arrive home. Standing in my kitchen, he says what I already know he's going to say. "I can't be what you need," he says. "You deserve more." He has decided what I want, and that he's not it. "I'm so sorry," he keeps repeating, in a condescending tone that I find infuriating. "I'm *hurting* you," he keeps insisting, and yes, that's true. But the implication is that I'll fall apart without him. Doesn't he get it? If there's one thing I know how to do, it's how *not* to have a boyfriend.

"People get hurt," I tell him. "They get over it." I'm so irritated it takes me a minute to figure out what's really happening: He's apologizing so profusely, so unrelentingly, that I finally realize he wants me to soothe *him*. He feels so guilty, he says. It's so terrible, so awful for him to be hurting me.

"I can't help you with that," I say, but I feel like yelling. *That's what fight club is for, jackass!*

I send Scott away with a box of parting gifts: a bottle of banana rum from Saba that I still regret not saving for myself, a jacket I was saving for Christmas, and a signed copy of *The Brief Wondrous Life of Oscar Wao* that Scott once said was the best book he'd ever read. I'd sent a hardback copy to the author, Junot Diaz, for an autograph. Scott leaves feeling guilty about these things, too, but he doesn't know what to do with himself if he doesn't feel like crap, so what's the difference?

It's less than twenty-four hours before he calls again, wants to meet me at a nearby park to talk. I know what's coming. Scott has always been in a relationship; he hasn't gone a month without one since he was fifteen years old. He needs that assurance. Needs someone to tell him, every day, that he's wonderful.

"I didn't sleep all night," he says. "I think I made a mistake."

"So what changed since yesterday? What would be different, if we got back together?"

"I don't know," he says. "But I don't want to not have you."

I wish I could say I walked away, but I didn't. And two weeks later, in my kitchen, it's the same story again, like an instant replay. He needs time on his own, needs to learn how to be by himself, he says. He's sorry, he says, again and again. He *wants* to love me.

That too-familiar sentence clarifies everything. He's waiting for me to shout, or beg him to stay. He wants roller coasters. He wants bees.

I send him from my kitchen for the second time after predicting with startling accuracy what happens next: five days later, Scott's entangled with someone else in the up-and-down, on-and-off, hot-and-cold chaos he identifies as love. Which isn't to say I'm not heartbroken.

Anger and situational depression collide over the following weeks: I do my share of crying myself to sleep, eating my feelings, and punishing myself with a lineup of romantic comedies on DVD. Thinking— every time the man professes his love—*yeah right*, or *fuck you*.

After those initial stages of grief pass through me, I stop in for a rendezvous now and then with Scott, when he's broken up with his girlfriend *for real this time*. I miss the sex, I'm not dating anyone, and I don't know how to be promiscuous. It seems a good compromise at first. But it takes only four or five of these rendezvous, over a space of as many months, for me to get worn out with Scott's inevitable, exhausting "what does this *mean?*" the next morning. He doesn't want a relationship with me. He's made that clear. I wish he'd save me the dramatic talk, let me drink my coffee and get on with my day. When I say this to Danielle, she's horrified.

"I feel like you have very male attitudes about love and sex," she says. "I don't get it. Don't you feel like sex means everything? Like it *must* mean he loves you? That's what we were always taught. When my husband had the stomach flu, I burst into tears on the fifth day he didn't touch me," she says, laughing at herself. "I was convinced he didn't love me anymore. You should've seen his face. 'Baby,' he groaned, all weak and pasty. 'I have the *flu.*'"

"Honestly?" I say, afraid that what I'm about to admit will mean I'm damaged or abnormal. "I'm not sure I feel *any* connection between love and sex. They've always existed so separately. Every time I've felt love, it was in the absence of sex. And any encounter that even approached sex happened in the absence of love."

So what I'm dreading more than the slow, painful shift into the platonic with Scott is everything I've been warned will happen, now that I've had premarital sex, now that that relationship has failed. Some days I wonder if or when I'll start to feel estranged from God and my sense of self. If I'll feel lost, or if my self-esteem will erode. If I'll feel like I've committed the third-worst sin in the world.

But every day I wake up still feeling like myself. It doesn't take long to realize I am, and always will be, who God made me. Who my parents and my LDS community made me. I'm a product of the best of their intentions, and all of their love. It means something to me, still—my Mormon upbringing. Even now that I'm not practicing, I respect and admire the system that taught me so much about integrity, charity, and love.

Which is why I've remained intentionally ignorant about the LDS church's involvement in Proposition 8—which last year overturned the previously granted right of same-sex couples to marry in California. I have turned off the television, flipped the radio station away from the news; I've hidden Facebook friends, thrown newspapers unread into the recycling bin, not wanting to acknowledge that the current prophet would—in response to a call from the Archdiocese of San Francisco—tell church members how to vote.

I don't want to believe that a letter was sent from Salt Lake, to be read aloud in every California ward, asking members to give time, give money, go door-to-door in a "pro-family" campaign, the results of which were inarguably antigay. I don't want to believe that church members would be asked to take away anyone's civil rights. That LDS volunteers went to other members' houses, armed with tithing records, to suggest an amount that could or should be given to the Prop 8 campaign. Particularly since I've always admired the church's policy of encouraging its members to vote according to their consciences. I've always believed in the words of the late prophet Gordon B. Hinckley: "Our membership in this Church . . . should never be any cause for self-righteousness, for arrogance, for denigration of others, for looking down upon others. All mankind is our neighbor."

But during a weekend visit to LA to see Sariah, I'm forced to relinquish my self-imposed state of ignorance. I'm forced to acknowledge what is true. At the Annenberg Space for Photography in Los Angeles, where we've come to see the Pictures of the Year International exhibit, I stop in front of a photograph of two men in their early twenties, with their arms around each other. I lean closer, drawn by what's illuminated in the background. It's nighttime in the photograph, and the Salt Lake temple shines majestic behind the two men, in direct opposition to the sign they hold in protest: HAPPILY MARRIED OCT. 26, 2008.

This couple moved to California from their Ohio hometown because they feared what would happen if they revealed their relationship there. I recently read an article that makes that fear seem founded: hate crimes based on victims' sexual orientation are at their highest in five years, and are increasing. The article detailed only a few of the thousands of such crimes reported last year: a lesbian in Richmond, California, gang raped by four men in two different locations; a gay student in Oxnard, California, shot twice in the head at a computer lab in his junior high school; a transgender woman in Colorado beaten to death with a fire extinguisher, whose assailant said he was proud to have "killed it."

Standing in the shadow of the photograph on the wall, I can't help but feel betrayed by the LDS church. In a time when such violence is rampant and rising, the LDS prophet—whose followers believe speaks directly as a mouthpiece for God—stood up to support the prejudice that drives it. To make clear that millions of God's children are not only unworthy of exaltation, but also unworthy of equality.

I feel myself grieving, inexplicably. Weeping for the wrongness of it— like I've had a part, somehow, in persecuting these men and those like them. And because I feel like something precious is being snatched from me. I can't explain it to Sariah: how I can still feel connected, how I feel further betrayed by these politics, this fight to keep millions of God's children apart from the rest.

The spires of the Salt Lake temple are blurred behind my tears, and all that's in my mind is a prayer: if the second-greatest commandment is to love our fellow man, where is that commandment in this? *Dear God, where is love in this?*

Driving away from the Annenberg, I look out the passenger-side window, concentrating on the white line racing beside us in the opposite direction. I'm still unable to talk, stunned by the fear that one day I'll look back in search of something beautiful, some cherished remnant of my faith, and nothing will remain.

Chapter 16

This hour I tell things in confidence,
I might not tell everybody, but I will tell you

—*Walt Whitman, "Song of Myself"*

When my name is called, I step onstage at the cabaret at Rich-ard Hugo House, grateful for the blinding stage lights. I can't see anything but a black void where the audience is, and a sign on the wooden podium: EAT THE MIC. With shaking, sweating hands, I smooth the typewritten pages in front of me and begin to read:

> *Of all the places I felt sure I'd never go, Planned Parenthood topped the list. Because they perform abortions and give condoms to kids, or so I'd been warned. Yet one spring afternoon I found myself in the waiting room between a candy-colored box of condoms and a teenage girl, clearly perplexed by the intake form. Her boyfriend kept sneering at her, whispering insults: "You don't know what a douche is? Geez, stupid."*
>
> *I imagined her bound for an uncomfortable, humiliating four minutes in the back of a borrowed Chevy Chevelle and had the urge to intervene, give her a big-sister lecture, make her see that a*

boy like this should not be anyone's "first." But what did I know? I
was a thirty-five-year-old virgin, preparing for my own first time,
which, incidentally, didn't happen until I was well into thirty-six.

I hear a collective intake of breath—and immediately, a more engaged silence in the room. The chairs in front of me, though I can't see them, are packed full of my fellow teaching artists. We are Seattle's Writers in the Schools, invited tonight to read on the theme "works in progress."

When I first heard the assignment—to read from new or unfinished work—I dismissed it outright. I didn't have anything new except the nineteen single-spaced pages sitting in my nightstand—evidence of a weekend-long emotional purge about growing up Mormon and remaining a virgin into my late thirties. The neat stack of pages had been languishing there for over a year; I couldn't go near them. Literally, couldn't open the drawer. Felt slightly nauseated when I thought about them.

The pages were inspired by, and subsequently abandoned, after a conversation with my friend Eric over sake bombs at the Fly Bar in San Francisco. "You're a writer with a story," he kept repeating, every time I tried to shut him down. I kept shaking my head no. Better to keep writing poems, I told him. I'd been telling myself the same thing in the two years since leaving the church. Better to filter my experience through character, parable, and punch line. Better to keep a safe distance from the first person singular, that terrible, truth-telling I.

Mine isn't the kind of story you *tell.* My story could hurt people, would make me too vulnerable. Besides, who would care about my religious crisis, which seems—oddly—more intimate than my body, more personal, and frightening to share. Who could relate to my sex life? How could I talk about it without seeming frigid, prudish, or fanatical?

"I'm afraid," I told Eric, shrugging. "Of shaming my family, of betraying the church." As if the church were a living thing; as if its heart could be crushed by the confidences I would break in the telling. And yet, that's what it felt like. Feels like.

When I opened the door to Hugo House—a creaky Victorian built in 1902, originally an apartment building, then a mortuary, then a theater, before becoming home base for much of Seattle's writing community—I was still undecided. Should I read what I've already published, what I've read aloud time and time again—those perfected, practiced, crowd-pleasing poems—or will I be brave? Will I force myself to stand onstage and say what feels impossible to admit: I was a virgin, until a year and a half ago.

I looked anxiously at the stage, and the ten or so square wooden tables packed full of other writers. My colleagues. They've published with more prestigious presses than I have. Their work has appeared in journals that continually reject me. They've won the grants and residencies for which I've been passed over, year after year. What if my work is less than, in comparison to theirs? What if I make a fool of myself in a way that isn't part of the routine?

These thoughts ran laps in my head until I took the stage. Until, blinded by the unrelenting glare of several halogen lamps, I felt anonymous enough to share my secrets. Because I couldn't see the audience, it felt for a moment like they had ceased to exist. Their absence gave me courage to begin. And I do fine, until I get to the part about my family.

"I tried for fifteen years not to lose hope," I said into the mic, hearing the words reverberate in the silence of the room.

The Gospel was the answer. It saved my parents, separately, differently, when they were young. Thanks to the Mormon Church, they escaped childhoods rife with abuse, alcoholism, and neglect. They found God, found each other, and were rescued by a community committed to family, forgiveness, and joy. Growing up, I was surrounded by love, and taught that I have a divine purpose. I felt

secure, fulfilled, purposeful, and connected. And further, I'd made
a commitment—how could I disrespect what my parents had
built for our family? How could I abandon God and his church
when in all ways but one, I'd asked, and had received?

This is when I break down. When I am overwhelmed by grief: by the
weight of the burden I've given my family, and the burden I carry,
because of it. They'll never understand why I rejected the best, most
beautiful thing they had to offer, like a gift. I wish that life could
have been enough; I wish I could have given them that in return.

I put a hand over my mouth to stifle the sobs threatening to burst
through. I step away from the mic and close my eyes, panicked. I can't
catch my breath, can't speak through the tightness in my throat, and
suddenly I am hyperaware of the audience. I can feel them looking at
me, all of them. I can feel them shifting in their seats, silent and staring.

Daemond, coach of the Seattle National Poetry Slam team, begins
snapping his fingers. His voice cuts through the dark void, through the
ragged breath trapped behind my hands, and the panic in my bloodstream. "You got it, girl. You got this."

The rest of the spoken-word crowd begins rubbing their palms
together—making the dry, papery noise that signals solidarity. The
people I'd been afraid of are looking at me, yes. But I've misinter-
preted the energy coming off them. They're leaning into my story,
waiting for the next sentence.

They call out encouragements until I step forward again, and claim
my place at the mic. "Here was empathy," I read. "Here—of all places—
was a path, opening. I would have an IUD instead of children; I
would have intellectual and spiritual freedom; I would write poems
and finally live inside my body. I would, for the love of God, feel a
man's hands on me before I die."

Saying the words aloud, I feel a final, freeing sense of catharsis.
Metamorphosis. A lightness so intense it's dizzying in the wake of their

applause. I'm keenly aware that this night has marked the end of being quiet, come what may. The end of being fearful of my own story, or others' reactions to it.

I can't concentrate on the final reader; my eyes are locked on a chair by the window. All I want is to sit there, alone. To slowly sip from the glass of bourbon in my hand, nurse it for an hour while staring at the rain, breathing out, letting go. But the room is a blur of noise after the reading. A maze of bodies and conversations. A soon-to-be award-winning novelist, Peter, is the first to corner me. "Send that out," is all he says. "Send it tomorrow."

My boss, Rebecca—a poet and director of education for the WITS program—asks if I ever read the Modern Love column in the Sunday *New York Times*. "It's my guilty pleasure," she says. "Your essay is perfect. It's perfect for them." Erin, another poet, clutches my arm. Her eyes are shining with held-in tears. "I couldn't breathe while you were reading," she says, and begins to tell me a story of her own. She's interrupted, not unkindly, by Storme, a poet and activist, who congratulates me for breaking free of the patriarchy, the indoctrination of my youth. I smile thinly, and remind myself: she thinks she's giving me a compliment. She doesn't know how offensive that word is, *indoctrinate*. As if God were absent from my faith, as if those of us who believe are no more than parrots, or drones.

The next day, from the 1970s-style couch at Freshy's, my favorite neighborhood coffee shop, I Google "modern love submission guidelines" and spend five hours revising the essay I'm no longer afraid to look at, read, or touch. Gretchen, who lives just down the street, happens to stop in for a quick break from her babies and her start-up business. She sits beside me and crosses her fingers while I hesitate over the send button—making a wish.

Gretchen closes her eyes, too, over a mug that pictures Corina, kissing her dachshund, Bebop. The caption reads *World's Greatest Lover*. Corina made hundreds last Christmas, and just as she planned, they're turning up all over town. I imagine Corina smiling down from the mug, also wishing me luck.

"Straight to the slush pile," I joke as I press send. I never expect anything beyond another form-letter rejection, "Dear Writer," to add to the thick stack in my nightstand. But always, in the back of my mind, is the what-if.

"At least I can say I tried," I tell Gretchen.

"It has to be someone," she says. "Why not you?"

And as if our collective, impossible wish were a premonition, I receive an e-mail the following week from Dan Jones: "re: submission—sex and the mormon girl."

DEAR NICOLE HARDY,

INTRIGUING ESSAY—I'D LIKE TO TALK TO YOU ABOUT IT.

My heart is in my throat at the first two words: "intriguing essay." My heart is pounding in my throat, and my eyes have gone blurry under a tidal wave of adrenaline.

ARE YOU AROUND TOMORROW FOR A PHONE CALL? IF SO, LET ME KNOW WHEN, GENERALLY, MIGHT BE A GOOD TIME TO TALK.

ALL BEST,

DANIEL JONES

MODERN LOVE EDITOR

THE NEW YORK TIMES

Every one of my pores has opened, releasing a clammy sweat. I am up and pacing and spinning in my living room. There is no one to tell. I am laughing, and crying, and I have to throw up and pee. There are too many liquids, too many, so many liquids in my body. I am spinning and shaking so much I can hardly dial the phone.

No one is home, no one is answering, everyone's at work, it's Monday mid-morning, and *holyshit, holyshit, holyshit* I have to *tell* someone. I have to say it out loud, so it will be real. I keep going to voice mail, and finally get so desperate I stand on my balcony, tilt my head toward the sky, and scream out loud. I scream and shake my hair.

But I *know* Gretchen is home. She has three kids and she works at night. She is killing me, screening her calls. After my fourth consecutive call, I yell the worst obscenity I've ever said, joyfully into her voice mail, "Call me *immediately!* I'm getting published in the New! York! Mother! Fucking! Times!"

The editor doesn't make a personal phone call to reject you is what I know for sure. Why can't someone *be here* to jump up and down with me, act like I've won the Showcase Showdown on *The Price Is Right*? Gretchen calls back in less than a minute, laughing into the phone. "I knew it!" she yells. "I knew it! I knew it!" There is more, even louder screaming when Melissa calls back, and a more serious conversation with Danielle. How will you tell your parents? she asks. And can you change your name?

At 8:00 PM, I put on every rhinestone I own—which is thousands—and strut into the Circa Christmas party—low-key this year, a small gathering at a bar across the street, for which I'm wildly overdressed. I buy a bottle of champagne, ask for ten glasses, and make a toast to Modern Love after which the girls erupt in a cacophony of cheers and catcalls.

Melissa has brought in a copy of last week's Sunday paper to show me the column, give me an idea of what mine might look like, in print. She's crying with pride, and I get a little drunk on purpose and later crash on Gretchen's basement couch, still dressed in my evening gown—but not before setting my alarm for 6:00 AM, at which time I rush home, brew a strong pot of coffee, change into yoga pants and my Wonder Woman T-shirt, and pull up the Modern Love archives: I'm not *about* to let Dan Jones know I've never read his column.

I start with a story about a fiftysomething woman in New York, who falls in love with a limo driver. And because she lives in a one-bedroom apartment and has a daughter, she details the heartwarming, hilarious tale of her courtship: noting the different cars he drove, the different places he parked for their secret rendezvous.

I read a humorous, beautifully constructed elegy for a husband who died of a rare, fatal disease. And a funny-sweet story written by the father of a boy who at age two epically fails to impress Michelle Williams's daughter—age three—at their favorite Brooklyn bagel shop. The last was called "Death Bear Will See You Now." Evidently, "summoned via text message, Death Bear will visit your Brooklyn apartment to remove painful reminders of your past." In a surprisingly poignant turn, a thin, delicate man in a bear mask shows up to exorcise the ghost of a woman's relationship past. He carefully packs up everything that will fit into his duffel bag, including the love letters painfully, reluctantly relinquished.

Waiting for the call from New York, I feel a brief wash of sadness over my own harrowing, hard-won letting go. And the futile wish that I could tell Jason, my teacher from Bennington, who died last year. This crazy thing that's happened, I need him to know. I've never had the heart to delete his e-mail address—I like seeing his name sometimes, unexpectedly. So I send a note into the ether and say a grateful prayer when it doesn't bounce back. I imagine Jason reading my essay in the hereafter—still wanting more from me, but proud that finally, I was able to write what I fear.

Christmas Eve eve, my mom and I are lying next to each other in her king-size bed, watching *Julie & Julia*. I'm loving Meryl Streep as Julia Child, indulging my years-old crush on Stanley Tucci, and finding the Amy Adams character more than slightly irritating. That is, until the Amy Adams character finds herself featured, against all odds, in the

New York Times. She is in line at a café, watching someone read an article about the blog she kept while working her way, page by page, through *The Art of French Cooking.* She returns to her apartment after work to find sixty-five messages on her answering machine—an editor at Little Brown, a literary agent, *CBS Morning News*, and on and on.

"What if that happened to me?" I joke, stuffing my face with popcorn, never considering it could. That's the Cinderella story, the thing that happens in movies, not in real life to real people. My mother doesn't respond. The last thing she wants is *CBS Morning News* to get ahold of me. She hasn't gone so far as to pretend my essay won't be available to a readership of millions, but she's absolutely *not thinking about it.*

So neither of us is prepared for the ways in which that scene foreshadows my immediate future. I have no idea that the Sunday *New York Times* goes online on Friday. I'm working my lunch shift, starting my sidework on a Friday around 2:00, trying to get done as early as possible, when my phone blows up. Text after text after text after e-mail after voice mail, notifications are ringing through. I rush to the wait station, even though it's my own rule that the staff can't have their phones on the floor. I'm worried that something terrible has happened, that someone has died or been in an accident.

It's the opposite kind of news, though the shock I feel takes the strength from my legs. I sit in an empty booth, a full forty-eight hours away from being mentally prepared for the world to know about my spiritual struggle, my decades of virginity, my visit to Planned Parenthood, my secret doubts and fears. "There are already fifty comments on the *NYT* page," Sariah texts. "How are you?" Danielle wants to know. "How is your family?" texts Melissa. By the time I get home, there are over a hundred e-mails waiting. Fan mail. Hate mail. *Your story is beautifully written, is honest, is moving, is a cop-out, is a bore. You should be proud, you should be ashamed, you're brave, a hypocrite, an inspiration, a sellout, a whore.*

Two days later, when the paper hits newsstands, friends arrive at my house at 6:30 AM with champagne, orange juice, pastries, and a stack of newspapers twelve inches high. Sitting at my kitchen table, seeing my name on the front page of the Style section, the rush of joy and disbelief strikes me speechless. Makes it hard to hear anything, see anything, except the square of newsprint in front of me.

I meet Willow's eyes, which, like mine, are brimming with tears. *This is how people must feel on their wedding day,* I think. Or when they hear their baby's heartbeat. This is how it feels to stand at the precipice of a different, dreamed-of life. To know, even as it's happening, that this is the day when everything will change.

From now on, it will be impossible not to believe myself when I say I'm a writer. Still, that thought does nothing to prepare me for what happens three hours later, when I'm rushing around, delivering pancakes and eggs over easy. I'm refilling coffee and running to the kitchen for sides of hollandaise between sips from the congratulatory thermos Corina has brought, filled with coffee and Frangelico. Meanwhile, every person at the bar and a few in the booths have a copy of the *New York Times* open in front of them.

I haven't considered that I'll *be there* when people read my essay. That I'll see their shifting expressions and body language, before and after. I didn't realize how intimately people will feel they know me, now—particularly the regulars I've waited on for nearly ten years. I didn't know to prepare myself for their curiosity, discomfort, surprise, admiration. A few have tears in their eyes. "Is this true?" they ask, and touch me lightly when I bend to drop their checks. I've not prepared myself for their tears.

But tonight will be the last, most trying test: how to survive the first calls from my family. I've told them not to read the essay. "Trust me, you don't want to. Please don't," I've said, again and again. They've been anxious from the beginning, since Dan Jones called to confirm he'd like to publish my piece.

My dad was in his car, outside the golf club, when I broke the news. "I told you," he crowed into the phone. "You're a *prose* writer!" It's true he's been telling me for years to switch genres. In the next sentence, he turned practical: he's proud of me, careerwise, he said. But he has some pretty serious reservations. He'd feel better if I could change my name, and if I didn't name the Mormon Church. Can't I say it's a conservative Christian church, and leave it at that? Why expose myself or the church to criticism? People will take any opportunity, he reminds me. He asks about contracts, payments, syndication. He tells me to keep my eyes open, in case the editors try to change my words, malign the church, subvert my intentions. Media cares about selling stories, he says, more than telling the truth.

When I got my mother on the phone, she was immediately tense. Afraid I'd opened myself up to be castigated, judged, or excommunicated. She doesn't understand why I'd *want* this story in the paper.

"I guess we're just different," she said. "I'm a private person. I don't even want people to know I went to the *store* today." She did her best to muster enthusiasm, but there are too many what-ifs for her to be comfortable. She feels vulnerable, because of what I've done. Frightened of the repercussions.

Despite my objections, my dad asked for a copy of my essay via e-mail before its official release—he needed to know what to expect, how to react, he said. But beyond that, he and my mother decided that no matter how difficult it is for them, they should try to understand my experience. They should try to know what I felt.

My dad calls in the evening to tell me what happened earlier, at church. Just before the Gospel Doctrine class he teaches every other week, his co-teacher approached to ask if he has a daughter who writes for the *New York Times*. My dad clarified, said I don't write for them, but yes, the essay is mine. "It was beautiful," said the woman. "You should be proud," she told him.

"I *am* proud of you," my dad said into the phone. "Though there were things in there no father wants to read." He says my mom would rather not talk about it just yet. Same for my brother, evidently, who sent a text this afternoon: "Read your piece. It was TMI."

It's Tuesday when my mother finally calls. She says the doorbell rang the day before, and through the peephole she saw a woman from the ward standing on her stoop. My mother didn't want to open the door. She was afraid of what this woman might say, worried that she might have come to pass judgment, or collect ammunition. Instead, the woman sat down and talked to my mom for two hours about her own children's struggles in the church.

"The church needs to serve its singles better," my mother tells me. "It needs to do better." Through the phone, I can feel her voice reaching toward me. I can feel the effort she is making. My eyes fill with tears at this small but grand gesture. She is looking for a way to acknowledge my experience. This is my mother, meeting me halfway.

Chapter 17

*I am come into my garden, my sister, my spouse: I have gathered
my myrrh with my spice; I have eaten my honeycomb with my
honey; I have drunk my wine with my milk: eat, O friends;
drink, yea, drink abundantly; O beloved.*

—SONG OF SOLOMON 5:1

Willow, Kevin, and I stand next to each other marveling at the
Coliseum the day after I arrive in Rome. I'm stunned by its
majestic architecture, its devastated beauty, and the night sky above
it—a magnificent, otherworldly shade of blue. As if it were the ocean,
in reverse. That depth. That wonder.

"I'd fly thirteen hours just to see this," I say, turning in a circle
with my arms outstretched. All day, I've been in a state of near ecstasy
over Italy in general. The anchovy pizza, the cappuccino, the celery—
how can it be so good? it's *celery*—the tomatoes sweet as strawberries,
the scents of lemon and jasmine wafting through the diesel-tinged air.
"I could go home *tomorrow* and feel like it was worth it."

"True words," sighs Willow, leaning closer into Kevin. They've
seen the Coliseum before, but still they're as spellbound as I am. Even
the vendors hawking cheap plastic replicas can't break the mood.

Eventually, the three of us wander up the street to a café for ricotta-stuffed zucchini flowers, and aqua frizzante—the one thing I can order in Italian without devolving into charades. The bartender makes us the best Negronis on God's green earth, and I feel myself sinking effortlessly into this foreign culture of pleasure. Already, I am sold on the lingering meals, long walks, late nights, and unpasteurized dairy.

Willow, who claims Italy as the home of her heart, will spend forty days and forty nights here with Kevin, to celebrate her fortieth birthday. She sent an e-mail to all of her friends, inviting us to join her at one or more stops on her sojourn through Italy. I am one of three who said yes—mainly because of my FOMO. No practicality stands a chance against a foreign adventure with friends. I didn't think twice about selling my grandmother's watch to pay for my plane ticket. I didn't know her, I reasoned. And if she knew me, she'd know how important it is that I see things like the Coliseum.

Like the marble Arch of Titus, which stands over fifty feet high and was built in AD 82 to commemorate Titus's military victories. "The year eighty-two!" I shout, poring over my guidebook two days after our visit to the Coliseum. "Eighty-two!" The days have been a whirlwind of eating, drinking, and walking. I've seen the Pantheon, and the Forum, and Circus Maximus, which looks a lot like an abandoned, unkempt football field. It's hard to imagine the drama of chariot races like those in *Ben-Hur*, but I do my best. We see catacombs, and Capuchin crypts where the bones of four thousand monks are displayed on walls like decorative molding, patterned like lace, or hung from the ceiling like chandeliers. We see Piazza Navona and Villa Borghese. We see Campo dei Fiore and Castel Sant'Angelo. We see the pope ten minutes after we joke about seeing the pope, as our bus rounds the corner in front of St. Peter's Basilica. I am caught up in the crush of tourists at the Trevi Fountain, and put off by the gore of much of the early Catholic iconography.

But to be standing and eating gelato in places where Caesar stood and ate. To see the antiquity, the hand-laid cobblestones of the city streets, the art, the religious history, and the deep, sculptural curls of the Roman men—so extraordinary I'm tempted to sink my hands in, just to see how far they'll go. All of it is so magical, I can't figure out what it is, nagging at me. What nearly imperceptible need keeps rising now and again to my consciousness.

It's not until our last day in Rome that I see the Sistine Chapel, and I realize what I've been feeling, or rather wanting to feel. Under the domed ceiling painted with frescoes, I picture Michelangelo lying on a tower of scaffolding, painting the scenes made iconic by postcards and wall calendars. I touch Kevin's sleeve, and point. There is God's finger touching that of Adam. That extraordinary image, in real life. I stand still and close my eyes, waiting to feel something spiritual, but it doesn't come.

The chapel is crowded with jostling teenagers and harried sightseers. People keep bumping me with their backpacks. Docents angrily clap their hands at intervals, attempting to maintain or restore an air of reverence. And afterward, walking through the enormous, linked rooms of the Vatican, I feel overwhelmed, and slightly uneasy. It's difficult for me to ingest—the extent of its opulence, so many square feet dedicated to the display of what's been seized, or plundered.

But in St. Peter's Basilica, I finally feel what it is I've been craving—what I was afraid I wouldn't have access to, outside my former religious structure. But standing with Kevin and Willow in front of Michelangelo's *Pietà,* that marble sculpture of Christ dying in the arms of his mother, I am overwhelmed by the spirit of God.

In front of us, Mary's body is too small to contain the thin, wasting body of her grown son, draped across her lap. His face, in the cradle of her arm, is turned into her shoulder. Her robe, in a pool around her, could be liquid, rather than stone. The energy of his death is palpable, inspires a hush among us, and the impulse to listen for his last shallow breaths beyond, or within, our own.

I forget about the bulletproof shield in front of the statue, that defense against zealots. I forget about the wave of tourists behind us. Nothing exists for me but the expression on Mary's face. She appears serene, until I realize my hand is at my throat. Until I find myself leaning toward her, wanting to reach out. Her face, and her body—protective, even as she is forced to offer up her son—reveal everything there is to know about sacrifice. About love, and the helplessness of being human.

When I turn to her, Willow's face is streaked with tears. She doesn't move to brush them away, just blinks to clear her vision. And Kevin, who has never claimed to believe, is also affected. I wonder if he is thinking of his own brother's death. How his mother must have felt, knowing she was powerless to save her son.

I leave Rome feeling edified, and inspired. Grateful to know that I will still have a way to worship. Art will be my church. And poetry. Music, history, nature, all of them will be my church. They will connect me to God and keep my spirit aligned with what is beautiful and true.

Three days later, on the island of Ischia, famous for its healing mineral waters, Willow, Kevin, and I eat a breakfast of cappuccino, prosecco, and cornetti in the shade of a tree made from two trees whose roots have twisted together—so both lemons and oranges hang from its branches. We toast to Willow and to age forty, overlooking the Mediterranean Sea.

Kevin takes out his guitar and plays something classical, Spanish-sounding. I notice how he and Willow look at each other and think how blessed I am, to be a witness to their love. Imperfect, as all things are. But in its presence, I'm inspired. Included, and beloved, as well. Woven into the music Kevin plays, I feel the words of scripture: "If we love one another, God dwelleth in us, and his love is perfected in us."

"*Cento di questi giorni,*" Willow says, as if she is reading my mind. *One hundred of these days.* We drink, and toast again: to growing old together. To the knowledge that there are many ways to make a family. We linger there for hours, above the gardens bursting with cactus and succulents. Peacocks roam the paths among honeysuckle and bright-orange birds of paradise, while Kevin is backlit in profile, playing "Who Knows Where the Time Goes." Willow says he could pass for one of the Italians, with his curly hair, regal forehead, Roman nose.

The next day, we travel by boat to Positano, where we think we are staying—a quaint village built into the side of a cliff. But our hotel turns out to be in a tiny village called Nocelle, high up in the hills. There is only one restaurant in Nocelle, called Santa Croce, where two young brothers wait on us. Their mother cooks.

"You must try a very special wine," one of the brothers says, and brings us a bottle of Morellino di Scansano. He decants it ceremoniously, with the aid of a candle. "You must try the potatoes," the other insists, when we order greens instead. "From my garden," he says, with a hand on his heart. "*Delicioso*, you must believe me."

Positano is a spray of delicate lights like stars below us, and the moon is like a spotlight illuminating the sea. I've known for a long time there is romance to be found even when one is not in love, even when candlelight shines on a party of three. I let my gaze linger on the town and the sea, reminding myself to remember this view, forever.

That night and the two that follow, Willow, Kevin, and I eat dinner beside a woman we've begun to call Italian Nicola. She's Nocelle's version of me: a woman content to travel alone, to spend hours savoring an exquisite view, a meal lovingly prepared, and a thick, beautiful book. When a British couple insists she join them, she kindly refuses, saying she is happy as she is. Seeing her, seeing my life from the outside, I feel a hopeful sense of peace. *If this is everything,* I think, *it is already wonderful.* But who's to say what more awaits Italian Nicola— what wonder, what possibility may lie in the next piazza, in the next town, or on the walk to her favorite café.

———

Five months after my return to Seattle, I wake to a moon too bright to let me sleep. I'd heard it was coming, on the weather report: a harvest moon, brighter than any in the past ten years. It seems wrong to close the curtains against it and the memories it inspires, of Nocelle and Positano. In my living room, I sit where I can see both the moon and its wide, shimmering reflection over Puget Sound. I flip on the television to wait out this rare bout of insomnia, and as if by divine intervention, *Big Night* is playing on whatever channel I was watching last.

I first saw this movie with Murphy, fifteen years ago, and I'm pleased by its repetition in my life. In my favorite scene, Stanley Tucci, as Secondo, makes eggs for his brother Primo the morning after the feast that failed to save their business. It's a long, silent scene, and it moves me every time I see it—such a simple, intimate gesture. But it's the villain, a rival restaurant owner, who delivers my favorite line. He yells in a heavy Italian accent at Secondo, who is about to lose everything. "Bite your *teeth* into the ass of life, and drag it to you!"

It's in this spirit that I plan my own fortieth birthday party, 1940s-style, in an underground, velvet-draped room in the basement of a place called Rendezvous. It was once a speakeasy—originally built in 1924 as a film-row screening room. Guests descend a long flight of stairs and find themselves walking back in time: entering a low-lit room with a built-in bar, scattered with cocktail tables. Two arched walkways separate the bar from the main room, where *Casablanca* would be playing, silently, on a blank wall—if the projector hadn't broken just this morning.

I've hired a favorite former high school student to be my nightclub singer. I've rented a regulation-size craps table: it's less authentic than roulette, but more fun. The bartender makes martinis and manhattans and French 75s. There is Moroccan-themed food, and a sheet of movie quotes on each table, along with cartons of candy cigarettes. Because you never know who will show up in a white tuxedo jacket. Who will pretend to light a cigarette and say, "You know, Rick, I have many a friend in Casablanca, but somehow, just because you despise me, you are the only one I trust."

Humphrey Bogart's coveted lines will be repeated by many throughout the night, with an affected air of brooding. "Of all the gin joints, in all the towns, in all the world, she walks into mine."

To a beautiful woman at the bar, someone will say, "I remember every detail. The Germans wore gray; you wore blue." Later, she'll respond to him, or someone else, "Kiss me. Kiss me as if it were the last time."

My mother is giddy, thrilling from her run at the craps table, her 30-to-1 win with boxcars or a hard eight or snake eyes. She is gleefully piling colorful chips on the felt in front of her, making one handsome man after another blow on the dice for luck. She keeps tugging on peoples' sleeves, asking, "Do *you* know why I keep winning?"

She squeezes me every time I walk by. "Happy birthday, Tootsiegirl. Love you." And then she's back to placing large, risky bets, in stark contrast to my father's conservative ones. I can't believe my family is still here, or, more accurately, that they've come at all. I invited them only to be polite. "It might get rowdy," I said, meaning, people will be drinking.

My dad replied that they wouldn't come, but thanks. My mother looked at him and declared boldly, "I think we *should* go." And even though I know she's the boss, my jaw dropped when they all showed up. "We're not staying long. I have a headache," my brother said upon his arrival. Which evidently *craps* is the cure for. Because here he is, in the wee hours, having fun in spite of his headache and the fact that his wife wanted to leave two hours ago.

Sometime close to midnight, I am mobbed at the bar, swept up by the Circa girls in a crush of perfume and curls and vintage-inspired dresses. I'm rushed into the other room before I have a chance to set down my French 75. And so it is that on the night of my fortieth birthday, my family—for the first time—is witness to me drinking an alcoholic beverage. They are unfazed, or pretending to be. My co-workers take to the stage, all satin gloves and matte red lips, singing a campy, vampy rendition of "Happy Birthday," à la Marilyn Monroe.

Gretchen is first to take the mic. "When I was a kid," she says, "the only thing I knew about turning forty was that it was the age my aunt died. And I thought, 'Well, she lived a long, full life.' The laughter that follows increases exponentially when she launches into a tipsy, tearful proclamation about my "commitment to diversity." Other friends stand up to make jokes and say sweet things, until my dad walks up to the stage.

The toast my father gives is the only one I can remember him making. He must have said something at my brother's wedding reception, but I don't remember it. In a culture of nondrinking, there is neither a culture of toasting. But here he is, standing up in front of fifty of my closest friends to say, "Nicole is the best daughter I could ever imagine." His bald head is ablaze under the glare of stage lights. "She's my favorite person in the world."

Immediately, I have to blink back tears. I didn't expect this, didn't expect to need to hear it. "Since she was a child she's known her own mind, and has gone wherever her dreams have taken her, without fear of failure. Maybe that's why she's never encountered it." He pauses for effect, and then says, "Who else would decide the *perfect* plan while pursuing her master's would be to sell everything and move to Grand Cayman to sell T-shirts and scuba dive? Better yet, it turned out just as she imagined.

"I admire her so much," he says, punch-drunk on Diet Coke and effusions of birthday joy. "I'm inspired by her." He pauses, not quite knowing how to finish. He raises his glass and says, finally, "What's not to love about my daughter?"

Then I'm mobbed with champagne kisses, *I love you*, from poets, writers, artists, and musicians, family, friends, co-workers, and customers. *I love you* is the chorus in my head, dancing with whoever will join me, until it's time to say good night. Scott is first to leave, he has an early flight, and I sink easily into his familiar embrace, the soft wool of his sweater. With his arms around me, I think of a story Jenna, one of the Circa girls, often tells about her grandmother—dreamy-eyed, prior to her passing. Jenna leaned close to ask, "What are you thinking about, Grandma?"

"Men," she answered, with a long, beatific sigh.

Scott kisses me on the cheek, and while I know we won't end up together, I'm still glad to have chosen him. We were perfect for each other, for a time: both of us in need of something it was a pleasure for the other to give.

Danielle is next to go; her husband and baby are waiting. John and Alphonsine have a ferry to catch. My family has church in the morning. The writers, the teachers, the Circa staff and regulars, my brothers, sisters, and soul mates, every good-bye kiss reminds me I am blessed.

Outside, Willow links her arm in mine as Kevin hails us a cab. He holds the door open, but I shake my head. "You first," I say, wanting a moment to breathe in the wet autumn chill, to memorize the city skyline and the long, silent stretch of Second Avenue glittering beneath the streetlamps. I look to the invisible stars, wondering what possibilities, what adventures might lie waiting for me in the next piazza, in the next town, or on the walk to my favorite café.

ACKNOWLEDGMENTS

Special thanks to Dan Jones, who plucked me from the slush pile; Susan Golomb, who championed my story; and Christine Pride, Kerri Kolen, and Elisabeth Dyssegaard, who brought order to the chaos. Thanks also to Eliza Rothstein, Krista Ingebretson, Allyson Rudolph, and Sam O'Brien, for managing the countless details. And Vermont Studio Center, the Helen Riaboff Whitely Center, Richard Hugo House, and Seattle's Writers in the Schools program, for their inspiration and support.

Thanks to those at Freshy's and Bird on a Wire. I may have starved without you. And to you who read, encouraged, critiqued and consoled: Eric Raymond, Sue Barr-Toman, Sariah Dorbin, Kim Puckett, Georgia Congleton, Willow Scrivner, Suzanne Morrison, Brian McGuigan, and Tommy Z. The South End poets, the Circa girls, and the Neptune 5—thank you for feeding me in other ways.

Thanks to Seattle writers Beth Branco, Carmela D'Amico, Sonora Jha, David Schmader, Jennifer D. Munro, Elissa Washuta, Rebecca Hoogs, Peter Mountford, Daemond Arrindel, and Erin Malone, who answered my (sometimes telepathic) calls for help.

Thanks most of all to my two families—the one I was given, and the one I found. In the immortal words of Barry White, you're the first, the last, my everything.